HOW TO TALK

SO LITTLE KIDS WILL LISTEN

A SURVIVAL GUIDE TO LIFE WITH CHILDREN AGES 2-7

HOW TO TALK
SO LITTLE KIDS WILL LISTEN

A SURVIVAL GUIDE TO LIFE WITH CHILDREN AGES 2-7

Joanna Faber & Julie King

With a Foreword by Adele Faber

Piccadilly
PRESS

First published in Great Britain in 2017 by
PICCADILLY PRESS
80–81 Wimpole Street, London W1G 9RE
Owned by Bonnier Books
Sveavägen 56, Stockholm, Sweden
www.piccadillypress.co.uk

A CIP catalogue record for this book is available from the British Library.

ISBN: 978-1-84812-614-5
Also available as an ebook

11

Printed and bound by Clays Ltd, Elcograf S.p.A.

Piccadilly Press is an imprint of Bonnier Books UK
www.bonnierbooks.co.uk

"A person's a person, no matter how small!"
                    —Horton the Elephant
                    (Dr. Seuss)

"The way we talk to our children becomes their inner voice."
                    —Peggy O'Mara

Contents

Contents

Contents

Foreword

Adele Faber

The first hint I had of the passion that would fuel the creation of this book came when it was my turn to carpool the authors to nursery school.

I put my daughter Joanna in the car, drove around the corner to collect Julie, and then two more blocks to pick up Robbie. Soon all three children were buckled up in the back seat, happily chattering with each other. Suddenly the mood shifted and a heated debate erupted:

Robbie: He had no reason to cry! He wasn't even hurt.

Julie: Maybe his feelings were hurt.

Robbie: So what? Feelings don't matter. You have to have a reason!

Joanna: Feelings *do* matter. They're just as important as reasons.

Robbie: No, they're not! You have to have a good reason.

I listened and marveled at these three little people. It wasn't hard to figure out where each of them was coming from. Robbie's mother was a serious, no-nonsense woman. Julie's mom, a piano teacher, loved talking with me about the discoveries I was making in my parenting workshops with the renowned child psychologist Dr. Haim Ginott. There was always so much for us to think about and try out with our children.

Sometimes bits of our discussions would find their way into the book Elaine Mazlish and I had decided to write together. We had each experienced such profound changes in our own lives and witnessed so many transformations in the lives of others in our group, it seemed wrong not to share our journey with as many parents as possible. Best of all, we had Dr. Ginott's blessing. He read our early drafts and offered his editorial support.

Fast-forward twenty-five years. Our first book, *Liberated Parents/Liberated Children: Your Guide to a Happier Family*, has been published. It wins the Christopher Award for "Literary Achievement Affirming the Highest Values of the Human Spirit." Seven more books soon follow. *How to Talk So Kids Will Listen & Listen So Kids Will Talk* and *Siblings Without Rivalry* become best sellers and are published in more than thirty languages.

The little girls I drove to nursery school are grown, married, and each has three children of her own. Each has lived abroad and explored different areas of study. I still have to smile when I remember Julie telling me about an exchange she had at her first internship as a law clerk at a legal aid agency. She was presenting a case for a lawsuit that appeared to be based on a simple misunderstanding.

"Can we get them together to talk? I'm sure if they could listen to each other's point of view they could come to an understanding."

The boss was impatient with her naïveté. "We don't do that. You can't talk to the opposing party."

It was at this point, Julie said, that she started to think she might be in the wrong profession.

And I have to smile when I remember a hurried phone call from Joanna after a frustrating day with the special needs children in her classroom.

"The kids won't stop fighting. It's chaos. I can't get through a lesson! What do I do?"

I drew a blank. "Well, you know what I usually do when I'm stuck, but . . ."

"Oh, you mean problem-solving. Okay, thanks. Bye!" and she hung up.

She swung into action the next morning, and we were thrilled to incorporate the amazing results of her new tactic when Elaine and I were writing *How to Talk So Kids Can Learn/At Home and In School*.

Finally, each woman found herself responding to the urgent need for parenting workshops in her part of the world: Joanna on the east coast, Julie on the west. After years of helping parents, many of whom had young children who presented a wide variety of challenges, they decided to join forces and produce a book of their own:

How to Talk So Little Kids Will Listen
A Survival Guide to Life with Children Ages 2 to 7

Elaine and I expect you'll be delighted and enlightened by all the discoveries you'll make as you turn its pages.

Happy reading!

How It All Started

Julie

My two-year-old son peed on the carpet under the crib . . . *again!* What to do? My degrees in public policy and law were of no use. I was surprised by how quickly I could be brought to my knees by a small person too young to drive a car—or tie his own shoes.

I didn't plan a career as a parent educator. I figured I'd be a mom on the side as I advanced my professional career. But when I was told that my first child had significant developmental delays, as did my second, I realized that parenting was not going to be an "on the side" activity for me. I found myself committed to endless rounds of appointments with medical specialists and physical therapists and advocating for children with neurodevelopmental differences.

Julie and Joanna in an earlier collaboration.

Lucky for me, I grew up with a best friend, Joanna, whose mom, Adele Faber, took a parenting workshop with the late, great child psychologist Haim Ginott. Her mom and mine are also close friends, and they tested out their new parenting strategies on us. Little did I know that these methods would become a lifesaver for me so many years later when I faced the challenges of parenting my own three children.

When the head of the Parent Education committee at my son's preschool was looking for someone to organize an event for parents, I volunteered to lead a workshop based on Adele's book *How to Talk So Kids Will Listen*. My first eight-week group was such a success that everyone insisted I continue to lead the group for another eight weeks, and another . . . and we ended up meeting for four and a half years! Through word of mouth, other people asked me to lead workshops, which snowballed into a career I had never imagined.

Meanwhile, my friendship with Joanna continued. In many ways she and I are quite different. She loves the outdoors and *dogs* (you will find many references to dogs throughout our book), while I love to sit at the piano playing classical music (which is why Joanna's references to pop music often go over my head). Yet I've always felt I can talk to her about anything, and she really listens and understands. Even though we now live on opposite coasts, we've spent the last year writing together and the result is this book.

Joanna and Julie today.

I hope you find this information as life transforming as I have, and I hope you have as many laughs reading it as we had writing it. I'll introduce you to my three kids in chapter five, where you can read more about the experience of parenting and teaching non-neurotypical children.

How It All Started

Joanna

I have a confession to make. I was raised by a mother who wrote best-selling books about parenting. My two brothers and I grew up in a family where my mother and father used a language of respect for their children's ideas and emotions. Even our most ferocious conflicts were resolved by problem-solving rather than punishment.

So parenting for me should be a snap. I have no excuses! Then again, I didn't think I would need any. Not only had I been raised by practically ideal parents, I had plenty of experience of my own. I have read and studied extensively in the field of child development and psychology. I have a degree in special education and ten years of experience working with both native English speakers and bilingual children in West Harlem as a teacher in the New York City school system. I was going to be a natural with my own kids.

I remember taking my first little baby to the supermarket, talking and singing sweetly to him about the apples and bananas. A fellow shopper leaned in and generously offered me some advice. "Enjoy him now, before he learns to talk." What an awful woman! I couldn't wait for my little darling to express his amazing thoughts to me in words.

Fast-forward a few years and there I was, back in the

grocery store. I now had three young children in tow, and on this day they were being particularly well behaved. The two younger ones were riding in the cart and the older one was helping me get items off the shelf. A grandfatherly man stopped, looked at these adorable kids, and said, "You are so good. I'll bet your mother never yells at you!"

It was a golden moment. My oldest looked at him wide-eyed and said, "*No,* she yells at us all the time . . . for no reason!"

What happened here? Who were these less-than-perfect creatures? And where was that ideal mom who would never "yell for no reason," no less, "*all the time!*"

What I discovered as a parent was that there is a certain twenty-four-hours-a-day relentlessness to caring for young children that makes it hard to think straight. Even though I thought I would be a natural, when it comes to handling all those constant needs and emotions day after day, night after night, there is no such thing as easy or perfect. Sometimes simple survival is a good goal.

As a new mom I certainly did not feel that I had much wisdom to share about raising children. I didn't even feel particularly competent. As a matter of fact, it seemed best to keep quiet about my own parentage. I kept a low profile and neglected to mention to the other moms in my social circle that my mother was a famous author. When my children were wailing, whimpering, or whacking each other, I preferred to deal with the situation without having to wonder if anyone was watching me and thinking, "Hmph, *her* mother wrote a book on parenting?"

It turns out that at least one person was watching and noticing. One day at a playgroup, my friend Cathy said to me, "Joanna, I have this book that you would love. It's just your style. It really reminds me of the way you talk to your kids. It's called *How to Talk So Kids Will Listen & Listen So Kids Will Talk.*"

At that point I figured it would be fruitless to feign ignorance. I admitted that my mother wrote the book. Cathy was delighted. She called out to the group of mothers, "Hey, guys, Joanna's mother wrote this great book and she never told us!"

And so I was outed, my secret identity revealed.

Soon after that, Cathy told me that she was in charge of organizing a lecture series for her church group, and she asked me if I would give a presentation about my experience growing up as the daughter of Adele Faber. As the date approached I began to hope for some disaster at the church. Nothing that would hurt anybody, just a little flooding or perhaps a well-timed power outage. What was I going to say to these people? I felt woefully inadequate to represent myself as a paragon of parenting. I didn't even want to think about it!

But they were expecting me to say something up there. The forecast looked good, no hurricanes or blizzards on the horizon. I was getting desperate. Finally it struck me that I did have something to offer. Cathy had noticed it when she commented on my style. I'm not the perfect parent; I get into plenty of conflicts with my children. But I do have skills to help get us through those conflicts, and I use them every day.

I gave my talk at the church. Afterward there was great enthusiasm among the parishioners about forming a parenting group. I found myself leading parenting workshops, and then giving more lectures, and eventually traveling across the country, giving presentations to parents, teachers, social workers, and health care providers.

The book you hold in your hand is the result of many requests by parents for more examples and strategies to use with very young children. Terrible two-year-olds, truculent three-year-olds, ferocious four-year-olds, foolhardy five-year-olds, self-centered six-year-olds, and the occasional semi-civilized seven-year-old. This work represents my re-immersion into the pool of knowledge that I grew up with and additional insights about making our way as parents in the twenty-first century. Part of this process included collaborating with my childhood friend Julie King, who encouraged me to lead when I felt like I was just finding my own way. The following work contains the very hands-on insights of Julie and myself and all the parents and teachers who trusted us and shared their stories.

We are presenting this work to you in two parts. Part one lays out the basic equipment you'll be glad to have in your toolbox when a youngster goes haywire. Part two addresses the specific challenges that we've found to be the most common themes of early childhood—eat, get dressed, get out the door, stop hitting, go to sleep!—and shows how the parents in our groups used these tools in various creative and unusual ways. We hope this book will provide you with a deep well of ideas that you can dip into and pull up by the cool, refreshing bucketful when you feel you've run dry!

A Note from the Authors

We struggled with the question of whose voice to use as a narrator. It quickly became clear that writing "I, Joanna . . ." and "I, Julie . . ." would not work. We tried to create a composite character with composite children, but it didn't feel authentic. We wanted to use real stories from our own families. As you'll see, while we collaborated on the entire book, we settled on writing in our individual voices. You will see the name Joanna or Julie under each chapter heading to let you know who is narrating that section.

All the stories told by characters in our book actually happened. Names and other identifying details have been changed, but in all cases real live children and real live parents and professionals really did say and do these things.

PART I

THE ESSENTIAL TOOLBOX

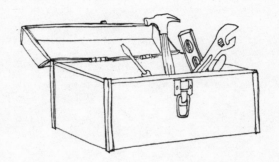

Chapter One

Tools for Handling Emotions . . .
What's All the Fuss about Feelings?

**—When kids don't feel right, they can't
behave right**

Joanna

Most of the parents in my workshops have been pretty impatient with this first topic: helping children deal with difficult feelings. They'd like to move right on to the second session: how to get your kids to do what you tell them to do! Not that we don't care about how our kids feel. It's just not generally the first priority for a frazzled parent. Let's face it, if they did as they were told, things would go so smoothly we'd *all* feel great!

The problem is, there's just no good shortcut to getting a cooperative kid. You can try, but you will likely end up knee-deep in a bog of conflict.

Think of those times when you're very glad you're not being filmed for reality television. The times when you're screaming at a kid so hard your throat aches; you've just told him for the hundredth time not to shove his little sister near the stove, or pull the elderly dog's ears—*"He will BITE YOU! And you will DESERVE IT!!"*—and your child remains oblivious.

3

I'm guessing those were times when you were feeling tired, stressed, or upset about something else entirely. If the same incident had occurred when you were feeling more cheerful, you would have shown grace under pressure. Maybe scooped up the little sister or the long-suffering dog, with a quick kiss or a scratch under the chin, and redirected your young savage with an understanding chuckle.

So what's the point of all this? The point is that we can't *behave* right when we don't *feel* right. And kids can't behave right when they don't feel right. If we don't take care of their feelings first, we have little chance of engaging their cooperation. All we'll have left going for us is our ability to use greater force. And since we'd like to reserve brute force for emergencies such as yanking children out of traffic, we've got to face this feelings thing head-on. So let's dig in!

Most of us don't have too much trouble accepting our children's positive feelings. That's pretty easy. *Gosh, Jimmy is your best friend in the world? You love Daddy's pancakes? You're excited about the new baby? How nice. Glad to hear it.*

It's when our children express a negative feeling that we run into trouble.

"What? You hate Jimmy? But he's your best friend!"

"You plan to punch him in the nose? Don't you *dare*!"

"How can you be sick of pancakes? They're your favorite."

"You want me to give the baby *back*? That is a *terrible* thing to say! Don't *ever* let me hear something like that come out of your mouth again!"

We don't want to accept negative feelings because they're so . . . well . . . negative. We don't want to give them any power. We want to correct them, diminish them, or preferably make them disappear altogether. Our intuition tells us to push those feelings away as fast and hard as possible. But this is one instance in which our intuition is leading us astray.

My mother always tells me, "If you aren't sure what's right, try it out on yourself." Let's do that. Consider your reaction to this situation:

Imagine you wake up feeling lousy. You didn't get enough sleep last night and you can feel a headache coming on. You stop to get some coffee before going to work at the preschool and run into a coworker. You say to her, "Boy, I don't want to go into work today and face all those loud, quarrelsome kids. I just want to go back home, take some Tylenol and spend the day in bed!"

What would your reaction be if your friend:

. . . denied your feelings and scolded you for your lousy attitude?

"Hey, stop complaining. The kids aren't that bad. You shouldn't talk about them that way. Anyway, you know you'll have a good time once you get there. Come on, let me see that smile."

. . . or gave you some advice?

"Look, you've got to pull yourself together. You know you need this job. What you should do is get rid of that coffee, drink some soothing herbal tea, and meditate in the car before school starts."

. . . or perhaps a gentle philosophical lecture.

"Hey, no job is perfect. That's just life. There's no use complaining about it. Dwelling on the negative is not productive."

. . . How about if she compared you with another teacher?

"Look at Liz. She's always cheerful about going to work. And do you know why? Because she is ultra-prepared. She always has really great lesson plans ready, weeks ahead of time."

5

. . . Would questions be helpful?

"Are you getting enough sleep? What time did you get to bed last night? Do you think you might be getting a cold? Are you taking vitamin C? Have you been using those Sani-Wipes they have available at the school so you won't catch germs from the kids?"

Here are some of the reactions we get when we present this kind of scenario in our group:

"I'm never talking to YOU again!" "This is no friend of mine!" "You have NO CLUE!" "I hate you! Go to hell!" "Blah, blah, blah." "SHUT UP!" "I'll never talk to you about my problems again; I'm sticking to topics like the weather from now on!" "I feel guilty for making such a big deal about this." "I wonder why I can't handle the kids." "I feel pitiful." "I hate Liz." "I feel like I'm being interrogated." "I feel judged; you must think I'm stupid." "I can't say it out loud but I'll tell you the initials . . . F-you!"

That last response perfectly expresses the intensity of hostility that we sometimes experience when someone denies our negative feelings. We can go quickly from unhappiness to rage when talked to this way, and *so can our children*.

So what *would* be helpful to hear in a situation like this? My guess is that some of your misery would be soothed if someone simply acknowledged and accepted your feelings.

"Ugh. It's awful to have to go to work when you don't feel well. Especially when you work with kids. What we need is a nice snowstorm, or maybe a very small hurricane that would shut the school down for just one day."

When their feelings are acknowledged, people feel relieved: *She understands me. I feel better. Maybe it's not so bad. Maybe I can handle it.*

Do we actually talk to our kids this way—correcting them, scolding them, interrogating them, and lecturing them when they express a negative feeling? The group has no trouble coming up with examples. Here are some of the most common.

Denial of feelings:

> *"You don't really hate school. You'll have fun once you get there. You know you like playing with the blocks."*

Has any child ever responded, "Oh yeah, you're right. You just reminded me that I *do* love school!"

Philosophy:

> *"Look, kiddo, life isn't fair! You've got to stop it with the 'He got more, hers is better.'"*

How likely is it that your child will reply, "Gee whiz, I was all upset, but now that you explained to me that life isn't fair, I feel so much better. Thanks, Dad!"

Questions:

> *"Why did you throw sand when I just told you not to?"*

What child says, "Hmm, why did I? I guess there's no good reason. Thanks for pointing that out. It won't happen again."

Comparison:

> *"Look at how Olivia is sitting quietly and waiting her turn!"*

Whose child would say, "Oh gosh, I will try to be more like Olivia!" It's more likely she'll feel like giving Olivia a bonk on the head.

Lecture:

> *"Why do you always want a toy as soon as your brother starts playing with it? You had no interest in it a minute ago. You just want to take it away from him. That's not very nice. Anyway, that's a toy for babies and you're a big girl now. You should be more patient with your little brother."*

And where is the child who responds, "Do go on, dear mother. I'm learning so much from this speech. Let me just jot down a few notes on my iPad so I can go over these points later."

Okay, okay, I hear you say. *But it's easy to be empathic with a grown-up friend. Grown-ups are civilized! Little kids aren't like that. They are way less logical. My friends don't keep me up at night. At least not most of them. I don't have to get my friends to go to school, or brush their teeth, or stop hitting their siblings. Pretending my child is an adult is not going to cut it. If an adult friend behaved like my child, she would not be my friend for long.*

All right, I get it. We can't treat our children like we treat our adult friends. But if we want their willing cooperation instead of their hostility, we need to find a way to use the same principle of acknowledging feelings when a person is in distress.

Let's peer into our toolbox and see how we can modify our stockpile for use with the younger set.

TOOL #1: <u>Acknowledge Feelings with Words</u>

The next time your kid says something negative and inflammatory, follow these steps:

1. Grit your teeth and resist the urge to immediately contradict him!
2. Think about the emotion he is feeling
3. Name the emotion and put it in a sentence

With any luck you will see the intensity of the bad feelings diminish dramatically.

Good feelings can't come in until the bad feelings are let out. If you try to stuff those bad feelings back in, they will marinate and become more potent.

For example:

When a child says, "I hate Jimmy. I'm never playing with him again."

Instead of, "Of course you will. Jimmy is your best friend! And we don't say 'hate.'"

Try, "Boy, sounds like you're really angry with Jimmy right now!" or "Something Jimmy did really annoyed you!"

When a child says, "Why do we always have to have pancakes? I hate pancakes."

Instead of, "You know you love pancakes! They're your favorite food."

Try, "Sounds like you're disappointed about pancakes for breakfast. You're in the mood for something different."

When a child says, "This puzzle is too hard!"

Instead of, "No, it's not. It's easy. Here, I'll help you. Look, here's a corner piece."

Try, "Ugh, puzzles can be so frustrating! All these little pieces could drive a person nuts."

You are giving your child a crucial vocabulary of feelings that he can resort to in times of need. When he can wail, "I AM FRUSTRATED!" instead of biting, kicking, and hitting, you will feel the thrill of triumph!

 **_All_ feelings can be accepted. _Some_ actions must be limited!**

I'm not suggesting that you then stand by and cheer as Junior slugs his friend Jimmy in the nose, or that you immediately start cooking up a mushroom and cheddar cheese omelet for your demanding toddler who has just complained about the pancakes. Just accept the feeling. Often a simple acknowledgment of the feeling is enough to defuse a potential meltdown. For those times when it's not enough, you'll find more tools in chapter two. (What? You're impatient? You want the entire book stuffed into chapter

I can see you're FURIOUS with your brother! I can't let you hit him!

one? I hear you! It's annoying to be strung along like this. If I could fit it all into one paragraph, I would.)

Like most great endeavors, this accepting feelings thing is easier said than done. I'm going to reminisce about a few (among many) of the times when I found it difficult to follow this seemingly simple path. To me the beautiful take-home lesson of these stories is that you can mess up endlessly and it's okay. You can fix it! You can wander from the path, get stuck in the bog, pull yourself out, scratch your mosquito bites, and move on down the road. The itchy spots will heal, the mud will wash off, and your journey will be pleasant again for the next little bit.

When a conversation was turning to conflict, my mother used to gesture wiping a slate clean and say, "Erase and start again!" But that's old school. She's from the generation of chalkboards. Have kids even heard of a chalkboard these days? Some parents in my groups have used the word *Rewind!* as they walk backward out of a room and then reenter with more accepting words. Even that has an old-fashioned sound now that cassette tapes have become a

Don't talk that way about your broth— ERASE!

11

thing of the past. What would be the modern equivalent of asking for a second chance? Perhaps yelling "Control Alt Delete!" or "Reset!" with the motion of a finger pressing an imaginary button?

The important thing is to give yourself endless chances, whatever imagery you choose to use. Here are a few examples from my years as a mom of toddlers where I managed to change course midstream and save my little parenting raft from upending in rough waters.

The Disappointing Sponge Creature

Sam, at age three, has little sponge eggs that you drop in warm water, where they hatch into little sponge animals. He has decided he will hatch one a day to make them last. He drives me crazy asking, "Is it the next day yet?" but sticks to his plan. On the third day two little horses come out attached by their noses.

Sam: What is it?

Me: (Needing it to be good.) Oh look, honey, it's a mommy and a baby horse.

Sam: No, it's not. You can't even see their faces.

Me: Yes, you can. See, they're kissing.

Sam: I don't like them.

Me: (Getting desperate.) I could draw their noses on with a pen.

Sam: I will never like them!

Me: (Foolishly persisting.) I could cut them apart with scissors so their faces will be easier to see.

Sam: *I WILL NEVER, NEVER LIKE THEM! THEY ARE BAD!!*

Me: (Finally seeing the light.) Oh, I see. You don't like the way their faces are squished together.

Sam: Yeah. I'm going to play with the penguins instead.

Why did I refuse to acknowledge his feelings for such a long time here? I just desperately wanted to make it better, fix the problem, protect my child from sadness and disappointment. Let's be honest, I wanted to protect *myself* from his sad emotions! Who enjoys a wailing child? But he just as desperately needed his disappointment to be heard before he could move on to happier feelings.

Here's another time Sam was disappointed and I had trouble accepting his feelings at first.

Where in the World Is (the Video Tape of) Carmen Sandiego

In this story, Dan is five and Sam is three.

Me: Dan, I taped *Bill Nye the Science Guy* for you.

Sam: Did you tape *Carmen Sandiego* for me?

Me: No.

Sam: Oh no! (Starts crying.)

Me: You didn't ask me to tape it. Dan *asked* me to tape *Bill Nye*.

(How many times has a nice reasonable explanation like that to a crying child worked for you?)

Sam: (Continues to cry, doesn't go for my logic.)

Me: (Irritated with him for being so whiny.) Sam, it's on every day of the week. You can see it tomorrow.

Sam: (Cries harder, heading for total meltdown.)

Me: (Switching gears.) Boy, you sound *so* disappointed! You really like that show a lot!

Sam: (Stops crying.) It's my favorite show.

Me: Tell me what you like about it.

Sam: I like the way the dancers flip around, and the machines make smoke, and they have to catch the bad guy. It's so cool.

And we proceed to have a nice civilized conversation about the coolness of Carmen Sandiego.

Why again, with all that I know, was it initially hard for me to just accept the darn feeling? Well, since you're asking, I'll tell you! I was sure my son was having an outsized reaction to a trivial matter. To me, a missed TV show does not qualify as worthy of a meltdown. But a child's emotions are just as real and important to him as our grown-up emotions are to us. The best way to help a child "get over it" is to help him go through it.

Here is one more story where I found it very challenging to accept the emotion.

Block Wars

I have that familiar sinking feeling as I watch my one-year-old, Sam, approach my three-year-old, Dan, who is building with blocks. Dan takes a guarding position.

Me: Dan, let the baby have a few blocks. He just wants to play with you.

Dan: No, no, I'm making something.

Me: Come on, Dan, he'll just play with them for a minute. You know how babies are.

Sam is upon the blocks. Dan shoves him and he falls down, wailing.

Me: Dan, what is the matter with you? Now you made the baby cry!

Clearly this is not a self-esteem-enhancing conversation. The good thing about being a parent is that if you blow it the first time, you almost always get another chance. In this particular case the same basic scenario recurred several hundred times, so I had ample opportunity to practice. Here I am in a finer moment:

Dan guarding blocks, baby approaching . . .

Dan: No! No! No!
Me (acknowledging and identifying his feelings): Oh no, here you are working on something special and the giant baby is coming to grab it. How frustrating!
Dan: Here, here, here!
(He swiftly tosses a handful of blocks to the floor to distract the baby and moves his creation to the coffee table.)
Me: Wow, you figured out what to do to keep that baby happy.

What made it so difficult for me to acknowledge my son's feelings the first time around? Well, because I was sure this desire to knock a sibling on his head over a few blocks was so wrong that I needed him to understand it *now*, and not indulge this aggressive impulse for even a split second. Yet it was only by showing respect for his strong feelings about his work that he was able to move past aggression. When I tried to dismiss his feelings, he had to fight his brother *and* his mother.

We do these things automatically—protect against sad emotions, dismiss what we see as trivial emotions, and discourage angry emotions. We don't want to reinforce negative feelings. To acknowledge them seems counterintuitive.

You may be wondering, "Isn't there a time when we have to explain to the child why he must do something, and don't children need to be told to respect other people's feelings?"

The answer is YES . . . but we're not there yet. Without having their own feelings acknowledged first, children will be deaf to our finest explanations and most passionate entreaties. My pint-sized next-door neighbor illustrated this very eloquently the other day. I had promised to take care of little Jackie so that her mother could get some important paperwork done.

Babysitting Failure

> **Jackie (three years old):** I want to go home.
>
> **Me:** You just got here. Let's stay in the yard for a while. We can play on the swings.
>
> **Jackie:** NO! Go home!
>
> **Me:** Your mom has to get some work done. We can have fun over here.
>
> **Jackie:** NO! (She runs back to her own house.)
>
> **Me (calling her mother):** Is Jackie okay?
>
> **Jackie's mom:** She's fine.
>
> **Me:** I'm sorry it didn't work out. Did she say why she wouldn't stay?

Jackie's mom: She just told me, "Joanna said, 'BLAH BLAH BLAH BLAH BLAH!'"

Hey, how dare she? I'm a communications expert!

But when I didn't acknowledge her feelings, all she heard of my effort to persuade her to stay was "Blah blah blah blah blah."

Children depend on us to name their feelings so that they can find out who they are. If we don't, our unspoken message is: "You don't mean what you say, you don't know what you know, you don't feel what you feel, you can't trust your own senses."

Children need us to validate their feelings so they can become grown-ups who know who they are and what they feel. We are also laying the groundwork for a person who can respect and not dismiss the needs and feelings of other people.

Okay, fine, can we move on now? you ask. *We need chapter two already!* I'm not going to insist that you stay here in chapter one. Skip ahead if you'd like. But I'm going to linger here a bit longer. This idea of accepting feelings is so big, so important, that I'm going to explore some variations on the theme before I join you up ahead in the next chapter. I'm betting that if I can spend more time accepting feelings in difficult situations, a lot of my conflicts will dissolve without even glancing at chapter two!

Here are some more ideas about how to make this powerful tool of accepting feelings work for you.

Sit on those "buts."

It is so very tempting to follow up a perfectly lovely statement accepting a feeling with the word *BUT*. We worry that our kids will think we approve of their negative behavior when we acknowledge a negative feeling. So we sabotage our good intentions by saying:

"I understand you are furious, BUT you cannot hit your sister!"

"I hear how upset you are about your brother wrecking your Legos, BUT you have to understand, he's just a baby."

"I know you want to stay and play, BUT it's time to pick up your brother."

"I know you're in the mood for chocolate chip cookies, BUT we don't have any in the house."

"But" takes away the gift you've just given. It's like saying, "I hear how you feel and now I am going to explain to you why that feeling is wrong." Imagine hearing someone say, "I am so sorry your mother passed away. But hey, she's dead, you're alive, tears won't change it; let's move on!"

If you feel a *but* bubbling up, you can replace it with this handy sentence starter:

The problem is . . .

"It can be irritating to have to deal with a baby when you're trying to build a spaceship! *The problem is*, babies don't understand about Legos."

"How disappointing to find an empty box when you're in the mood for cookies! *The problem is,* it's too late to go shopping."

The problem is suggests that there is a problem that can be solved without sweeping away the feelings. Perhaps you will find a table where you can set up the Legos out of reach. Maybe you will add cookies in big red letters to the shopping list and stick it on the refrigerator.

Toni, a no-nonsense mom in one of my parenting workshops, complained that she wasn't happy with this phrase. "It's not always a problem!" she protested. "Why does everything have to be a big problem? So, there are no cookies right this second. Get over it!"

I had to think. *Darn it, that's my go-to solution and this woman is rejecting it. I have to accept her feelings about it. I'd better come up with something else quick.* Thankfully a phrase my mother used came to me. "Ahh, try this," I offered.

Even though you know . . .

"*Even though you know* it's too late to go shopping for cookies, you'd sure like to have some right now!"

"*Even though you know* it's time to pick up your brother at the bus stop, it can be exasperating to have to leave the playground when you're having fun." (As a bonus, you've taught him a new vocabulary word!)

Even though you know is not off-putting because it gives your child credit for understanding the problem, while at the same time letting him know that you empathize with how strongly he feels.

TOOL #2: Acknowledge Feelings with Writing

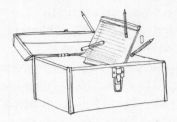

Seeing their feelings and desires written down in black and white can be very powerful, even for prereaders. Carry paper and pencil when you go shopping so that you can add to your child's "wish list." It will come in handy when you are on that unavoidable, dreaded shopping trip to the toy store for a birthday gift for *somebody else's child*, and your own child is presented with thousands of temptations and absolutely no understanding of financial limitations. Instead of explaining to your child why she should not whine for a new toy because she just had her birthday last month and she shouldn't be acting like such a spoiled brat (has *that* speech ever worked for anyone?) you can write down everything she wants on her wish list. It is satisfying to a kid to have a physical list of her desires. And you can keep it posted on your bulletin board and refer to it when holidays and birthdays come up.

"But won't that contribute to their feeling that every desire must be gratified?" asks Toni, the straight-shooter in my group.

"On the contrary," I countered. "How many times have we given in and just bought some stupid thing we don't need to avoid a public tantrum? Writing down wishes is a different way to avoid a tantrum, without spoiling your child. Think of it as an opportunity to accept feelings while limiting actions."

Having their feelings acknowledged actually helps children accept that they can't always get what they want. In the toy store you can say, "Oh boy, that is a really cool unicorn! You like the sparkles on his mane . . . and the pink and orange stars on his rump. Let's write it down on your wish list." Who knows, maybe she'll save her allowance, or request it from Aunt Bertha on her birthday, or perhaps in a few weeks or months her tastes will change and it will drop off the list. The important thing is that she has a parent who listens to how she feels when she yearns for something, and that helps *her* develop the important life skill of deferred gratification.

And how about when one child needs something and we have another child without any need. Do we spend the extra money resentfully just to preserve the peace? Put up with hurt feelings and wailing? With this skill, we can honestly empathize:

"Even though you know you don't need new PJs, it's still hard to see your brother get a new pair. Let's write down the colors you like so we'll know what to buy when you need them."

After a session on acknowledging feelings, Michael, a dad who is almost always eager to experiment, reported back to the group.

Michael's Story: Cookie Magic

My two-year-old, Kara, wanted chocolate chip cookies. I wrote the word *COOKIE* on a piece of paper for her inside a circle that was supposed to look like a cookie. She added the dots for chips. She was amazingly content to carry around that piece of paper. It was like the word was a magical talisman. Usually she doesn't give up when she wants something, no matter how many times we tell her we just don't have it in the house.

TOOL #3: Acknowledge Feelings with Art

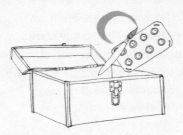

Sometimes words, written or spoken, are not enough to express a strong feeling. If you are feeling creative, try art. You don't have to be Rembrandt—stick figures will do.

Maria is the mother of one-year-old Isabel and three-year-old Benjamin, a child who has major meltdowns many times a day.

Maria's Story: Train Wreck

Benjamin is obsessed with trains these days. He loves to make elaborate tracks and crossings and push the trains uphill and down, but sometimes the trains or the tracks fall apart. It's amazing how quickly Benjamin can melt down into a major tantrum, and then the trains and tracks go flying. The other day I was at the train table and sure enough, the trains crested the hill and started falling apart on the way down. There was this pause, and I could see Benjamin was about to lose it, but since I had just taken the workshop I did *not* say "It's okay, we can fix it, don't worry." That's what I'd normally say, and then he'd scream and throw things. This time I said, "This is frustrating! You don't like the trains coming apart."

He looked at me and didn't scream.

I had a blackboard next to the table, so I grabbed it and said, "Let's draw how you feel."

I drew a sad face. "Is this how you feel?"

He nodded. I made a tear coming out of the eye and he said, "Draw another one."

I drew more tears. He reached for the chalk and I could see him get a little glimmer in his eye. He drew some gigantic tears. Then I drew another face that wasn't quite as sad. Benjamin had the hint of a smile at this point so I drew a happy face. He started giggling. We went back to playing with the trains. Tantrum averted.

Anton is on the autism spectrum, and it can be particularly hard for him to have his expectations thwarted. His mother, Anna, shared this story with the group.

Anna's Story: The Tragic Nap

I had promised Anton that we would stop at this really cool playground on the way home from his aunt and uncle's house. But we left late and by the time we passed the playground Anton was asleep in the car and I certainly wasn't going to wake him. I was hoping he would sleep through the night, but of course he woke up when his dad was carrying him in from the car. When he realized that he missed the playground, he started crying and saying "You lied, you lied!"

I tried to be patient. I explained to him that he was sleeping, but that made him madder. Finally I said, "You really like that playground. Even though you were sleeping, you still wanted to play there. You wanted us to wake you up!"

"Yeah!"

I grabbed a piece of paper and a pencil and I started drawing. "What's your favorite thing at the playground?"

"Swings," he said, so I drew them.

"Put in the big slide." I drew that, too. He drew a snowball on the slide.

"How about the bridge?"

"Yeah!"

I drew that. Then I put a cat on the bridge, and a boy. He wanted to tape the picture on his wall, so we put it over his bed. It was a good save to the evening!

Michael was enthusiastic about giving the art solution a try. He came in with this story.

Michael's Story: Fire Balls

I went to wake up four-year-old Jamie for preschool. He burrowed down under the covers and said he was not getting up, not going to school, he hated school!

I gave him a little back rub and said, "I can see you are *not* ready to get up. I'm going downstairs to make breakfast, and you can come down when you're ready. I'll have a paper and crayons for you so you can draw me a picture of how bad school is."

In about five minutes Jamie came pounding down the stairs and flung himself into his chair at the kitchen table. "Where's the paper and crayons?"

Oops, I guess I didn't really believe he would go for it. I quickly grabbed the supplies for him. He started drawing furiously. I looked at it and asked him, "What are these big red things bouncing all over the page?"

"Those are the fireballs at the school," he said emphatically.

He sounded so convincing, I actually asked him if there were really fireballs at the school.

"NOoooo!" he answered as scornfully as a four-year-old can say that word.

"Then he ate breakfast and went to school happily. Never found out anything else about those fireballs."

Sometimes pure art is not enough. Maria's three-year-old son Benjamin often gets so angry he hits himself and his mom. Here's what happened when she invited him to draw his feelings.

Maria's Story: Performance Art

Benny was mad because he didn't get to go with his dad this weekend. He was moping around and kicking things. I got out a pad and some crayons and said, "Show me how mad you are."

Benny said "No!" and threw the crayons down. It wasn't working but I needed a story for the group, so I kept on trying.

I took the crayon myself and said, "You are this mad!" I made angry marks, kind of attacking the paper. The crayon ripped through, which really got Benny's attention. He grabbed the crayon and started slashing at the paper. That was satisfying to him. Then he grabbed the paper in both hands and began to rip it into little pieces. I kept saying things like, "Wow, you are this mad!"

When the paper was completely shredded, he looked at the pile and started giggling. "Look how mad I was, Mommy."

"Yeah, you were *really* mad. That poor paper. It looks like a tiger tore it up."

He walked off and asked for a snack. I gave him some apple slices. Every once in a while for the rest of the day he walked over to the pile of paper and said, "Look how mad I was!" with great delight.

VERY IMPORTANT POINT

Match the emotion. Be dramatic!

Some of the parents reported that when they tried to acknowledge feelings, their kids seemed to get even more furious. It just wasn't working. I asked them to give me an example.

Toni said, "I told my son, Thomas, 'You seem angry.' Thomas reacted with annoyance, 'I don't *seem* angry. I AM angry!'"

When I heard Toni's calm soothing tone, I said, "Aha! Your words are telling me you understand, but your tone is telling me to calm down. There is nothing so infuriating as being told to calm down when you're angry." Sarah, another mom in the group, immediately agreed. "Those are two words my husband is *never* allowed to say to me. If he dares, I will rip his head off!"

"Imagine this. You call me and say, 'What a horrible day. The kids were totally hyper and it was pouring rain outside, so they were climbing the walls. I finally got it together to take them out to the movies, and it turned out the paper had the wrong time so we had to go home and everyone was whining and crying.'"

In the most irritatingly calm, soothing, singsong voice I could muster I said, "Oh, you seem frustrated. It's okay to feel frustrated with your kids sometimes."

The group reacted with rolling eyes and threatening shakes of their fists.

"Okay, okay, give me another chance! Is this better?" This time I spoke with real emotion, "Oh my gosh, how *frustrating*! Sounds like one of those horrible days when everything is against you."

This time I heard the word "Yes!" muttered by several people, and I felt a little safer. Always good to have the tools to soothe an angry crowd.

"That would at least be an acceptable start," snapped Toni. "I don't like all this sugary, fake stuff."

It's important to be genuine when you acknowledge feelings. Nobody likes to feel manipulated. Reach inside and find that emotion. Be real!

My group went home and went to work. The next week they reported some big changes.

Maria's Story: All Terrain Bicycle

You already know that Benjamin melts down over the littlest things. I realized that I often take this kind of fake soothing tone with him out of fear that I'll send him over the edge. It never works! Last night he had a meltdown over having to put his new big-boy bike away at dinnertime. The way he was screaming you'd think he had a life-threatening injury. This time instead of trying to calm him I got loud. I said dramatically, "You want to keep riding your bike!"

He said, "Yes," with a trembling lip, holding back tears.

I said, "Who cares if it's dinnertime? I bet you'd be happy to eat while riding!"

Another "yes" from Benny.

"I bet you'd like to ride that bike in bed when it's time to go to sleep! You'd ride it in your dreams."

"Yes" again, but now he'd stopped crying and was looking at me with curiosity.

"You'd be happy to ride your bike underwater at your swimming lesson tomorrow!"

Now he was laughing. And just like that, our little guy came in to dinner.

Michael's Story: Born Free

My wife, Jan, has trouble dressing our daughter in the morning. Kara is only two, but she can really put up a fight. She'll twist and wail because she likes to be naked. It's a real wrestling match. Jan tries to gently acknowledge her feelings and explain why she has to be dressed to go to preschool, but it hasn't helped.

After our last session Jan decided to try a more dramatic tactic. I heard her yell, "You like to be a nudie!! Nude all night and nude all day! Nude in the house, nude in the car, nude at school!"

Then I heard Kara yelling, "NUDIE, NUDIE, NUDIE!"

I guess Jan was putting her clothes on the whole time because she came downstairs fully clothed and Jan said it was a breeze to dress her.

TOOL #4: Give in Fantasy What You Cannot Give in Reality

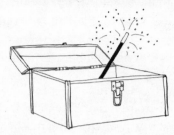

Sometimes a child wants something that it is impossible to provide. Your first impulse is usually to explain *why* she cannot, or should not, or must not have her heart's desire. That's the rational approach.

And how does that work for you? Not well, you say? Your kid isn't going for your logic? As soon as you begin your explanation she covers her ears and screams? You are not alone! A child in emotional distress is unlikely to be soothed by well-reasoned discourse.

A terrific tool for moments like these is to give a child in fantasy what you can't give in reality. When your child is crying in the car because he's thinking about the candy you didn't buy him at the mall, it's not the right time for a lecture on tooth decay. Admit it! Candy tastes good! *Wouldn't it be nice if we could eat candy every day and nothing bad would happen to our teeth? What would we have for breakfast? M&M's or lollipops? And how about lunch?* Encourage your kids to chime in. I recall a memorable ride home when my three boys happily imagined a world where the car itself was made out of sweets and even the road was paved with candy. You could take a rest stop and nibble on the bumper, or crumble off a little piece of pavement if you felt like having a snack.

Sarah is a preschool teacher in our group. She is also the mother of seven-year-old Sophia, five-year-old Jake, and Mia, who just turned three. She reminisced about a stressful time in her life when fantasy pulled her through.

Sarah's Story: The Pink House

We had been renting a one-bedroom apartment and now with a second child, space was getting tight. We were finally making the big move. We had closed on a house. We were excited but anxious because we were stretched to our limit with the closing costs, and we were second guessing ourselves all the way to the bank. As I was driving Sophia to preschool one morning she started whining, "I hate the new house!"

I know that little kids don't like change, and that it was natural for her to be upset about the move, but that didn't stop my instant irritation. I snapped at her to stop whining. Then I launched into a lecture about how the old apartment was way too small, and in a bad neighborhood, and in the new house she would have her own bedroom.

I went on and on until I glanced over and noticed that she was crying. That brought me up short. "Boy, you really don't like the new house. You would choose a different house."

She said, "YEAH!"

"What if you could choose any house you wished? What would your house be like?"

"PINK!"

"Ohhh, a pink house."

"Yes, it would have pink walls, and a pink roof, and a pink bed."

"How about some pink grass on the lawn?" I offered.

"Moo-oom, no such thing as pink grass. But there could be pink flowers."

We spent the rest of the ride happily listing all the things in the house that could be pink. The mood was saved. Later on we did buy some pink sheets for her bed. I was able to deliver a happy child to school, instead of a miserable, weepy one.

At the next session, Sarah shared this story from her preschool class with the group.

Sarah's Story: Endless Hours

Last week in our block room a child was reluctant to begin cleaning up. Instead of giving him the standard clean-up lecture, I acknowledged his feelings by saying, "It's frustrating to have to clean up when you're not finished with what you're building." He just looked at me. So I tried giving him a wish for more time in fantasy. "I wish you had a hundred more hours to play."

He responded, "I wish I had a hundred million billion more hours to play!" Then he started putting blocks away. Amazing.

Maria's Story: A Penny Saved

Benjamin found a penny at the park and put it in his pocket. We were driving home and he wanted the penny, but he couldn't get it out of his pocket because he was strapped into his carseat. He was starting to scream and cry about it. Normally I would have told him, "It's okay, we can get it when we get home," which would not have helped. Or I would have tried to fish out a coin to give him while I was driving, which would have endangered the people in the next lane. But this time I remembered the idea of giving a wish in fantasy. I said, "That is so frustrating! You know what I wish? I wish I had a button right *here*." I pointed to a spot on the dashboard.

Benjamin stared at the spot. "And whenever I pushed that button, heaps and heaps of pennies would come pouring out over here." I pointed to the light in the ceiling of the car.

"Not just pennies, but every kind of coin, even coins from other countries, and they would all fall right into your lap. And you would have so much money, you could buy anything you wanted. What would you buy with all that money?"

"A really big teddy bear!" Benjamin said.

"How big? As big as you?"

"Yeah!"

At this point he was really into the story and very happy. He didn't lose it over the penny, which is pretty amazing if you know my son!

 **Resist the urge to ask questions of a distressed child.**

You may have noticed that we don't respond to a child's distress by asking questions: Are you sad? Did that make you angry? Why are you crying? Even gentle questions can feel like an interrogation when a child is in distress. He may not know why he is upset. He may not be able to express it clearly in words. Often when questioned like this, even adults can feel threatened. We have the feeling we are being asked to justify how we feel and that our explanation may not live up to the asker's standards. (*Oh, is* that *all it is? You shouldn't be crying about* that!) By making a statement instead of asking a question, we accept the feelings without requiring any justification. You don't have to figure out the cause of the feelings in order to empathize. You can say, "You seem sad." "Something upset you." Or even just, "Something happened." That kind of phrase invites your child to talk if she feels like it, but also gives comfort if she doesn't feel like talking.

Toni, mother of six-year-old Thomas and four-year-old twins, Ella and Jenna, was skeptical but willing to give it a try.

Toni's Story: The Gauntlet

For the past few weeks, Thomas has been cheerful in the car on the way to school, but once we get there, he sits on the curb and refuses to go in. When I ask him what's wrong he says, "Nothing!" Sometimes he'll jump up and run in as soon as one of his classmates arrives.

Thomas isn't very big on answering questions when he's upset, but I really wanted to find out what was happening. I waited until after dinner when he was in a relaxed mood to say, "I notice you're not too happy when we get to school. Something makes you not want to go in."

Thomas nodded slowly. Then he explained that if he goes in at the same time as the second graders they call him a baby, and he is *not* a baby. (He really prides himself on being the big boy in the family.) He likes to wait until all the second graders are in, or at least wait for a friend so he doesn't have to go in alone. I didn't realize it was so complicated to get into school. I have more patience for him in the morning now that I understand what's going on in his head.

Sarah's Story: . . . And Then What?

Jake came in all red-faced and teary after playing with the neighbor children in their backyard. Clearly he was very upset. In the past I would ask him, "What's wrong?" or "What happened?" And I always got the standard responses, "I don't know," or "Nothing."

This time, instead of questioning him, I tried making a statement to show I understood how he felt. I said, "Jake, you look mad and sad at the same time." Well, that opened a floodgate. He told me a long, complicated story about one of the neighbors pushing him off the swing, and then there were some "bad words" like *stupid* and *dummy* exchanged, and then there was threatening with a stick. He went on and on and then he looked at me and, well . . . I didn't know what to say next!

The problem is that being a parent doesn't end at the third frame like the comics in this book. Don't panic. Read on.

TOOL #5: Acknowledge Feelings with (Almost) Silent Attention

(Don't just say something. Sit there!)

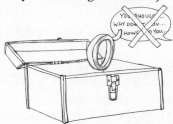

This brings us to a small and unimpressive-looking tool of great power. The tool of (almost) silent attention. You can continue to listen to your child, responding with an empathic, "Ugh!," "Mmm," "Ooh," or "Huh." Often that's all you need. By lending an attentive ear and firmly squeezing our lips together, or letting out a sympathetic grunt, we can help our children find their own way through their feelings. The gift we can give them is to not get in the way of their process by jumping in with our reactions: advice, questions, corrections. The important thing is to give them our full attention and trust them to work it out.

Sarah reported back on this tool.

Sarah's Story: Sibling Squabbling Zen

Well, I did it! My seven-year-old daughter came in just before bedtime to complain about her younger brother . . . again. I have very little patience left at this time of night. All I can think is "Can't it be over?" He had come into her room, he had touched her toys without asking, he had teased her, and so on. Usually I try to tell her that he's just a little kid and she should be more patient, which results in her repeating the charges in a louder and more emotional voice. This time I just said, "Mmm ... ugh ... oh ... I see ..." right out of the script. It was nothing short of miraculous. After about five minutes she said, "Okay, I'm going to read now," and kissed me goodnight. I didn't have to solve anything. I feel freed!

Michael's Story: Very Bad Day

Jamie came home from school and said, "I had a horrible day and everybody hates me." Normally I would have argued with him. How can a preschooler have a horrible day when all they do is play games and paint and have story time? It's not like they have to fill out tax forms or get stuck in traffic! And it's not true that everybody hates him. I would have started listing all the people who love him: his parents, sisters, grandma and grandpa, friends.

This time I just gave my most sympathetic "Ugh" and put my arm around him. He sat down and told me that his friend Max was really annoying. Again I bit my lip so as not to remind him that he could be annoying too sometimes, and that Max was his best friend. He proceeded to tell me a long, sad story about how he and Max used to play Star Wars together, but now Max was playing Ghostbusters with a new friend and didn't want to play with him anymore. And that he, Jamie, didn't want to play Ghostbusters, because that was stupid, and how do you play that game anyway, and now all the kids are playing it. He talked himself out and then wandered away for a snack.

I was amazed because he's never talked to me like that before. I had no idea preschoolers had such complicated social lives. I felt sad for him, but I think he'll be able to work it out. He was certainly much cheerier after telling me all his woes.

• • •

It was the end of a session and we had almost run out of time, but Toni insisted on telling this story before we left.

Toni's Story: Sisters Are Doing It for Themselves

We were coming back from getting take-out from a burger place and Ella really wanted to start eating in the car. We were all tired and Ella's whining was driving me nuts. I explained that she could have the food just as soon as we got home, but we were not going to have it in the car because of the mess. We were going back and forth and getting nowhere when her twin sister, Jenna, said, "I know, Ella. Sometimes it's hard to wait."

It was a watershed moment. I said, "You're so right! Sometimes it *is* hard to wait, isn't it?"

Ella said, "Yeah. It's hard to wait."

Things were calmer for the rest of the drive home. Jenna understood that her sister needed empathy, not reasoning, and it was just funny that a four-year-old knew what to do when her own mother didn't. I consoled myself that she was modeling an empathetic response from me on a previous day. They already know at age four what I'm just learning now!

At the end of this chapter you'll find a handy reminder page to copy and stick on your favorite reading surface. Sure, you've done all this reading, but that doesn't mean that you can think straight when you're in the trenches, under fire. When the baby is crying, the milk is spilled, the toast is burning, and the dog is running off with the diaper, you'll need to be able to review your options at a single glance!

INSTEAD OF DISMISSING THE FEELING

ACKNOWLEDGE FEELINGS WITH WORDS

Tools for Handling Emotions

ACKNOWLEDGE FEELINGS WITH WRITING

ACKNOWLEDGE FEELINGS WITH ART

GIVE IN FANTASY

INSTEAD OF LECTURING...

EMPATHIZE WITH A WORD OR SOUND

REMINDER: Tools for Handling Emotions

1. Acknowledge Feelings with Words

"You were looking forward to that playdate. How disappointing!"

"It can be so frustrating when train tracks fall apart."

2. Acknowledge Feelings with Writing

"Oh no! We don't have the ingredients we need! Let's make a shopping list."

"You really want that underwater Lego set. Let's write that down on your wish list."

3. Acknowledge Feelings with Art

"You seem so sad." (Draw a stick figure with big tears, or simply hand over a crayon or pencil.)

"You are this angry!" (Make angry lines or rip and crumple paper.)

4. Give in Fantasy What You Cannot Give in Reality

"I wish we had a million billion more hours to play."

5. Acknowledge Feelings with (Almost) Silent Attention

"Ugh!" "Mmm." "Ooh." "Huh."

- *All* feelings can be accepted. *Some* actions must be limited!

- Sit on those "buts." Substitute: "The problem is . . ." *or* "Even though you know . . ."

- Match the emotion. Be dramatic!

- Resist the urge to ask questions of a distressed child.

Chapter Two

Tools for Engaging Cooperation ... Feelings
Schmeelings, She Has to Brush Her Teeth

—Getting kids to *do* what they have to *do*

Joanna

Enough with all the talk about feelings. It's lovely to know
we're enhancing our children's confidence and sense of self,
but does that actually get us through the day? Not entirely.
We have to get our kids to *do* things—get in the bathtub;
brush teeth; sit still so I can get your shoes on; climb into the
carseat ... *now*, or we're going to be late; go to bed, *PLEASE*!

And sometimes, it's more important to *not* do things—
don't hit your sister; stop throwing your food; don't take those
shoes off when I just got them on; don't stick your fork in the
electrical outlet; don't eat the lollipop that just fell in the dirt;
stop pulling the dog's tail; don't climb the refrigerator—those
are shelves, not steps. Endless reminding, nagging, cajoling,
demanding. That's the reality of being a parent.

So our kids get told what to do. All day long. *That's* the
reality of being a kid. And they should listen, because we're in
charge and we're just trying to do what's best for them, and
keep them from killing themselves, or at least protect them
from stinkiness, rotted teeth, malnutrition, and exhaustion.

The problem is, nobody likes to be ordered around. A
parent in one of my groups put it succinctly: "Even if I *want*

43

to do something, as soon as somebody tells me to do it, I don't want to do it anymore."

I recently experienced this phenomenon of irresistible contrariness as an adult, when I saw a stack of books at my local library with a note taped to the wall behind them. The note read, DO NOT TOUCH THESE BOOKS. I presumed there was a reasonable explanation. No doubt the books had not been put into the system yet. Still, I couldn't help myself. I veered toward the stack, stuck out my finger, and *touched* the books. "Hah, so there!" I felt a spark of childish glee.

It's human nature. We're stuck with it, and our children are no different. We resist being told what to do. Direct orders provoke direct opposition. When we give children commands, we're working against ourselves. Where we had hoped to inspire obedience, we've just stirred up rebellion in their little hearts.

I like to start this workshop session with a few *commands* for the participants:

"Hey, you two in the back . . . No talking!"

"Don't touch those books! Do you see your name on them?"

I toss in some *blame and accusation:*

"Who left this bag in the doorway? Someone's going to trip on it."

And on to some *name calling:*

"You forgot to bring a pencil again? You're such an airhead."

"Don't interrupt. You're being rude!"

A few *warnings*:

>"Don't balance your laptop on the edge of your knees like that. You're going to drop it."

>"Don't move the chairs while you're on your cell phone. Pay attention to what you're doing or you're going to hurt somebody."

Some *sarcasm*:

>"One blue sock and one green sock. Nice! Did you unplug your brain this morning?"

A few *rhetorical questions*:

>"Why do you keep your bag in such a mess that you can't find anything?"

>"Why can't you wait your turn to speak?"

A *threat*:

>"Listen, people, if these side conversations don't stop immediately, we're not going to get through all the material and I'm going to have to keep you here for an extra half hour."

And of course, a *lecture*:

>"You're ten minutes late again. This is becoming a pattern with you. Do you realize what happens when you're late? You're holding up the whole class. Everyone else made the effort to get here on time. Some of us are paying babysitters so we can sit here waiting for you. How would you feel if someone did that to you? You know, being punctual is a life skill. And it's a skill you better learn if you want to be successful in life. You need to start making a little more effort. Get yourself organized ahead of time. Don't leave everything until the last minute."

The group stares at me murderously. "So," I force myself to ask cheerfully, "is anyone feeling cooperative?"

The staring continues. I'm getting the silent treatment. I'm feeling a little uneasy, so I try a different tack. "Do we really talk to kids this way?"

Finally someone speaks, "Sure we do!"

"Can anyone think of examples of what we actually say to children?"

Now the floodgates open. Here are some of the responses from the group.

Commands:

"Is that your bag? Well, pick it up. Now!" "Clean up those blocks." "Stop making that noise." "Turn off the TV." "Leave your brother alone." "Wash your hands." "Don't touch the stove." "You just interrupted her. Say you're sorry!"

Blaming and accusing:

"If you had screwed the top on the apple juice first instead of trying to grab the last cupcake, it never would have spilled."

Name calling:

"Hey, come help with this cleanup. You helped make the mess. Don't be so lazy." "Your friends always share their toys when you visit them. Don't be selfish." "You're pulling the cat's tail. That's just plain mean."

Warnings:

"Careful, you're going to get hit by a car." "Stop wiggling, you'll fall off that stool." "You'll make yourself sick if you eat all that candy." "Watch it, you'll burn yourself!" "Get down from there, you're going to fall!"

Sarcasm:

"You left your backpack at your friend's house? That was smart." "You knocked down your little sister just so you could be first? That was nice."

Rhetorical questions:

"Why would you pinch the baby like that?" "Why did you throw the ball in the kitchen when I just told you not to?" "Is that what you're supposed to be doing right now?" "What is the matter with you?"

Lectures:

"It's not nice to grab. You wouldn't want anybody to grab something from *you*, would you? Then you shouldn't grab from anyone else. Nobody's going to want to play with you if you keep this up. You need to learn to be more patient."

Threats:

"If you don't put these toys away by the time I count to ten, I'm throwing them in the garbage." "If you don't get in the car right now, I'm leaving without you." "If you don't finish your vegetables there'll be no dessert." "If you don't get your seat belt on and stop fussing I'm not taking you anywhere." "Get your helmet on now, or the bike is going back in the garage."

The group was a little taken aback by their ability to compile such an impressive list so easily. But they weren't ready to throw out the entire arsenal.

Toni was the first to protest. "What you're calling a threat, I call a consequence. I'm just telling my child what will happen if he doesn't listen. He needs to know!"

"It's so tempting to toss in a threat," I agreed. "It does seem kind of, umm, informational. *If you do this, I'll do that.* The problem with a threat is that it can come awfully close to sounding like a dare.

When a parent says, 'If you throw sand one more time, you're going straight home!'

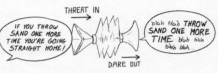

the child doesn't seem to hear the whole sentence. What the child seems to hear is, 'Throw sand . . . *one more time!*'"

The threat has become an irresistible challenge.

"What if you use the word *please*?" Sarah asked. "That's simply good manners. I tell my children what they need to do, but I say it politely."

Sometimes, to soften the sting of an order, we toss in a *please* at the end. The problem here is similar to that of wings on an ostrich. They seem like the right sort of attachment, but nevertheless, that bird is not going to fly. It's just too heavy. *Please* is best reserved for standard etiquette like, "Please pass the salt." When you "ask" a child to *please* hold still . . . or get in his carseat . . . or put away his blocks . . . you're not really making a gentle request. You're not truly willing to accept "No thank you!" as an answer.

"If I started the session by telling you all to 'Please sit still and stop talking,' how many of you would feel warm and cooperative?" I asked the group.

No one raised a finger.

Someone sighed. The feeling in the room was clear. *Everything we say is wrong!* It was time to move on before these people got too frustrated with me and staged a rebellion of their own. I plunged ahead.

"So what *can* we do when we need the cooperation of a small, illogical, and unruly creature such as a human child? If we can't tell him what to do, what's left?"

TOOL #1: Be Playful

The first tool I have for you is not one that can be used in all weather. You have to feel at least partly sunny. Even though it's a part-time tool, I'm offering it to you as a first resort because of its unusually powerful effect. Let's call it the art of being playful. What's that, you say? You don't *feel* playful when children are being uncooperative? And what does that word mean, anyway? Isn't it a bit vague?

All valid criticisms. And yet, if you try it, you just might find you like it. So *if* you're in the mood, read on.

One technique, sure to be a hit with the seven and under set, is to **make an inanimate object talk**.

Lonely shoes can whine, "I feel cold and empty. Won't somebody put a nice warm foot in me?" Hungry toy boxes can demand, "Feed me blocks! I want the green crunchy ones!" Cups can screech, "Don't leave me out here by myself! I gotta get in the sink with my buddies." Toothbrushes can use their best tough-guy voice, "Lemme in dere. I think I seen

a germ hiding behind
dat molar." All of these
clamoring objects will
bring a smile to a child's
face and a more willing
attitude toward participating
in the mundane chores of life.

Another playful technique is to **turn
a boring task into a challenge or a game**.

Instead of, "Look at this mess. You're supposed to put your
dirty clothes in the basket."

Try, "How many seconds do you think it will take to toss
all your dirty clothes in the laundry basket? . . . Twenty?
Oh dear, I don't think so. That is way too much work to
do in just twenty seconds. Okay, I guess it's worth a try.
Ready . . . set . . . go! . . . Holy cow, you did it in ten! You
beat the clock."

Instead of, "Get in the car now. I don't want to have to ask
you again."

Try, "We have to get all the way from the door to the car.
Let's try hopping. It won't be easy!"

Instead of, "If you don't get into pajamas right now, there
will be no story time."

Try, "Do you think you can get your PJs on with your eyes
closed?"

Beyond talking objects and making a game out of a chore, the
field is wide open. Experiment with your silly side. Instead
of just telling a child what to do in your regular voice, talk

like a duck, or a sports announcer, or your child's favorite cartoon character, or sing it with a country twang. Devise ways of leaving a friend's house that involve avoiding lava, quicksand, or alligators. Instead of telling a classroom of preschoolers to sit still and be quiet, have them freeze like statues. Tell them they're "as still as an iceberg," or "as quiet as a little mouse hiding in the grass from a cat." Give them an "energy pill" (a single raisin carefully placed in the palm) to give them the strength to clean up. Almost any tedious task can be transformed if it's infused with the spirit of play.

The group looked at me with various expressions, ranging from intrigued to annoyed. Michael was smiling. I could tell he was already coming up with a wild idea. Maria looked a little bit exasperated. "Aren't there times when a child should just do what his parent tells him to? Do I really have to make every little thing into a game? You're making me feel tired!"

In my experience, if you can muster up a little playfulness, it actually takes less energy than having to deal with all the whining and resistance you get from a direct order. It also sets a nice tone. Even if orders are more efficient, the mood will be brighter with playfulness. It makes people feel more loving and cooperative.

You're also teaching kids how to turn a tedious task into a pleasant activity. We can grumble and mope over a sink full of dirty dishes, or we can put on some lively music, work up the suds, and dance and sing our way through the mess. That's a valuable life skill.

Michael's Story: Clothing with Character

Kara hates to get dressed in the morning. Now my wife and I offer different characters to dress her. Roger

Robot (that's me) uses a mechanical voice and jerky motions. "This . . . arm . . . must . . . be . . . inserted . . . in . . . sleeve."

Then there's Kermit the frog, who talks in a Kermit voice. Mrs. Meanie (that's my wife) is rough and screechy: "What? A child without clothes? That is terrible! Get over here now!" Gentle Jennifer (also my wife) is extremely sweet and says things like, "Oh dear, could I possibly put this sock on your poor little foot. Oh, I'm so terribly sorry, I bumped your poor little toe with my nose." Silly Sally always gets it wrong and has to be corrected by my daughter. "Does this sleeve go over the toes? I think the sock should be on your ear, right?"

Obviously my wife's favorite character is Mrs. Meanie and unfortunately she doesn't get too many requests for that one. But Kara is excited to get dressed in the morning now. She doesn't run away from us anymore. That's maddening when we're running late, which is pretty much always.

Toni's Story: Fly Away Home

I've always had a heck of a time getting the twins out of the car and into school in the morning. They get engrossed in arguments with each other, they insist on counting each step they take, or picking up pebbles, whatever it takes to make us late. Last week they were talking about dragonflies, so I said, "Let's pretend we're a family of dragonflies and we're flying to our home in the classroom." We all spread our "wings" and "flew" through the parking lot and into school. It worked so well, I did it again the next day. Then we pretended to be butterflies, then ladybugs, then hawks. The next week, as soon as I got out of the car, the security guard in the parking lot raised his eyebrow at me and asked, "What are you this morning?" I felt a little embarrassed, pretending to fly in public, but hey, it beats yelling at the kids.

Maria's Story: The Very Hungry Nail Clipper

Benjamin always objects to having his fingernails clipped. He doesn't like to sit still. Last night I pretended the nail clippers were talking to him. "Oh Benjamin, I'm so hungry. Won't you let me have a little bite of your pinky nail?" He stuck out his little finger, and the nail clipper had a delicious snack: "Oh, thank you. Yum, yum! This is such a tasty little nail. May I have another one?" He stuck out his other fingers. Then he had a very serious conversation with the nail clippers about his dinosaurs while I finished clipping his nails. The nail clipper was very interested in the biting abilities of the vegetarian and carnivorous dinosaurs. Benjamin was happy to expound on his favorite topic.

TOOL #2: Offer a Choice

The second tool for engaging cooperation is to substitute a choice for a command. Choice, you ask? What choice? There is no choice. She has to get dressed, she's not going to school in her pajamas. He has to wash his hands, he's not eating a sandwich right after playing with frogs. She's not riding her bike without a helmet. It's simply not negotiable!

I'm not suggesting that you make uncomfortable compromises or that you put a three-year-old in charge of the whole show. I'm just saying that human beings, including small ones, like to have some input and control over their lives. There are plenty of options we can offer our children, short of handing over the car keys and the credit card.

Instead of, "Get in the car, now!"
Try, "Would you like to bring a toy or a snack for the ride?"
"Do you want to take giant steps to the car or do you want to skip to the car?"

Instead of, "If I have to tell you one more time to get into that tub . . ."
Try, "Do you want your bath with bubbles or boats?"
"Would you like to hop to the tub like a bunny, or crawl like a crab?"

Instead of, "Get your homework started. No more excuses!"
Try, "Would it be easier to get your homework over with right away and be free of it, or would you rather have a snack first?" "Do you want to do it in the kitchen while I cook dinner, or in your room where it's quiet?" One parent had great success with, "Do you want to do your homework on top of the table or under the table?" (I think you can guess which her daughter chose.)

Instead of, "Pajamas now!"
Try, "Do you want to put your pajamas on the regular way, or inside out?" "Do you want to jump five more times

before putting on your PJs, or ten? Okay, let's make them big ones. *ONE . . . TWO . . . THREE . . .*"

Each of these statements says to your child, "I see you as a person who can make decisions about your own life." And every time your child makes a small decision, she's getting valuable practice for some of the bigger decisions she'll be making down the road.

Joanna's Story: Choice Cuts

This choice thing doesn't always go according to script. When I told Dan that he was not allowed to give the carpet a haircut with his scissors, I followed up with a perfectly reasonable choice. "You can cut paper or cardboard. You decide."

Dan's response: "NO!"

Sometimes a parent must persist. "I don't want my carpet cut. What *else* can you cut?"

Now I had his interest. He looked around. "I can cut string, I can cut tissues, I can't cut the laundry. I know! Weeds!" He ran outside to trim the dandelions.

Notice that I put Dan to work making up his own choices. Why should I have to do all the mental gymnastics?

Toni's Story: Picture Perfect

We had our relatives over for a family reunion. My cousin wanted to get a group photograph, but her four-year-old daughter refused to cooperate. She wouldn't sit with the group, no matter what her mom said. I don't know why. I think she just started out not wanting to sit still and then it became a battle of wills.

I went over to her and said that I needed her to decide if we should take the picture with everybody standing or with the kids sitting on the picnic table. She stopped in her tracks and stared at me. Then she said, "Picnic table," and went over and sat down. I was the hero of the day!

Michael's Story: A Tub of Trouble

I've been offering Kara choices about the tub. It worked really well to ask her if she wanted a carrot stick or an apple slice while she took a bath. I know it sounds unusual, but she likes to eat in odd places. The mistake I made was the day we had pancakes for dinner. Kara still had a pancake in her hand, so I asked if she wanted a plain bath or a bath with pancakes. You know which she chose. Don't do what I did. Pancakes dissolve surprisingly quickly in water. And I don't even want to talk about the syrup! It was a pretty big mess.

My wife was mad when she got home and saw the bathtub. But you'll be proud of me because I accepted her feelings! I said, "I can see that you're really upset about this mess! I'm taking care of it as soon as Kara's asleep. Just back out slowly and pretend you never saw this."

Joanna's Story: Kids Take Over

Three-year-old Dan and his friend Chris were playing with plastic animals. The tiger and lion were fighting. Dan was pressing the tiger down on Chris's hand, which was holding the lion. Chris was using his other hand to press down on Dan's hand.

"Let go! You're hurting my hand!" cried Chris.

"*You're* hurting *my* hand. I *have* to hurt your hand because you're holding my hand down."

"But *you're* holding *my* hand down!"

Neither boy was willing to yield. Voices were becoming

angry and tearful. I sighed. I'd have to step in and break up the wild animal fight. Just as I started to open my mouth to interfere, I heard Dan say, "Christopher, here are our choices. We can keep on playing with the animals and not hold each other's hand down . . . or we can play with something else. Which do you *choice?*"

Christopher replied, "Let's play with something else." They both got up and left the animals in the dirt.

 **Don't turn a choice into a threat.**

When giving a choice, *it's important that both options are pleasant!* Satisfying as it may be to say, "You can come with me now, or I can leave you here for the wild dogs to chew on. You decide, honey!" try to resist that impulse. Also not qualifying for the child's choice award is this father's statement, in which both options are unpleasant. "I can spank you with my right hand or my left. It's up to you!"

TOOL #3: Put the Child in Charge

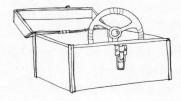

A common complaint among parents of toddlers is, "He won't do what he's told because he just wants to be in control!"

My response is, "Then let's *put* him in control." Whenever you can put your child in charge of his own behavior, you come out ahead. Whether you're a toddler, a teen, an adult, or an entire country, you probably react badly to being controlled. Human beings of all ages yearn for autonomy and independence. How about that Boston Tea Party? If it had been a bunch of toddlers we would've called it the Boston Temper Tantrum. So let's think about how we can put our kids in control.

Anna gave me a quizzical look. "But wait, isn't that like letting the animals run the zoo?"

"Well, yes, sort of. But it doesn't mean that there are no boundaries. You can put the lions in charge of their own turf without inviting them into the snack bar and gift shop. At least not until they're ready to exercise a certain level of restraint."

As a parent you can define the job that needs to get done, but let your child be in charge of the details. Delegate! It's less work for you in the long run, and your child will enjoy some independence.

For example, if you find yourself arguing with your child every morning about whether or not he needs a jacket, you may want to make a temperature chart.

Joanna's Story: You Don't Need a Weatherman to Know Which Way the Wind Blows

When Dan was five, he refused, on general principal, to wear a coat. The dialogue was boring and predictable.

"You need a coat. It's cold outside."

"No, it's not."

"Yes, it *is*!" And so on.

One afternoon, when I was feeling artistic, I sat down

with some paper, a pack of markers, and a large, outdoor thermometer. I called Dan over. "We need some pictures for this thermometer."

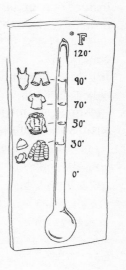

We made a bathing suit and stuck it to the thermometer at the 90-degree mark. We made a coat and taped it to the 40-degree mark. Hat and mittens at 32, ready for snow! Then we filled in the rest with a T-shirt at 70, sweatshirt at 60, and a jacket at 50. We covered the drawings with clear tape to make them rainproof and hung the thermometer outside. A good hour's work.

But well worth it! From now on Dan was the weather master. Instead of telling him what to wear, I asked him to check the thermometer so that he could tell *me* what to wear. Once he was in charge, his protests dissolved.

Sarah was bursting to speak. "I have another good way to use this tool. You can put kids in charge of time! You know how we're always nagging our kids 'Ten minutes left to play' or

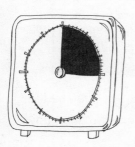

'Hurry up, we have only five minutes 'til the bus comes,' and they never seem to get it? We have this handy little timer in our classroom. When you twist the dial it shows a slice of red. So if you set it for 30 minutes, half the clock face is red. Fifteen minutes, a quarter of the clock face

59

is red. The slice of red gets smaller as the time gets used up, so the kids can *see* time go by. That way we can put them in charge of taking turns, or knowing when it's time to clean up, instead of nagging them. I've actually heard them warn each other, 'We have to hurry. There's only a sliver of red left!'"

I wish I'd had one of those timers when my children were young. Time is such a difficult concept for children to grasp. It's this abstract, invisible, intangible thing that adults are obsessed with. We live in a world of minutes and seconds ticking by at an alarming rate. A world of, *Go, go, go, we're going to be late!* Kids inhabit a different world. Their world is, *Oh, hey, look at that spider hanging from the ceiling. . . . Ooh, we could pull these cushions off the couch. . . . I wonder if a dog will lick applesauce off the carpet.* We get furious with them for not sharing our urgency. I love the idea of putting a child in charge of time.

Joanna's Story: On the Nature of Time

Years ago I had the following conversation with my son's four-year-old friend Noah:

> **Me:** Noah, Dan has to leave in five minutes.
> **Noah:** How much time is five minutes? Is it long or short?
> **Me:** Well, that depends on how you feel. If you're having fun it feels like a short time. If you're in pain, like if you had a clothespin stuck on your nose, it feels like a long time.
> **Me (a few minutes later):** Noah, why do you have a clothespin stuck to your nose?
> **Noah:** So we can play for a longer time.

TOOL #4: Give Information

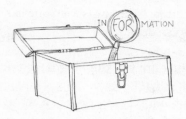

You don't always need elaborate preparation to put your child in the driver's seat. Often it's enough to give her simple information instead of an order. Here's how it works. You give your child information. Then she has a chance to figure out for herself what to do. Not only do you avoid the natural resistance that comes from a direct order, you're also laying the groundwork for your child to develop the ability to exercise self-control, *whether or not there's an adult telling her what to do.* A valuable lesson indeed. You're offering your child useful knowledge for the future, in place of a rule that might be followed only when you're around to enforce it.

Instead of, "Stop banging on that keyboard. You're going to break it!" (To which the inevitable reply is an offended, "No, I'm not!")

Give information: "Keyboards are delicate. All they need is a very light touch."

Instead of, "You left the cap off the glue stick again. Great!"

Give information: "Glue sticks dry out very quickly when they're not capped."

Instead of, "Get your seat belt on, or I'm not driving you to your friend's house."

Give information: "The law is everyone has to be belted in before we can drive."

Instead of, "What are you thinking? Don't leave the cheese on the chair like that!"

Give information: "The cheese is in reach of the dog."

Part of the beauty of using this tool is that it's not too irritating when it doesn't work. When you give a child a direct order—"Buckle your seat belt, now!"—and she doesn't comply, it's infuriating. But when you give her information and she doesn't act on it, you can move on to another tool without feeling the sting of direct defiance. You'll be in a better mood to try something else.

Maria's Story: Air Mail

We were coming home and Benjamin wanted to get the mail from the mailbox. He carried it inside and immediately threw it up in the air. Instead of my usual, "Hey, that's not okay! You need to pick it all up," I said, "Benny, the mail belongs on the desk." He gathered it all up and put it on the desk.

TOOL #5: Say It with a Word (or a Gesture)

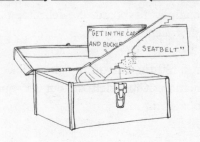

Much of what we say to our children when we're trying to control their behavior is a repeat performance. They've heard it all before. Many times! Let's face it, kids tune out lectures. Grown-ups are no different. Which would you rather hear as you leave this room at the end of the workshop session?

"You guys left the chairs out again. How many times do I have to tell you? There's no maid to clean this classroom after we leave."

Or:

"Chairs!"

"If you said it the first way I'd be tempted to throw the chair at the back of your head," said Toni.

"I will remember that!"

"Hey, I only said I'd be tempted," Toni reassured me. "I *probably* wouldn't actually do it. But seriously, I can hear the difference. When you say 'chairs!' you're giving us the benefit of the doubt. You assume that if you just point out the problem, we'll be glad to fix it. The other way is disrespectful. You're implying that we're lazy, thoughtless people."

"Yes! You cut to the heart of the matter. It's more than a tool. It's a whole different attitude. You're assuming that your child can tell herself what to do."

What happens when your four-year-old hears you say, "Apple core"? She has to think. *Apple core? What about an apple core? Oh, I left it on the couch. I guess I should put it in the garbage.* The child tells herself what to do. She doesn't feel bossed around. Now she won't be tempted to throw the apple core at the back of your head.

Just be careful that the one word you use is a noun, not a verb. A verb is more likely to sound like a command. Sit! Come! Quiet! Better for dog training than for child rearing.

I asked the group for useful examples. Suggestions came flying:

"Seat belt." (Instead of, "Buckle your seat belt, now.")

"Jacket." (Instead of, "Pick your jacket up off the floor and hang it on the hook.")

"Light." (Instead of, "How many times have I told you to turn the light off after you leave the bathroom?")

Toothbrushing gesture.

Finger to lips gesture.

Handwashing gesture.

And finally, one of the nicest things about the one-word statement is that you can use it when you're feeling happy and relaxed, and you can use it when you're angry. If you've asked your child not to leave her apple cores on the couch a hundred times already and you just sat down on a slimy, rotten core and are feeling the wetness seep through the seat of your pants, you can stand up and roar, "APPLE COOOORE!" It's therapeutic for the parent and not likely to cause long-term psychological damage to a youngster. You expressed your feelings strongly without resorting to character attacks, name-calling, or threats.

Sarah's Story: A Word to the Wise

It's very hard for me not to lecture the kids about leaving food out. It's a pet peeve. Wanna hear my speech? "You left the milk sitting out *again*. I've already told you, if you're *old* enough to take your own snacks out of the refrigerator, then you're *old* enough to put them away. We're going to have a whole carton of sour milk. Do you realize how much milk costs?" I can really go on!

The kids always come back with an excuse.

"It wasn't me." "I took it out, but Jake used it last."

"I don't care who used it last, just put it away!"

"No fair! Why aren't you telling him to do it? You only tell me!"

This time I just pointed and said, "Milk."

Sophia said, "Oh, sorry," and put it away.

Five minutes later Jake left his orange peels on the counter and I did it again. I pointed and said, "Compost."

Jake said, "Oh, yeah," and grabbed the peels and put them in the compost without a hint of protest.

It was really quite amazing. They were so cooperative when I left out the lecture. My irritation dissolved and I ended up feeling very warmly toward them.

TOOL #6: Describe What You See

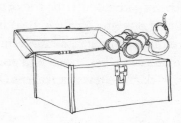

Sometimes a single word is not enough. You may need to string a few together. If you can restrict yourself to a simple description, without adding an irritating command or accusation, you may find your child willing to help out.

Instead of, "Don't walk away and leave your jacket on the floor. I'm not going to pick it up for you."
Describe: "I see a jacket on the floor."

Instead of, "You're making a big mess. Clean that up or the paints are going away."
Describe: "I see paint dripping."

Instead of, "Get back here! You're half naked!"
Describe: "I see a boy who is almost in his pajamas. He has the shirt on, and soon . . . the pants!"

 **Appreciate progress before describing what's left to do.**

As you may have noticed in the last example, when you describe what you see, it helps to describe the positive instead of focusing on the negative. Describe the progress that you see before pointing out what's left to be done. Instead of, "I see you haven't finished the cleanup," you can say, "I see almost all of the cars and blocks have been put away! There's only one dump truck and a few road pieces left to go."

TOOL #7: Describe How You Feel

As parents and teachers we expect ourselves to be endlessly patient with children. To take deep breaths, count to ten, visualize world peace. To stay calm and in control at all times. It's not realistic! We're humans, not robots. It's not a good idea to pretend to be calm until we explode (and most of us *will* explode eventually).

It can be helpful for a child to know what another person is feeling. Kids need to know when their parents or teachers are frightened, frustrated, or angry. It's hard for them to figure out what's going on when our words don't match our emotions.

When you describe how you feel, you're not only giving children important information, you're also modeling a vocabulary of emotions that *they* can use when *they* are frustrated, upset, or scared.

Michael's Story: A Pressing Concern

I was ironing a shirt when Jamie asked me to help him make a peanut butter and jelly sandwich. Normally I would have stopped ironing to do it. I'd have to unplug the iron and put it away so Kara couldn't touch it. But then I realized I didn't want to do that, so I told him, "I'll get frustrated if I don't finish this shirt first. I can help you as soon as I finish ironing the sleeves."

Jamie said, "Okay, Dad," and then he stuck around to watch me iron. I would never have thought to tell him my feelings before this class. It's so strange to me that I didn't learn to say things like "I'm frustrated" until I was thirty-four years old, and my son already knows that at four. He's way ahead of me!

Joanna's Story: No-Fear Mountaineer

My son, Dan, had no sense of fear as a child. My attempts to impress upon him a sense of his own mortality rolled off him like water off a duck's back. When we hiked I often found myself warning him not to go too near the edge of a drop-off because "You could fall and get hurt."

His standard reply? A breezy, "No I won't."

It worked much better to tell him, "I get scared when I see a boy so close to the edge. I worry about broken bones! I'm okay if you go up to this point, but no farther."

If he's in his usual agreeable mood, he's happy to oblige. If he's not, I just have to move him to a less precipitous area! He cannot be convinced to be afraid, but he's generally willing to make accommodations for his nervous mother.

Maria's Story: Cain and (Is)Abel

Ever since I had a second child it's been like Cain and Abel in my house. When Benjamin hurts Isabel I go crazy. I usually start yelling whatever comes into my head. "Don't shove your sister! She's just a baby! You hurt her! That's mean!" He reacts very inappropriately. Sometimes he actually laughs in my face.

This week I've started telling him my feelings instead. "When I see one child hurting another child I get very upset!"

I have to admit it works! He stops and he doesn't laugh or run away. Last night at bedtime *he* told *me* his feelings. He was jumping on the bed saying, "*I'm . . . angry . . . at . . . you!*" with one word for each jump.

I could guess why. Isabel had a fever and was on my lap all day. I told Benjamin, "It's annoying to have a sick sister! She gets all Mama's attention."

He jumped until he collapsed on the bed with me admiring each jump. "Oh my gosh, you almost touched the ceiling. You almost flew like a bird. You almost went to outer space!"

I told him, "You're getting good at putting your angry feelings into words instead of hitting. That's not easy to do."

He crawled into my lap and gave me a hug!

I feel like this kind of language is helping us get back to the close connection we had before Isabel was born, when he became the rough older brother and I became the angry mother.

 **When expressing anger or frustration, use the word *I*, avoid the word *you*.**

When Maria expressed her angry feelings to Benjamin in that last story, she did it in a particularly skillful way. She completely avoided the word *you*. She said, "When *I* see one child hurting another *I* get very upset!" What she didn't say was, "When I see *you* hurting your sister . . ."

When expressing annoyance, irritation, or anger, it's important to banish the word *you*.

The *you* is accusatory. As soon as a child hears *you*, he feels defensive. He may respond by arguing, laughing inappropriately, running away, or getting angry in return. If we can avoid *you* altogether, we're much more likely to get a cooperative attitude.

There's a world of difference between, "Look at this mess you made!" and "I don't like to see food on the floor!"

To the first statement, a child is likely to respond, "I didn't do it!" "Why are you yelling at me? It was Johnny's fault." "Who cares?" The second statement allows a child to think to himself, "Uh oh, Mom really doesn't want crackers on the carpet. I'd better pick them up."

When you see a child doing something dangerous, it doesn't usually help to say, "Stop that, you're going to hurt yourself!" You will most likely get the classic reply, "No I'm not."

It's more effective to describe your feelings without the word *you*: "I get scared when I see people jumping around near the stove while I'm cooking. I worry about burns."

When your child demands, "Give me juice!" don't bother telling her, "You're rude!" Calling her rude is not going to help her learn to be polite. She'll just learn to say, *"You're* rude, too!"

It's more useful to tell her how you feel. "I don't like being yelled at! That doesn't make me feel helpful. I like to hear, 'Mom, can I have some juice, please?'"

Kids often respond well when we give them the words

they can use to get what they want. The younger the child is, the more explicit you can be about giving him the language you prefer to hear.

 **Express strong anger sparingly. It can feel like an attack.**

Even if you use the perfect wording, it's difficult for a young child to handle strong negative emotions from an adult. Use words like *angry* and *furious* sparingly. It's easier to hear words like *upset*, or *frustrated*, or *I don't like it when* without feeling attacked.

I remember a workshop member telling me she was frustrated that we always ended the workshop late. She explained that she often had to miss the end of the session because she needed to get home in time to relieve her babysitter. I was chagrined. I thought I was being accommodating by starting late, but it turns out I was making it more difficult for this mom who had to leave on time. I apologized to her and resolved to announce to the group that we would honor our start time.

But what if this mom had approached me by saying that she was *furious* with me for starting late? I'm sure my reaction would have been different. I would have felt attacked and perhaps wondered if she might be a bit unbalanced. I might have even tried to avoid her in the future.

Save your outrage for those times when it is unavoidable. Your kid smacked you in the nose, covered the cat in molasses, flushed your wedding ring down the toilet. Fury is not a useful everyday seasoning for a relationship!

TOOL #8: Write a Note

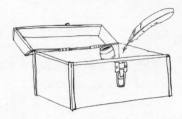

When you find yourself repeating the same plea again and again until you're sick of your own voice, it may be time to write a note. Don't worry if your child doesn't know how to read. The written word has a mysterious power that spoken words do not. A note can be more effective than a nagging voice.

Joanna's Story: An Invitation to Bathe

One repeat battle in my home that was eased by note writing was the dreaded bath time. You can bodily throw a child in the tub, but it takes a toll on your back. And my kids found so many different ways to resist and procrastinate, I'd be weary and irritable before even starting. I found myself wondering, "Why *are* children expected to be clean? How much can I get away with? Days? Weeks? Would their teachers notice?"

I solved this particular dilemma with a formal notice. I wrote out an "appointment card" for bath time. I offered various options: the 6:00 p.m. slot, the 6:15 slot, and the 6:30

72

slot. The 6:00 p.m. slot was on special offer, with bubbles. The 6:15 slot offered a happy hour with carrots and rubber fish. All the child had to do was check a box with a marker. They each happily did so after giving serious thought to their options. I was amazed at how well it worked. All I had to do was brandish the card and say, "Your 6:00 p.m. bath is ready, sir!"

Sarah's Story: Hours of Operation

I try to get up earlier than the kids so I can have my coffee and read the paper for twenty minutes before going into action. I really need that transition time. But Mia has been sneaking downstairs early. When I tell her it's not time to come down to the kitchen yet, she fools around, putting one foot in the kitchen and then running back to the stairs. She has this kind of cute, playful look on her face. I'd throw myself in front of a bus for my daughter, but I can't stand it when she does this. I just want those few minutes!

This week I wrote a note on a big piece of paper and strung it across the bottom step. It said KITCHEN OPENS AT 7:00. When Mia came down, I asked her, "Did you see the sign?"

"Mommy, I don't know how to read."

"Do you want me to read it to you?"

"Okay."

I read it to her. She got her timer. I set it for her and she went back upstairs and waited until 7:00.

TOOL #9: Take Action Without Insult

None of these tools will work for every child in every situation. You're still in charge of the zoo, and you do what you have to do to keep it afloat. (Let's imagine the zoo is on a boat, to make this metaphor work. It could be kind of like Noah's ark.) The final tool of this chapter is to take action without insult.

If your child refuses to wear his bike helmet in spite of your brilliant use of playfulness, choice, and information-giving, you can say, "I'm putting the bike away for now. You're in no mood to have your head squeezed by a helmet, and I can't let you ride without one."

If your child keeps pounding on your touchscreen, in spite of your protest that it is delicate, you can remove it, saying, "I see you have a lot of energy. I'm worried that the screen could break. Let's find something to play with that can take some rough treatment."

If your child can't resist throwing gravel in the park, in spite of your efforts to offer tempting alternatives, you can say, "I'm taking you home now. I don't want anyone to get hit by a rock, even a little one."

If your child wants to help put pancake batter in the pan, but despite friendly reminders you can't convince him not to jump around at the stove, you can say, "I can't cook with you now. I'm too worried about burns."

If your child refuses to get in his carseat, "I can see the seat belt is uncomfortable. You feel freer without it. I can't take you to your friend's house without the belt buckled." Or, "I don't want to be late for work. I'm buckling you in. I know how much you hate it!"

If your student is flicking the paintbrush full of wet paint at his seatmates, "I can see you're in no mood for keeping paint on the paper right now. I can't let you splatter the other kids. Let's move you to the Play-Doh table. You can squeeze it, pound it, roll it, or smash it flat!"

Notice that in all these examples the child isn't being scolded or accused. The adult is describing her own feelings and actions. She's standing her ground, enforcing a limit, or stating her values.

It had been a long session. The group was looking a little glassy-eyed. I heard a sigh. Finally Anna expressed the feeling that was in the air. "This is so much work. I mean, everything here is such a song and dance. Choices, playfulness, making weather charts, and buying special clocks. Where does it end? When can I just tell my kid what to do and he does it?"

I shrugged. "It is kind of a three-ring circus. Kids are exhausting. Little kids are exceptionally exhausting. For me it's more fun when we're all tired and cheerful, instead of tired and irritable. These tools all help you achieve the former. And it does get easier. The older they get, the more they can be in charge of themselves, especially if they've had the practice of making choices and being in charge of their own behavior when they're younger."

And for those times when you don't have the patience or energy to come up with a really terrific tool, you still have credit in the bank from all those times you *did* make the effort. The payoff for taking that extra step to engage our kids' cooperation without orders, bribes, and threats is enormous. Study after study has found that young children who are not constantly ordered around are much more likely to cooperate with simple requests from a parent—for example, cleaning up toys when asked—than children who are micromanaged and controlled much of the time. They're also more likely to cooperate with another adult, such as a teacher, *and* more likely to follow rules when no adults are present to control them. Self-control can only be developed by practice, not by force![1]

Tools for Engaging Cooperation

INSTEAD OF A THREAT...

DESCRIBE HOW YOU FEEL

BE PLAYFUL

OFFER A CHOICE

PUT THE CHILD IN CHARGE

TAKE ACTION WITHOUT INSULT

Tools for Engaging Cooperation

INSTEAD OF...

SAY IT WITH A WORD

DESCRIBE WHAT YOU SEE

BE PLAYFUL

GIVE INFORMATION

WRITE A NOTE

REMINDER: Tools for Engaging Cooperation

1. Be Playful

- *Make it a game.*

  "Can we get all the cars into the box before the timer beeps? Ready . . . set . . . go!"

- *Make inanimate objects talk.*

  "I'm an empty sock. I need a foot in me!"

- *Use silly voices and accents.*

  "I . . . am . . . your . . . robot . . . Must . . . buckle . . . seat . . . belt . . . now."

- *Pretend!*

  "We need to climb this slippery mountain into the carseat."

- *Play the incompetent fool.*

  "Oh dear, where does this sleeve go? Over your head? No? On the arm? This is so confusing! Thank you for helping me!"

2. Offer a Choice

> "Do you want to hop to the tub like a bunny, or crawl to the tub like a crab?"

3. Put the Child in Charge

> "Johnny, would you set the timer and let us know when it's time to leave?"

4. Give Information

> "Tissues go in the trash."

5. Say It with a Word (or a Gesture)

> "Trash!"

6. Describe What You See

> "I see most of the blocks put away in the toy box. There are only a few blocks left to go."

7. Describe How You Feel

> "I don't like food thrown on the floor."

8. Write a Note

> "Put me on your head before riding. Love, your bike helmet."

9. Take Action Without Insult

"I'm putting the paint away for now. I can't let you splatter the other kids."

- Don't turn a choice into a threat. Make sure both options are acceptable to you and your child.

- Appreciate progress before describing what's left to do.

- When expressing anger or frustration, use the word *I,* avoid the word *you.*

- Express strong anger sparingly. It can feel like an attack.

Chapter Three

Tools for Resolving Conflict ... Avoiding
Combat on the Home Front

**—Replacing punishment with more peaceful,
effective solutions**

Joanna

What do you do when a child deliberately does something
you've just told him not to? He steals the candy, pulls the
dog's tail, pinches the baby, upends the egg carton just to
see the beautiful sight of a dozen raw yolks oozing out of
their smashed shells into the crack between the stove and
the counter. What happens when you've tried all the tools
in chapter two, but your child continues to defy you? Kids
can be so frustrating, so irritating, so *enraging*,
that the impulse to punish is hard to resist.
You've read this book, you've
studied it, and now you want
to throw it at them.

Wait! Lock yourself in the
bathroom and take a look at this
chapter before you start flinging and
the pages start flying.

Consider this scenario: You take your
children to the park one sunny afternoon.
Before you leave the house you remind your four-year-old

that he needs to hold your hand in the parking lot and stay in sight at the playground. And don't forget to take turns and play nice.

What do you do when little Buckaroo decides to ignore those rules? He squirms away and zips through the parking lot, weaving between the cars. Once in the playground, he runs around with the stroller, bashing it into the playground equipment. At the top of the slide he impatiently shoves his two-year-old sister who is taking too long to work up the courage to go down.

Should he get a smack on the bottom? Should he lose out on a treat from the ice-cream truck? Should he be sent to his room for a time-out when he gets home, to contemplate his crimes?

Most adults agree that *something* must be done! A child cannot be allowed to put himself in danger and freely terrorize all those around him. People say, *"Kids need consequences. There's a time and a place for punishment, and this is the time and place!"* *"This kid is just not getting it. He needs to be taught a lesson."* It feels like common sense.

Before we start dutifully doling out consequences and punishment, I'd like to take a moment to define our terms. Just what do we mean by natural or logical consequences? And what lessons *are* we teaching when we punish?

Let's start with natural consequences. We can't *give* a child a natural consequence. The only truly *natural* consequences are the ones found in nature. They happen without us having to do anything. If you pull a dog's ear, you may get bitten. If you stick your hand in a fire, you get burned. If you step off the edge of a cliff, gravity will cause you to plummet to the ground below.

As for logical consequences, the "logic" is highly debatable. If you continually arrive late for my workshop, despite my warning that lateness is unacceptable, I may find it "logical" to lock you out of my classroom. Or perhaps it would be more "logical" to keep you locked *in* after class for the same number of minutes you were late. Or maybe my "logic" demands that you miss out on the snacks. As you may be starting to suspect, these are not true exercises in logic. They're really more of a free association, where we try to think of a way to make the wrongdoer suffer. We hope that the suffering will motivate the offender to do better in the future.

Let's be honest. From the point of view of the child, getting a consequence and getting a punishment are two different names for the same thing. Even if we modernize it by calling it a natural or a logical consequence. The traditional parent may say, "You are being sent to your room . . . losing your computer privileges . . . getting a spanking . . . as a *punishment* for your behavior." The modern parent may say, "You are being sent to your room . . . losing computer privileges . . . getting a spanking . . . as a *consequence* of your behavior." The child is experiencing the same emotional distress or physical pain no matter what label we paste on our actions. Either way, our intent is to find some way to make the child suffer, or at least feel bad, in the hope that she will be discouraged from repeating her unacceptable behavior.

For the purposes of this discussion, I'm going to use the term *punishment* to refer to any unpleasant experience imposed by an adult with the intent of changing a child's behavior.

CONSEQUENCE

PUNISHMENT

I asked my workshop group why people punish kids. Here are their responses.

Michael: Listen, some boys are hardheaded. I was a pretty wild kid. I didn't listen to my mom when she told me not to do something. She had to hit me just to get my attention!

Toni: We can't give up our authority as adults just to be nice. I don't advocate physical abuse, but sometimes punishment is the only thing a child understands. A smack on the bottom is worth it, if it stops a child from running into the street.

Sarah: I don't believe in punishment as a regular, everyday tool, but kids have to know there's a limit, don't they? As a teacher I don't necessarily know *why* a child is acting out, but that doesn't mean I can give him a pass on following the rules. We would never hit a child at school, but they can lose privileges, or be sent to the time-out corner.

Maria: Sometimes a child does something dangerous or hurtful, but he doesn't seem to care. Giving him a consequence makes him "feel the pain" so that he won't do it again, even if he isn't old enough to understand why. They need to know they can't just get away with doing anything they want.

"Now I want to hear the other side of the story," I say to my group. "Can you remember being punished as a child? Did it inspire you to change your bad behavior?"

A big grin spread over Michael's face. Clearly he was having some fond memories of past misadventures. "Oh no! Getting in trouble was much more fun than punishment was bad. It was totally worth it to be spanked. My mom didn't hit that hard."

Toni looked like she was trying to suppress a smirk. "I remember getting grounded for lying about a sleepover. I learned to lie better the next time. I was pretty sneaky. When I got older I used to climb out the window."

"I don't actually remember getting punished as a child," said Sarah. "I guess I was that good little girl who always wanted to please. But I can tell you that the kids in my pre-school who get put in the time-out corner and lose privileges are the same ones week after week. I have to admit, it doesn't seem to change their attitude."

"One time my little sister and I shoplifted candy together," said Maria. "My mom found the candy and punished me, but my sister got off free because she was younger. I had to miss my best friend's birthday party. I remember being outraged at the injustice of it. I don't think I shoplifted again, so I guess you could say it worked. But I was angry at my sister for a long time. I got back at her. I would tease her until she tried to hit me, so she'd get in trouble with my mom."

Anna looked distressed. "I hate to say it, but punishment did work for me. My father didn't spank softly. He hit hard, with a belt. Sometimes my mother made me kneel on rice with bare knees. It was painful and humiliating. It stopped me from doing anything that I thought might get me in trouble. But I was a miserable, terrified little kid. I don't want my own kids to feel that way."

These experiences illustrate some of the problems with punishment. While it may produce quick results, it can lead to many pitfalls:

- When you've committed yourself to using punishment to solve a conflict and the punishment isn't harsh enough to be effective, you're in a dangerous position. You may find yourself locked in to using harsher and harsher punishments.

- The punishment doesn't address the underlying problem. A child in preschool who has trouble socializing with other children may be punished for shoving or biting, but that doesn't help him acquire the social skills he needs to get along with his peers.

- Often a strong-willed child who is punished becomes more determined to defy authority. Studies find that kids who are punished are *more* likely to misbehave in the future. Punishment actually increases the undesired behavior.[1]

- Punishment can distract a child from the important lesson she needs to learn. Instead of feeling an urge to fix the problem or make amends, punishment prompts a child to think selfishly. What television shows will she be forced to miss? What dessert will she have to give up? She's likely to be filled with resentment instead of remorse.

- Even when punishment does work to eliminate an unwanted behavior, the victory may come at a high cost. A child who is punished harshly can develop other problems, from fear and timidity to aggression toward other children.

- And finally, the punishments we mete out to our children give them a blueprint for how to approach conflict in their lives. We have to ask ourselves if we want them to use these methods on their peers and siblings.

This last point was graphically illustrated to me when Dan, at four years old, kept poking his little brother in the head no matter how much I *explained* that this was not a pleasant sensation. I could not fathom the pleasure he took in this activity. Finally, at my wit's end, I yelled, "*DAN, YOU ARE NOT UNDERSTANDING ME! I have to show you what this feels like.*" Fueled by the intensity of my frustration, I gave him a forceful poke on the head. "Do you like that?"

He cried. "No!"

"Okay, then . . . *Don't. Do it. To your brother!*" Point made.

The very next day I heard his logical little voice from the living room speaking calmly to his younger brother. "Sam, I have to show you what this feels like." Hysterical wailing from Sam. Okay, wrong point made.

It is kind of stunning how much our kids really do want to emulate us. And how much they focus on our overall strategy. It's a tired old phrase but true: children will do as you do, not as you say.

The key question is: *how do we want our children to approach conflict*? Do we want them to think about what they should do *to* the other person—take something away or inflict pain—or do we want them to think *what can I do to solve this problem?*

Sounds a bit idealistic, doesn't it? What about that child careening through the parking lot and shoving his sister on the playground? What can a parent actually *do* with all this philosophy in the face of an out-of-control child?

We need practical tools to put philosophy into action.

Here's how it might look when we apply our tools to the young ruffian who pushed his little sister at the top of the slide.

TOOL #1: Express Your Feelings . . . *Strongly*!

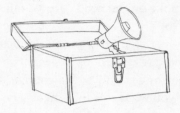

"*HEY*, I don't like to see people being pushed!"

Sometimes that will be enough. You've avoided the command: "Stop that right now!" You've avoided character attacks: "Bad boy! That's mean!" You've avoided threatening: "If you don't stop it right now, there'll be no ice cream for you!" You stayed away from all those reactions that cause natural resistance.

But it still might not be enough to stop your wild child. He's having fun and he doesn't truly understand the possible repercussions of pushing a little kid at the top of the slide. Heck, he was just helping her get going.

TOOL #2: Show Your Child How to Make Amends

"Your sister got scared when she was pushed. Let's do something to make her feel better. Do you want to offer her some apple slices, or do you think she'd like to play with your sand bucket?"

The quickest way to change a child's behavior and *attitude* is to get him involved in fixing his mistake. *The best way to inspire a child to do better in the future is to give him an opportunity to do better in the present.* A punishment makes him feel bad about himself. Making amends helps him feel good about himself, and helps him to see himself as a person who can do good.

TOOL #3: Offer a Choice

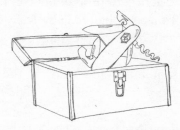

"We're going to give the slide a rest for now. I can see you're in no mood to wait for a turn. You can swing on the swings or you can dig a big hole in the sand. You decide."

Sometimes a youngster needs help to redirect his energy. A choice can help him move on to a more acceptable activity.

TOOL #4: Take Action Without Insult

If your little firecracker continues to pose a hazard to himself and others, you may have to take action:

"We're heading home. We'll try the playground another day. I'm too worried about children getting hurt right now."

"Aha! So you *do* believe in consequences!" I hear you cry. "What was all that fine talk about how consequences are really punishments, and punishments are bad?"

Here's how I see it. I take action in order to *protect*, not to punish. I take action to protect my child from harm, to protect others from being harmed physically or emotionally, to protect property, and to protect my own feelings.

I may have to snatch my child's arm in the parking lot or require that he ride in the stroller to protect him from being hit by a car.

"I'm buckling you in so you won't get hurt by a car. I know you don't like it! As soon as we get out of the parking lot, you can be free!"

I may have to remove him from the playground to protect other children from being hurt by his rambunctious behavior.

> "I'm taking you to the grassy field. Let's bring the ball. We need a place to play where a person can run around without worrying about bumping into anybody."

I may take away the stroller to prevent him from breaking it.

> "I'm putting the stroller in the car so it won't get broken. Let's find something else to play with. Something tough that can take a good banging!"

I may even place a moratorium on trips to the playground until we come up with a better plan to protect myself from a stressful outing.

> "I'm not taking you to the playground today. I don't want to end up getting mad and yelling again. We need to come up with a new plan first."

Notice that we are giving a very clear message to the child that we are not acting to punish, but to protect. We don't say, "You behaved badly at the park yesterday, so you don't get to go today." We don't say, "You were too rough with the stroller, so you've lost the privilege of pushing it." *We focus on safety and peace of mind for the present, and solutions for the future.*

It's a lesson kids can take forward with them into adulthood. When you have a problem with an adult—say, for example, you have a friend who's always borrowing things and returning them late or broken or not at all—you probably don't think about how you can punish that person. You think about how to respectfully protect yourself. You don't say, "Now that you've given me back my jacket with a stain on it, and broken the side mirror off my car, I'm going to . . . slap you." That would be assault. Or ". . . lock you in your room for an hour." That would be imprisonment. Or ". . . take away your smart phone." That would be theft. You'd probably say something like, "I don't feel comfortable lending you clothes anymore. I get very upset when they come back damaged. And, I can't lend you my car, which I just got repaired. I need to have it in working condition. In fact, I'd appreciate some help with the repair bill!"

Your friend may very well learn a lesson from your actions. He learns that you have a limit and that he has stepped over that limit. If he wants to do any borrowing in the future he'll have to change his behavior. Not because you did something to make him suffer, but because you acted firmly to protect yourself.

Of course, children are different from adults, and sometimes a whole lot wackier. Here are more examples of how to **take action** with children when all your other tools have failed.

> "I'm putting the blocks away for now. I can't allow throwing. I'm too worried about broken windows and broken heads."
>
> "I'm separating you from your brother! I can see how angry you are and I don't want either of you to get hurt."
>
> "We're leaving the library. I can't let books be pushed off the shelves."
>
> "I'm putting the food away. I can see you're not hungry and I don't like food to be smeared on clothing."

Taking action to protect yourself and those around you is an essential life skill for adults and a powerful way to model for our children how to deal with conflict. This approach is a world apart from the tactic of thinking up ways to cause discomfort in the hope that a lesson will be learned.

"But what about that lesson?" you ask. "What about the next time we go to the park? If I just keep gently preventing my child from causing harm—to himself, to others, or to property—what is going to inspire him to change his behavior? With no punishment, isn't he 'getting away with it?'"

Don't close the book yet! We have a tool for you that will be more effective than punishment in motivating your child to change his behavior in the future. This tool is invaluable when you have an ongoing problem that resists a quick fix. It can't always be used in the moment. Some situations are unsalvageable. But as you drag your child screaming and kicking from a store or playground, you will have this comforting thought in the back of your mind: *Later, when things calm down, I'm going to try problem-solving, and the next time will be better!*

Here's the way it works.

TOOL #5: Try Problem-Solving

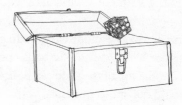

One of the keys to successful problem solving is to wait for a time when the mood is right. It can't be done in the midst of frustration and anger. After the storm has passed, invite your child to sit down with you.

The first step of problem-solving is to acknowledge your child's feelings. This is the most important step, and the most frequently skipped! Without acknowledging feelings first, you won't get far. Your child needs to know that you can see things from his point of view and understand what he's feeling, or he won't be open to any of the suggestions that follow.

> "I can see that you don't like your hand held in the parking lot. You'd rather be free to run!"
>
> "You certainly don't like having to wait a long time to go down the slide. It's annoying to be blocked by a little sister who can't decide whether to go down or not."

If your child has something to add, continue to listen and reflect feelings. "Ah, so you hate it when I squeeze your hand. And you wish you could have the playground all to yourself sometimes!"

The second step is to describe the problem. Here's where you can talk about *your* feelings or other people's feelings. Unfortunately this part has to be short. You can't go on and on, or you'll sink the ship before it sails.

> "The problem is, I worry about cars hitting children in the parking lot."
>
> "Being pushed at the top of the slide can be scary to a little kid. She could fall and get hurt."

The third step is to ask for ideas. For this step you're going to need paper and pencil. Be sure to write down *all* ideas, no matter how outrageous. If you start rejecting ideas at this stage of the game ("Oh no, that would never work!") your child will quickly lose interest. As a matter of fact, it's nice to start out by putting some truly preposterous ideas on your list.

> "We need some ideas so we can go back to the park and have a good time without people getting mad or scared or hurt. What can we do?"

- Make the cars disappear.
- Fly over the cars like a bird.
- Instead of holding hands, hold on to a belt.
- Instead of holding hands, hold on to the stroller and help push it.
- Pretend Mommy is lost. Hold her sleeve and lead her through the parking lot.
- Squirt water on the slide so nobody else will use it.
- Put a sign on the slide that says NO BABIES. They can use the swings.
- If a kid is scared, offer to go down the slide together.
- If the slide is crowded, go to the climbing house.
- If the slide is crowded, jump down from the ladder, get out the bucket and shovel, and go play in the sandbox.

The fourth step is to decide which ideas you both like and cross out the ones that neither of you like.

> "Hmm, it would be nice to fly like a bird, but I don't think I can do that. How about helping push the stroller? Oh, you like the idea of leading me by the sleeve. Let's circle that one."
>
> "I guess we can't really put water on the slide. That would make people mad. And we can't keep the babies away. The park is for everyone. How about the climbing house idea?"

The last step is to try out your solutions. Get a magnet, stick your list of ideas on the refrigerator, and wait for opportunity to strike. Bring your list to the park. Take it out before you leave the car and double check the plan with your child.

> "So, you're ready to lead me to the playground? Okay, grab my sleeve, I'm ready to follow!"

Chances are that if your child participated in coming up with solutions, he'll be eager to try them out. You'll find yourself at the park, feeling good, with a cooperative child who is getting valuable practice in solving the thorny problems of life. You skipped the whole punishment phase of the parenting journey and went directly to solving the problem.

But what if it doesn't work?

Then it's back to the drawing board. You need new ideas. The beauty of problem-solving is that, unlike punishment, it offers endless possibilities. If you're committed to punishment and your child continues to misbehave, all you can do is punish more severely. You might hit him harder or take away more privileges, but chances are you won't get any closer to your goal of having a cooperative child. And you'll create a lot of ill will in the process. With problem-solving, you can always go back and brainstorm some more. When you put your heads together, you're bound to come up with something that will work for both of you.

If nothing is working, you may have to reconsider your basic expectations.

When children are not ready to behave in a way that is safe for themselves and others, we default to managing the environment. We don't expect babies to keep their fingers out of electrical sockets. We cover them. We don't build playgrounds next to highways and expect toddlers not to run into traffic after a rolling ball. We fence in the playground. We don't leave bowls of chocolate bars in the middle of the table and expect preschoolers (or their parents!) to *eat just one*. We give one to each person and put the rest out of sight. We give babies board books so they won't rip the pages out with their chubby, determined fingers. If Grandma has a house full of fascinating, delicate china dolls displayed on low shelves, you don't expect to spend a relaxing time there with your two-year-old. You invite Grandma to visit her granddaughter at your house.

Library Mayhem

When Dan was almost two, the library was a very interesting place. He loved books. No, not in that way. Not to read! He loved the physics of shelved books. His favorite

activity was to race down the aisles, pushing on the spines of the books as he sped by, so that the books on the other side fell down with a series of satisfying clunks. Then he'd race down the next aisle to see the result of his experiment with mass and gravity. I decided that library visits would be suspended for a while, until my little scientist became more interested in what was inside of books.

Blocked

On Dan's second birthday, my parents proudly presented us with a wonderful gift: a full set of large wooden blocks. I'm sure they envisioned a creative explosion of architecture. Castles, skyscrapers, roadways with bridges and tunnels for toy cars to traverse, entire cityscapes. Dan had other ideas. He found it fascinating to launch these heavy, rectangular projectiles into the air. He thrilled to the soaring arc and the crashing finale. After trying numerous approaches, I conceded defeat. In the interest of protecting the structural integrity of our windows and our heads, I packed the blocks in boxes and stored them in the basement. They reemerged when Dan was three. Construction projects resumed, now firmly rooted to the ground. A wonderful gift. It's all in the timing!

But let's assume that you are asking for behavior that is age appropriate and within your child's skill set. Here are some real life examples of parents using alternatives to punishment. Although you may wonder if skipping the punishment lets a child off the hook and deprives him of learning to take responsibility for his actions, you'll notice that in all these examples, the opposite is true.

In this first story, learning that he has the power to make amends gives a child the courage to face a mistake.

Michael's Story: Truckful of Trouble

I walked into the living room to find that Jamie had been using his dump truck to transport flour. There was a huge mess all over the floor. I yelled, "Who made this big mess?"

Jamie said, "Trouble!" and ran and hid behind the couch.

I saw that I had scared him, and that made me feel bad. So I said, "Oh no, we have a problem. What should we do to fix it?"

He stuck his head out and yelled, "Water!" He ran to the kitchen and got a wet paper towel.

Jan and I usually get upset with Jamie because when we scold him he tries to run away instead of saying he's sorry. But with this new approach, I see his whole attitude changing. The other day he was in the living room flipping through the pages of a book of animal photographs while I was in the kitchen. He came running in looking very worried and said, "Daddy, I ripped a page. What should we do to fix it?"

I gave him tape. I think in the past he would have closed the book and hidden it.

And then there are times when it's enough for a parent just to express her feelings strongly.

Maria's Story: Escape Artist

We have a fenced yard, so sometimes I let Benjamin play outside while I'm working in the house. I keep an eye on him through the window. Yesterday I looked out and saw him climbing the fence. I've punished him several times for that very activity with a smack on the bottom and a time-out. There's a busy road on the other side, so it's very dangerous. This time I yelled as loud as I could, "I see a boy on a fence and I'm afraid he'll get hurt!" Benjamin jumped down and ran over to me. I hugged him and said, "That made me very, very scared!" He said, "Sorry, Mommy!"

• • •

Sometimes you'll need an assortment of tools in combination. In this story see if you can spot *acknowledging feelings*, *expressing feelings strongly*, *giving choices,* and *taking action*.

Joanna's Story: Slip Sliding Away

We were at an outdoor birthday party at a public mini golf course with a large group of seven-year-old boys. There was a dancing area with a live band. A light drizzle had made the dance floor slick in spite of the canopy covering it. Kids in our party realized that they could take a running start and go *sliiiiding* across the wooden floor. What fun! Except that other people on the dance floor were clearly uncomfortable with this activity. Parents were grabbing their toddlers so they wouldn't get knocked down by these wild boys. Some elderly people were flinching in fear of being toppled. I looked to the parents of the birthday boy to lay down the law. After all, it was their party. They seemed reluctant to ruin their son's special day by chastising him.

I felt too uncomfortable to ignore the mayhem, especially since my own son was participating.

I yelled out in a loud voice, "Hey, no sliding on the dance floor! I can see it's really fun. The problem is people are dancing here and they don't want to be knocked down. You can dance on the dance floor, or slide somewhere else, off the dance floor."

Some of the kids stopped, including mine. A few kept running and sliding, including the birthday boy. I grabbed each of those kids by the arm and repeated the choice. They went running off to play elsewhere and a few people on the dance floor mouthed *thank you*!

These boys weren't trying to terrorize anyone. They were just having some lively seven-year-old fun, oblivious to the needs of others. I acknowledged their feelings and let them know how other people felt, without attacking their character. I gave them a choice. And I took action by stopping the ones who couldn't quite manage to stop themselves. Nobody's feelings were hurt and the party proceeded with everyone in a merry mood.

And then there are those trying times that call for the more elaborate activity of problem-solving.

Joanna's Story: Dirty Kid

Bath time had become an enormous battle. It was so unpleasant that I'd allowed the intervals between baths to grow from a few days to more than a week. How long could I stretch it before people started to notice? The sticking point was the washing of the hair. Five-year-old Zach hated it. I had tried humor, choices, giving information, and was now using the default option—force. I had to do it. Nobody else was sending their kid to kindergarten with sticky, smelly hair. I would start out trying to carefully rinse the shampoo out of Zach's hair, and then as he struggled and refused to cooperate in any way, soapy water would get in his face and he would start to scream. Since he was already mad as a hornet, I'd just hang on to his slippery arm and dump more water on his head to finish the job. Much sputtering and more screaming would ensue. No mother-of-the-year awards here.

I decided to try problem-solving.

I sat down with Zach one evening and heaved a big sigh. "Boy, you really don't like having your hair washed. If it were up to you, that would just never, ever happen!"

"Yeah! The water blurs my face. And you get soap in my eyes!"

"That sounds really unpleasant. No wonder you don't like it."

"I hate it!"

"I can tell. And I hate fighting with you about it and making you sad and mad. The problem is, I'm supposed to send you to school with slightly clean hair. It's one of my jobs as a mom. We need ideas for how to do this better."

I took out a piece of paper and wrote at the top THE PROBLEM WITH WASHING HAIR.

Underneath I entered Zach's main complaints, reading out loud as I wrote: WATER BLURS FACE, SOAP IN EYES

Then I wrote my complaint: STICKY HAIR.

And underneath that I wrote SOLUTIONS.

We looked at each other. I figured I'd go for a lighthearted mood. "Well, I guess you could wait for the rain and just go stand outside and get clean that way."

I wrote my suggestion down with a little stick figure in the rain so Zach would have a picture to go along with the words.

Zach got into the swing of things. "I could be a fish! They don't mind being under water."

I wrote it down, with a picture of a fish.

"Or I could be a cat! They never have to take baths."

I wrote it. Luckily fish and cats were both within my limited drawing ability.

Zach was still on a roll. "I could wait until I'm as old as Sam. He doesn't mind washing his hair."

Sam was eight years old. I drew a stick figure with a number 8 over his head.

I was thinking that I'd better turn the conversation toward something a little more realistic or it might be three long years before Zach's next bath. That would *really* be stretching it!

I wrote down a suggestion that Zach could stand in the tub and bend over to dunk his hair in the water, then quickly put a towel around his head so the water didn't drip in his face. I wrote that Zach could rinse off by himself, using the detachable showerhead. Zach countered with the suggestion that I take him to a pool because he didn't mind water on his face at a pool.

"Hey, wait a minute. Why is that? Why *don't* you mind getting water in your face at a pool?"

Original pictures, drawn by stressed parent.
NOT an artist's re-creation!

"Because I wear goggles in the pool."

"Ohhh."

A breakthrough! "What if we get some goggles for the bathtub?" I wrote it down.

We looked over our list. Standing out in the rain got a check mark. All the other ideas were crossed out as being unrealistic or unpleasant, except for the goggles. That held promise. In the months that followed, all hair washing was done with goggles. Occasionally water seeped through, but it seemed to be okay because even if the solution wasn't perfect, it was ours. What a relief!

Problem-solving doesn't always have to be a laborious, time-consuming, multistep activity. Sometimes it's a simple shift in perspective. Instead of thinking, "How can I control this child?" we can think of our child as being on the same team and invite his help and participation.

Julie's Story: Dirty Mother

When Rashi was a newborn and Asher was three, it was a challenge to take care of my own essential needs. Taking a shower often didn't make the cut.

One morning Rashi was taking one of his unpredictable naps and it struck me that with a little luck I might be able to take a shower before he woke up. The problem was that if I left Asher unsupervised, he was sure to make a beeline for the crib and do *something* to wake the baby.

I found Asher in the kitchen holding his Magic Mitts—plastic discs covered in velcro that you strap on your hands and use to catch a fuzzy ball.

"Mommy, you throw the ball!"

Darn it. Asher had other ideas for this precious nap period. If I wanted to be clean I was going to have to be skillful. Rashi was a light sleeper.

"Oh, you want to play with the Magic Mitts now."

"Throw it!"

"I want to take a shower now. What should we do?"

Asher thought for a moment. "I can get the tape player and listen to *Sesame Street* in the bathroom."

"I like that idea. Let's do it!"

I got my shower that morning. A clean victory!

• • •

Here's another story where an attitude of problem-solving led to a quick fix.

Joanna's Story: The Trouble with Trikes

It was one of those miserable, cold, rainy days that parents of young children dread. Outside, the unpaved driveway was a sea of mud. Luckily two-and-a-half-year-old Danny was having a fine time riding his tricycle in the kitchen. The problem was that he only wanted to ride it unnervingly close to six-month-old Sam, who was on the floor trying to crawl.

"Dan, not so near the baby!" "Dan, you'll hurt his little fingers." "Dan, I'm going to have to put the trike away if you keep doing that."

Dan ignored my warnings and threats, supremely confident of his ability to pilot around his helpless brother. I didn't really want to put the trike away. It was keeping him happy and occupied. So instead of making good on my threat I decided to try something new. I knew he was still too young for problem-solving. He wasn't even talking much yet. But I felt like I had nothing to lose. I said, "Danny, I can see you're enjoying riding your trike in the kitchen. And Sammy is enjoying watching you." (That was the accepting feelings part of the formula.)

"The problem is, I'm worried about his little fingers being hurt by the wheels." (That was the describing the problem part.)

"What should we do? We need an idea!" (That was the asking for solutions part.)

Danny gazed thoughtfully into the distance and pronounced, "Danny ride ovah heah."

He pushed his trike to the other side of the kitchen, away from his brother. I was astounded. My terrible-two-year-old was perfectly willing to cooperate as long as he could be the idea man. After that incident, *"Danny have a idea!"* became an oft heard phrase in our house.

And another problem-solving fix, not quite so quick.

Joanna's Story: Miss Liberty Pitches In

It wasn't until Danny was two years and eight months old that we had our first formal problem-solving session, complete with pencil and paper and a list of ideas posted with a magnet to the refrigerator door.

I remember his exact age because I was so eager to have a child who could deposit bodily fluids in a potty, that I was counting the months. Heck, I was counting the minutes. We talked about "that feeling you get" when the pee wants to come out, and how hard it is to stop what you're doing and get to the bathroom, pull down your pants, and sit on the potty in time. We spent a few housebound, winter days practicing, with Dan sitting on the potty at random intervals waiting for the magic to happen.

Finally, it all came together. I had a boy who was toilet trained. My first ever! And then a few weeks later, he lost interest. The bloom was off the rose. The potty was old news. He would clutch his crotch while playing and insist that he did "NOT need to go to the bathroom!"

When he could hold it no longer, he would let loose a stream on the carpeted floor. Then he would run to the kitchen, drag the stool to the supply cabinet so he could reach the foam action carpet cleaner, and enthusiastically scrub away at the carpet. My toilet training triumph was crumbling before my eyes.

I got out my pencil and paper and started in, reading aloud as I wrote.

"Dan does not like to stop playing to go to the bathroom!"

"Mom does not like pee on the carpet."

"What are you doing?" asked Dan.

"We need ideas for this problem," I announced.

I wrote numbers one through four along the margin of the page. I was feeling hopeful. I looked at Dan. He looked back at me. I knew I was supposed to let the child go first, but this child wasn't saying anything. I realized I hadn't thought this through ahead of time. I didn't have anything creative or clever to offer. But I had started this and I was going to go with the flow, even if it was just an ooze.

I read aloud as I wrote, "Number one, Mom will remind Dan in a friendly way to go to the bathroom."

Now Dan was ready to jump in. "Number two, Dan will clean the floor with carpet cleaner."

I gritted my teeth and wrote it down without protest. Next I offered, "Number three, Dan can wear diapers if he doesn't want to pee in the potty."

Dan was gazing vacantly around the room. His eyes lighted on a green plastic Statue of Liberty souvenir I had purchased on one of my school trips. "The little green man will tell me, 'peepee in the pot.'"

I thought, *Oh well, this is not working.* But I forged ahead. "Let's look at our list and see which ideas we like and which we don't like."

Number one: the friendly reminder. Dan strongly objected. We crossed it out.

Number two: Dan liked this one but Mom didn't. The

carpet was getting too smelly. There's only so much action in that foam. We crossed it out.

Number three: Dan was happy to go back to diapers, but Mom objected to her own idea. We crossed it out.

Number four: the little green man. It was all we had left. I had my doubts but I managed to sound enthusiastic as we both put big check marks on number four.

I posted the list on the refrigerator and waited for the next crotch-clutching incident. It happened at dinner time. Dan was squeezing and wiggling, making no move to get up. I picked up Miss Liberty, held it to his ear, and whispered, "Peepee in the pot," in my best raspy, bronze statue–like voice. Dan took the statue and whispered something back (I never found out what) and then jumped up and went to the bathroom!

For the next few months I carried that "little green man" everywhere with me. It was my emissary to my son's bladder. No longer did I have to suffer the embarrassment of a teenaged grocery clerk telling me, "Excuse me, Ma'am, your son needs to go to the bathroom," while I shrugged helplessly. Now I could whip out the little green man and off we'd trot to the lavatory.

There was one bit of social awkwardness when my Swedish friend spotted me clutching my statue. "My, aren't we patriotic. Should I be carrying the Swedish flag?"

And while we're on the topic of toilet training, here's a much shorter problem-solving session with my youngest son, Zach. As you will see, I didn't follow the correct protocol: accepting feelings, describing the problem, and asking for ideas. Nevertheless, we muddled through.

Going Natural

> **Frustrated Mother:** Zach, let's give the potty a try.
> **Recalcitrant Two-and-a-Half-Year-Old:** NO!
> **FM:** It could be fun to see if you can fill the pot with pee. Then you wouldn't have to wear a diaper.
> **RTAHYO:** I'm not "instrested" in that.
> **FM:** You do it when we're outside. You know how to stop playing and pull down your pants and pee in the bushes.
> **RTAHYO:** That's because I'm peeing on leaves. I LIKE to pee on leaves!
> **FM:** Okay, let's go get some leaves.

We go outside and pick leaves. We bring them in and nestle the leaves into the potty. Zach immediately pulls down his pants and pees on the leaves.

> **FM:** You did it!
> **RTAHYO:** I *told* you!

Fortunately there is an endless free supply of fresh leaves in our yard. Potty training is on!

Problem-solving can take on endless variations. It can be an activity for two or a group effort.

Sarah's Story: Stop Means Go

My three kids get really wound up at about 5 o'clock in the evening. They like to play this crazy game where they go hurtling through the house, chasing each other and generally crashing into things. It hardly ever ends well. At first they're all excited and happy, but my youngest, Mia, usually ends up getting hurt. Or at least upset enough to feel like she's hurt.

I've tried to stop them in the past. It's just so stressful, waiting for the disaster and the tears. They always protest that they're having fun and everyone is laughing. Sure, until they're not!

I tried the problem-solving approach. It was easier than I thought. Here's how it went:

Me: You guys love chasing each other around the house. It's fun. The problem is I get upset because a lot of times someone ends up crying. I think we need some ideas for how you can have fun without anybody getting hurt or even scared.

Mia: When I say stop, Jake and Sophia don't stop.

Sophia: That's because you're *laughing* when you say stop! You just want to win all the time.

Jake: Yeah, you act like a baby.

Mia: I'm not a baby, stupid-head!

Me: Hey, no name-calling. We're trying to think of ideas here! Maybe "stop" isn't a good word because sometimes people say "stop" when they're just playing and sometimes they say "stop" when they're scared or hurt. It can be confusing. Maybe we need a better word that means "really stop, I'm not kidding around."

Mia: (She climbed up on a chair and put her finger in the

air to make her pronouncement.) I know! We can say
"PAUSE THE GAME!"

Sophia and Jake agreed. "Stop" will mean go. "Pause the game"
will mean stop. They went back to running around. Whenever
Mia started to feel a little bit overwhelmed, she wielded her
new power. "Pause the game!" Every time she said it, all the
children froze. They didn't seem to mind the new twist to the
activity. Then she'd yell, "Play!" and they'd go back to running.

This is absolutely better than threats and ultimatums.
It's teaching them how to play together and be more aware
of each other's point of view.

 **Show respect for the conflict. Don't min-
imize the problem.**

When there's ongoing conflict between kids, we get worn
down. We just want it to go away. "Stop already! It doesn't
matter!" But all our attempts to sweep the problem under
the rug do not result in peace and harmony. We keep tripping
over that lumpy rug.

The battle over the TV remote control may seem petty to
you. Who cares whether the kids watch a show where various
objects are blown up in the name of science, or a cartoon
about a fruit-dwelling sponge creature?

Keep in mind, this conflict matters just as much to your
children as any dispute with a coworker, friend, or relative
matters to you. Children need practice resolving their "childish"
disputes so they can become grown-ups who can peacefully
resolve their adult disputes. This is the work of childhood.

Instead of saying, "Oh please, again with the remote? You're being silly. It's not worth fighting over."

You can say, "This is a difficult problem. Two children want to watch two different shows."

You'll have to resist the urge to take sides. "You always get your way. Just let your little sister watch her cartoon so she doesn't make a fuss." Avoid the temptation to solve their problem for them. "Let your brother watch his show today and then you can watch yours tomorrow."

But you can't just walk away, either. (Sorry if you were hoping for that!) Unless your kids are already experienced problem-solvers, they'll still need your help and guidance.

 **Remove the disputed object temporarily.**

When the disputed object is in one child's hand it will be hard for them to think clearly. The struggle will continue. You'll need to say, "I'll put the remote control up on the shelf for now, while we figure out what to do. I bet if we put our heads together we can think of a solution that feels fair to both of you."

Your next job is to listen and reflect back each child's perspective. You'll find yourself saying, "Oh, so all day you've been looking forward to watching the explosion show. They're going to blow up a whole stack of watermelons and you don't want to miss it."

Then you'll turn to your other child and reflect her feelings. "Ah, so you feel like you never get to watch your cartoon. It's not fair. Your brother always grabs the remote and you have to miss your sponge guy. And he's really funny!"

Back to the first child, "I hear you saying that the sponge

cartoon is on every day, sometimes twice a day, and your show is only on once a week. This is your only chance to see it!"

Then you'll say, "Hmmm, what can we do so that both of you get to see the show you like? Should we take turns? Should we make a schedule and have certain days for each person to decide? What do you guys think will work?"

Your kids will be pleased with themselves when they come up with their own plan. What's more, they'll be learning to fight less and negotiate more when they have conflicts in the future.

The Trouble with Rewards

What about rewards? you ask. *If you didn't have time for problem-solving, couldn't you offer a reward? That's a positive solution, isn't it? And positive is good, right?*

Let's take a moment to think about how it feels to be offered a reward in return for a change in behavior. Imagine that you've been turning out some delicious late-night dinners for your family on your night to cook. You're pretty pleased with yourself. Between work, shopping, cleaning, and supervising kids, it's remarkable that the family is getting healthy, home-cooked meals instead of take-out pizza. But your spouse isn't happy and says to you, "I need you to make dinner earlier on week nights so I can get to bed earlier. Listen, I'm going to offer you a reward. For every five nights that you get dinner on the table by 6 p.m., I'll take you out to a restaurant of your choice. I made a sticker chart so I can track your successes!"

What's wrong with this scenario? Why do we suddenly have the urge to serve dinner at midnight . . . burnt?

Well, first of all, does your spouse even care about *your* feelings? Does he not recognize the effort you put into all this food production? Does he realize how difficult it would be

to get it all done earlier? And what if you get dinner on the table early four nights in a row, and then mess up on the fifth? Do you have to start from square one because of a single misstep? Is it even worth the effort? What about that reward? Maybe a new car would be a better incentive. Maybe you should be getting rewards for all the other things you do around the house. A new pair of boots for folding the laundry, a flat-screen TV for cleaning the toilet.

Rewards have many pitfalls. They don't address the cause of the problem. They are used to manipulate the other person rather than work with her, which can lead to resentment. They are subject to inflation. And they have a dark side. A reward is offered with an implied threat: If you don't do what I say, you'll miss out on something good.

Most people would prefer a partner who is willing to work with them to solve a problem. Someone who might say, "Gee, I really appreciate all these delicious meals. My problem is, I'm frustrated with the late nights. I feel like I'm not getting enough sleep. Is there anything we can do to get dinner on the table earlier? What could I do to help make that happen? Let's think of some ideas!"

Here's a report from the frontlines of a reward gone bad.

Sarah's Story: Gum Grievance

I had a bunch of tedious errands to run and three young children to drag along. I promised them each a stick of chewing gum once they got to the grocery store if they could cooperate at the bank and post office. The kids were excited. *Yes, gum!*

But my youngest and liveliest daughter, Mia, could not control herself. She managed to sit quietly at the drive-through bank, happily watching the vacuum tube suck up the deposit slips. But by the time we got to the post office she was out of her carseat and crawling around the van causing mayhem. No gum for her! The well-behaved siblings got their treats, and Mia cried and raged all the way through the grocery shopping. It was a miserable day.

What went wrong? The corollary to "you can have this wonderful thing if you do as I say" is "you can't have this wonderful thing if you *don't* do as I say." The reward slips its mask and reveals itself as a punishment in disguise. And more important, it doesn't help a little girl stay in a carseat. If Sarah had talked to her kids about how boring errands are and how difficult it is to stay belted in for a long time, then challenged them to come up with ideas for how to amuse themselves and one another while imprisoned in their carseats, they might have had more success. They could have come up with games, songs, or stories to make the car ride more bearable. And what's more, they would have been learning important skills for dealing with adverse circumstances. More time-consuming than offering a stick of gum, but more useful in the long run.

The same is true for siblings fighting, toilet training, good grades in school, or eating broccoli. No promise of reward will help a child learn how to get along with a younger brother, figure out when his bladder is full, learn addition facts, or enjoy healthy food.

If this sounds overly idealistic to you, consider the latest research on motivation. An eye-opening study found that when people are offered large monetary rewards to complete a challenge, their creativity and engagement in the task plummets. Rewards helped people perform well on some very simple mechanical tasks, but as soon as they needed cognitive skills, rewards interfered with their ability to function. These surprising results have been replicated in study after study. It turns out that the three factors that motivate people most strongly are a sense of autonomy (the drive to be self-directed), mastery (the intrinsic drive to develop competence), and purpose (a sense that our actions are meaningful and have value).[2]

"So we're not supposed to use any kind of incentive, ever? You're making my life more difficult!" complained Anna.

I'm not saying you shouldn't use incentives. Just use them for your kids the way you use them for yourself. You might tell yourself, *After I get through this sinkful of dirty pots and pans, I'm going to sit down with the paper and a nice cup of tea.* It helps to give yourself something to look forward to when faced with an unpleasant task.

In the same spirit, you might tell your children, "Let's think of a good snack we can have on the ride home. That way we can look forward to getting into the car, even though it's sad to leave your friend's house."

The difference is that you're not saying "*if* you get in the car, *then* I'll give you a treat." You're planning your exit strategy *together* as a team.

You can let them know that fun activities await them when chores are finished.

"*As soon as* we get our teeth brushed, we can have bedtime stories."

"*As soon as* the blocks are put away, we can go to the park."

You've avoided the unpleasant and manipulative "*If* you do this, *then* I'll give you that" statement, and replaced it with information.

The Trouble with Time-Outs

Toni had her hand in the air. "Okay, so no punishments and no rewards. What I want to know is, how do you feel about time-outs? Are you going to take that away from us too?"

I hated to be the eternal naysayer. I took a deep breath and shrugged sadly. Toni threw up her hands in mock despair.

Usually when people ask me what I think of time-outs, they want to know what they're doing wrong. Why is this technique not working for them? It doesn't seem to lead to improved behavior and it's difficult to enforce. How do you make a child stay in a time-out chair? My answer is that the reason time-outs aren't working for you is that time-outs don't work.[3] The main weakness of the "time-out" is that it doesn't address the problem. Let's say your son shoves his little sister away from his blocks, and you grab him by the shoulder and rush him to the time-out chair. What do you think he'll be saying to himself as he sits in that chair?

We'd like to imagine that he's thinking, *Gee, this chair time is helping me realize that I should show a lot more love and tenderness to my dear sister. After all, we do have shared genetic material. As the older child I should learn to be more patient, even when she's irritating me.*

Unfortunately it's more likely that his thoughts will run along the lines of, *It's not fair. I hate her. She pushed me first. She's always ruining everything. Mom always takes her side.* Or he may be thinking, *I'm mean to my sister. I'm a bad person.*

And that's if you can get him to stay in the chair in the first place!

If our intent is to foster a better relationship between siblings, time-out is not the answer.

So what can you do? First you can comfort your daughter and express your feelings strongly to your son. "I don't like to see people pushed! Even when you're angry!"

You can invite your son to make amends, if the mood is right. "Ella is crying. How can we make her feel better? Can you find her a toy? Or do you think she'd like a pretzel?"

Once the drama is over, you can have a conversation about how difficult it is to build with blocks when a little sister is around. A big brother needs ideas for what to do next time so he won't end up hurting his sister. Maybe he can play with blocks in his room. Maybe he can make a tower for her to knock down. Maybe he can have a special word that he uses when he needs you to come and help very quickly. Any of these solutions will help him to see himself as a responsible older brother who can coexist peacefully with a little sister.

This is not to say that you won't sometimes have to separate a child from a situation that is overwhelming him. If you really want to use the phrase *time-out* in a positive way, you can say, "*We* need a time-out so nobody gets hurt! Quick, Thomas to the kitchen, Jenna to the living room!" You may even say, "I'm getting frustrated. *I* need a time-out. I'm going to my bedroom for a few minutes to calm down!" This kind of time-out is intended to protect, not to punish. It's a way of letting our children know that sometimes we need to take a break before we can solve a problem.

I watched my neighbor use this technique with her three-year-old daughter, who would often become overstimulated when playing with other children and behave roughly with the smaller kids. Her mom would say warmly, "Jackie, come over here and sit with me for a little while. We need some time-out." She'd sit with her arm comfortingly around her daughter for a few minutes, then ask her if she thought she was ready to go back to playing. There's a very different feeling to that kind of time-out. It doesn't say, "I'm banishing you because you were bad." The message here is, "I'm on your side. It's not easy to play with a bunch of kids. Let's take a break together." Some people call this a *time-in*: taking a break *with* a child, and refreshing the sense of connection between the two of you.

Michael's Story: Sad Sister

Jamie and Kara get into a lot of conflicts, which almost always end up with Kara crying. Of course, she's only two and Jamie is four, so there's really no contest. Jan and I used to remind him constantly that Kara is just a baby and he needs to be patient with her. Jamie doesn't want to hear it. I can see it in his face even if he doesn't say anything. *No fair, you always take her side.* We also were giving him time-outs for being rough with her. That didn't make things better either, but it was all we had.

Now that we've been using the problem-solving approach I see a real change in Jamie. They still have fights, but when Kara cries, I say to Jamie, "Oh no, Kara is sad. We need an idea to make her feel better." It's hard to believe, but it actually transforms him. He gets very serious. "I think she needs her teddy bear to hug," or "Can we give her some apple slices with cinnamon?" He's really thinking about how to make his sister happy. And he's more patient with her in general. At first I thought the "no punishment" thing was a bit over the top, but this is the better way!

 **You don't have to wait for a problem to occur in order to use problem-solving. When possible, plan ahead!**

Here's a story that involves prescient parenting—solving a problem *before* it happens. When we know we're headed for trouble, like the proverbial Boy Scout, we can be prepared! We don't have to wait for disaster to strike. When you plan ahead *with* your children, so much the better! Toni managed to turn a dreaded ordeal into a well-choreographed success, with some creative, preventative problem-solving.

Toni's Story: The Opposite of Winging It

My in-laws were having a family reunion and they expected us to be there. They don't have any memory of what it's like to have young children. They actually insisted it would be a nice vacation for us. The thought of five and a half hours on a plane with my kids was daunting. I had to prepare them if we were going to survive!

I lined up the kitchen chairs so they could practice walking down a narrow aisle. I gave each of them a backpack to carry, and I walked behind them and announced when we reached our row. Then I had them sit in chairs, one behind the other, and stuff their packs under the seats. I told them to kick the seat in front of them and notice how annoying it felt, especially while trying to draw or read. We practiced sitting in the chairs, keeping our feet off the chairs in front of us. We repeated the whole routine every day for three days before the flight.

Then we made a list of things you can do while stuck in a seat. It included reading, drawing, and a game called a Million Questions—they didn't like the idea of only twenty questions. I took them to the library and they each picked out a book for me to read and to the dollar store to pick out their own "magic" coloring books, activity books, and more food! They each packed a bag full of loot for the trip.

I knew I would need some surprises up my sleeve so I also collected a bunch of things to pull out during the flight. I stuffed my pockets with stickers, finger puppets, and little packets of goldfish crackers.

The flight went smoothly. The kids didn't kick the seats or throw their toys, and they were excited about all the new things in their backpacks. The flight attendant actually complimented me on how well-behaved my kids were. If she only knew!

The minute we got to my in-laws' house, Jenna threw up. Turned out she had a stomach virus. My husband and I spent the entire "vacation" taking turns in the hotel room. I think we'll wait a few years before our next family trip.

And then there are those parenting moments when everything falls apart. You didn't know the bridge was out, and you're on track heading at full speed for the ravine. The train wreck is unavoidable. Creating a family atmosphere of seeking solutions rather than inventing punishments will still stand you in good stead in the long run.

The Cliffhanger

Five-year-old Zach had a fit at bedtime when I finished reading a chapter and told the kids it was time for sleep. He wasn't used to chapter books and had a hard time accepting that we couldn't finish the whole book in one sitting. But he still wanted to join in on his older brothers' story time. "It's a two-hundred-page book!" I protested. "I can't finish it in one night, and besides, Sammy's already asleep."

"But it's a cliffhanger!" he screamed. How could I leave him like this, not knowing the ending to the story? In a fit of rage he grabbed an empty plastic seltzer bottle (you can see how neat my house is) and flung it at my head. His aim was true. The lovely story time ended with me yelling, "I will never read you a story again!" while my husband carried Zach, hysterically sobbing, off to his bedroom, away from his raving mother. There was just no salvaging the situation. I was furious. *Is this supposed to be part of motherhood? Having projectiles lobbed at my head? Good thing it was plastic, not glass! Good thing I'm not a single mom right now.*

Problem-solving? Punishment? Forget about it. Survival is all we're striving for here.

The next night at dinner I said, "I don't know what to do. I want to read more of the book, but I don't want screaming and I don't want bottles thrown at me."

My husband laid down the law. "Everyone has to promise to go to bed without fuss when the chapter is over." I'm very dubious about extracting promises from children. Apparently Zach was just as reluctant to commit to a promise. "What if it's a cliffhanger?" His older brothers had taught him that word and he relished it!

Ten-year-old Dan had an idea. "I know! We can make predictions, like in school."

Zach was intrigued. "What's a prediction?"

His two brothers launched into a spirited explanation with many examples. Later that night, after I finished reading the agreed-upon chapter, I closed the book with a sense of trepidation. *What will happen this time? Would Zach hold it together, or are we in for another explosion?* Zach sat straight up and said, "Okay, now it's time for predictions. I predict that they will lock Lassie up even more tightly but she will still escape and go back to her family."

Then he trotted off to bed. I was truly amazed at both his equanimity and his accuracy.

There's no telling what solution kids will come up with when a problem is put in their hands. When the solution is their own, it will usually work for them. And when you have multiple kids, you have multiple problem-solvers instead of just multiple problems.

When we use problem-solving in place of punishment, we are truly modeling the attitude we want our kids to take toward conflict in their lives. Not "I'm a bad kid who doesn't deserve a bedtime story." Not "I'm a failure as a mom because I screamed at my kid," but rather, "How can I fix my mistake?" "How can I make things work better?" "What should I try next time?"

The larger message is: When there is conflict between us, we don't need to put our energy into fighting each other. We can combine forces to search for a solution that respects the needs of all parties. The child is an active participant in solving his problems. This will stand him in good stead in the years to come.

Punishment has a short shelf life. Little kids grow quickly. It's difficult to physically punish a child who is larger and stronger than you are. As children become more independent it becomes harder to enforce punishments. How do you ground a teenager or take away his screen privileges without becoming a prisoner of your own punishment?

This cooperative approach to conflict will grow with your child. As youngsters mature, their ability to problem-solve grows with them. When your children are out in the world you won't be able to keep them safe by force. The most powerful tool you can wield is their sense of connection to you. The fact that you are willing to consider their feelings and solicit their opinions will keep their hearts and minds open to your feelings and opinions.

Tools for Resolving Conflict

INSTEAD OF:

EXPRESS YOUR FEELINGS STRONGLY

HELP YOUR CHILD MAKE AMENDS

OFFER A CHOICE

YOU CAN DRAW ON PAPER OR CARDBOARD BOXES. YOU DECIDE.

TAKE ACTION WITHOUT INSULT

I'M PUTTING THE MARKERS AWAY FOR NOW.

I SEE IT'S TOO TEMPTING TO USE THEM ON THE FURNITURE.

TRY PROBLEM-SOLVING

STEP 1: ACKNOWLEDGE FEELINGS

YOU REALLY LIKE TO DRAW IN A LOT OF PLACES.

STEP 2: DESCRIBE THE PROBLEM

THE PROBLEM IS, I DON'T LIKE MARKS ON THE FURNITURE.

Tools for Resolving Conflict

STEP 3: ASK FOR IDEAS

WRITE ALL IDEAS WITHOUT JUDGMENT

STEP 4: DECIDE WHICH IDEAS TO USE

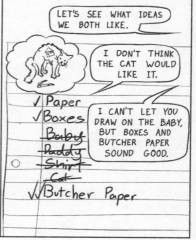

REMINDER: Tools for Resolving Conflict

1. Express Your Feelings . . . Strongly!

"*HEY*, I don't like to see people being pushed!"

2. Show Your Child How to Make Amends

"Your sister got scared on the top of the slide. Let's do something to make her feel better. Do you want to offer her some pretzels? Do you think she'd like to play with your sand bucket?"

3. Offer a Choice

"We're going to give the slide a rest for now. I can see you're in no mood to wait for a turn. You can swing on the swings or you can play in the sandbox. You decide."

4. Take Action Without Insult

"We're heading home. We'll try the playground another day. I'm too worried about children getting hurt right now."

5. Try Problem-Solving

Step One: Acknowledge your child's feelings
"I can see that you don't like your hand held in the parking lot. It makes your fingers feel squeezed."

Step Two: Describe the problem

"The problem is, I worry about cars hitting children in the parking lot."

Step Three: Ask for ideas

"We need some ideas so we can go back to the park and have a good time without people getting mad or scared. What can we do?"

Step Four: Decide which ideas you both like

"So you like the idea of holding on to my sleeve and leading me to the playground. Let's circle that one."

Step Five: Try out your solutions

"Here we are at the parking lot. Grab my sleeve and show me which way to go!"

- If nothing is working, you may have to reconsider your basic expectations.

- Show respect for the conflict. Don't minimize the problem.

- Remove the disputed object temporarily.

- You don't have to wait for a problem to occur in order to use problem-solving. When possible, plan ahead!

Chapter Four

Tools for Praise and Appreciation . . .
Not All Odes Are Equal

—Ways to praise that will help, not hinder

Julie

You've read the chapter title, and I know what you're thinking: *Really? Does everything have to be complicated? Sure, we all need help with children who scream and hit and run away in parking lots. But praise?*

Sorry to say, praise can be complicated. Research and observation suggest that it's not a matter of how much praise we dole out, but *the way we praise* that makes the difference.

Consider these scenarios:

1. You're an elementary school teacher. After a tough morning with a group of wild, quarrelsome, unfocused kids, there is a momentary lull. When your supervisor walks in, the kids are quietly listening to a story. The supervisor says: "You are the best instructor here. You have excellent control of your class."

What is your reaction to this praise? Are you glowing with pride of achievement? Or are you focusing on your weaknesses: *Are you kidding me? I couldn't control an elderly basset hound on a hot summer day. I just got lucky. I don't know if I should even be in this profession.*

2. You don't have any formal musical training, but you've always liked to sing in the shower. You decide to take it on to dry land and join a choir. After the first few sessions, you're still struggling. The harmonies are difficult and you can tell that much of the time you're not singing the right note. You say to the choir director, "I don't know if I should keep on with this. I'm just not getting it."

He replies, "Don't worry, you're doing fine! You sound really good out there."

Would that praise help you feel more confident? Or would you wonder, *Is he mistaken, or is he lying? Maybe he just didn't hear me because he was listening more to the sopranos. Maybe he's trying to make me feel better. Or maybe he just needs my membership fee for his next car payment.*

3. You spent weeks working on a proposal for a new reading program at your child's school. You send it to the director and wait eagerly for his response. The next day you get an email saying, "Great job. Thanks."

Are you elated that the director admired your ground-breaking ideas? Or are you wondering if he *really* liked it? Did he notice all the thought you put into your presentation, the way you backed up your ideas with the latest research, and solved the problem of funding? Or is he just checking off his to-do list—*clear email inbox*—before he goes home for the weekend?

4. You enjoy basketball. It's a fun way to get a workout, but you're only a fair player. You're shooting baskets at the gym and just as you finally sink one, some guy you don't know walks in and says, "Nice! You have a perfect jump shot!"

What's your reaction? Do you want to play a pickup game

with this guy, or are you more likely to hurry home before you dispel the good impression with a series of bungled shots?

What are we trying to accomplish when we offer our children praise? Most people say something like, "We're trying to make them aware of their own strengths." Or "We want to encourage them to do more of the same." Or "We want them to feel confident . . . or try even harder." It seems only natural that if we're trying to boost self-esteem, we'll tell our children frequently and enthusiastically, "You're great, smart, wonderful, beautiful, the best!"

But when we use words that evaluate, we often achieve the opposite effect. As you probably noticed when reading the scenarios above, praise that judges or evaluates can create problems.

It can make us focus on our weaknesses rather than our strengths. *I'm not really that great. You should have seen me ten minutes ago.*

It can make us doubt the sincerity of the person offering the praise. *Does he really mean it or is he just trying to make me feel good? What does he want from me?*

It can feel dismissive. *Did he even look at all that work I did? Maybe it wasn't worth the effort.*

It can make us feel threatened. *What if I can't do it again?*

It can even cause us to give up completely—to stop what we're doing and walk away.

I observed this

phenomenon at a music festival a few years ago. A group of jugglers were encouraging the public to try out the tools of their trade. I noticed a young boy, who was more persistent than most of the adults around him, managing to keep several beanbags in the air at the same time.

"Hey, look at that kid," I said to my husband. "He's really good!"

The boy looked up at me with a startled expression, put down the beanbags, and walked away.

What happened? Why did spontaneous praise from a bystander cause him to stop?

This boy was deeply engrossed in the process of learning something new and challenging. Suddenly he is being judged. Now, instead of focusing on the task at hand, he has to worry that he may fumble the next throw and have this bystander judge him as inadequate. Better to quit while you're ahead. What a miserable thing I did to this poor kid!

The first rule of praise is that it's not always appropriate to praise.

When a child is engaged in an activity, there is no need to disturb her concentration by looming over her and offering unsolicited comments. Give her space! Think about how you would feel if you were cooking dinner with your partner sitting a few feet away saying, "Nice technique slicing those onions. Good choice of cooking oil. The carrots are very evenly diced. You're displaying a very effective grip on that can opener." How many minutes could you put up with that before screaming "Leave me alone!"

But what about those times when kids *do* want a reaction? They run up to us, sticking their crayon drawings under our noses, saying "LOOK! Do you like it?" What kind of response will inspire rather than discourage?

Tools for Praise and Appreciation

TOOL #1: Describe What You See

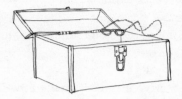

A more useful way to praise is to resist the impulse to evaluate and instead to simply describe what you see (or hear or notice with any of your five senses).

Instead of, "That's a beautiful picture!"
  Try, "I see green lines that are zooming up and down the page. And look how they connect all these red shapes!"

Instead of, "Good job!"
  Try, "I see you picked up all the cars and all the books, and you even picked up the dirty socks! I see bare floor. That was a big job."

Instead of, "Excellent work."
  Try, "I see you circled every single picture that begins with the letter *B*."

Instead of, "Good job following directions."
  Try, "You found your spot in the circle as soon as you heard 'circle time.'"

Instead of, "Nice try."

> Try, "That ball reached the fifth row of tiles on the wall. It's getting closer to the basket almost every time!"

> Or, if you're not in the mood for a lot of words, you can simply say "You did it!"

All of these statements let a child know that you noticed and appreciated something he did—without evaluation or judgment, which could discourage him from future efforts.

Sarah's Story: Fish Tale

There's a little girl at preschool who's always showing me her drawings. "Teacher, teacher, look!"

I say, "Very nice, that's beautiful."

Then she drops it on the floor and walks away. It's pretty much scribble, so there's not much else to say.

This time I said, "I see wiggly lines on the top and lots of blue on the bottom. It reminds me of the wind and sea."

She looked very intently at her own picture and pointed to a tiny squarish scribble that I hadn't noticed. "Do you see that? That is a little tiny fish!"

She went back to the craft table to draw more tiny "fish."

It seemed that my looking at the picture closely made her appreciate it more herself and want to work harder on it.

 **Consider asking questions or starting a conversation instead of praising.**

"Oh, look what you made! Tell me about this."

"How did you get the idea to do this?"

"How did you make this?"

"Show me how this works."

"This makes me think about outer space. What does it make you think about?"

"I wonder what you're going to make next."

Michael's Story: A Boy's Best Friend

I tried starting a conversation, and I almost got more than I bargained for. Jamie showed me one of his animal drawings and instead of the usual "Very nice," I said, "Oh, look at this! It makes me think of how much you like dogs."

"Yeah. This is the dog I'm going to have when I'm five years old. It'll have brown fur and I'm gonna teach it to sleep in my bed. And his name will be Slinky Dog. And he'll go to school with me every day . . ."

He went on describing his day with his dog and all the things he would teach it (to make his bed) and feed it (half of his peanut butter and jelly sandwich). I never knew he had such elaborate plans. I'm hoping he forgets about this by the time he turns five.

TOOL #2: Describe the Effect on Others

We all want our kids to be good citizens. We'd like to encourage their efforts to help others. But we need to beware the temptation to judge their character. Stick with description!

Instead of, "You're a good girl."
> You can say, "You carried those grocery bags all the way to the kitchen. That was a big help!"

Instead of, "You're the best big brother!"
> You can say, "The baby loves it when you make those funny sounds. I see a big smile on her face."

Instead of, "You're such a thoughtful little girl!"
> You can say, "You helped Johnny zip up his coat. Now he'll be nice and warm when he goes outside."

Instead of, "Good boy. I knew you could be nice to the kitty if you tried."
> You can say, "I hear Sparky purring. She likes that gentle petting."

Michael's Story: Go-Getter

My two-year-old, Kara, was asking for blueberries. I was ignoring her because I was trying to finish a work email. Finally my four-year-old, Jamie, dragged a stool over to the refrigerator and got her the blueberries. I said, "Wow, Jamie, you just made two people happy. You made Kara happy because she got her blueberries, and you made me happy because I got to finish my work."

All week Jamie's been jumping up to get things for me and his sister. He's usually very demanding—"Get me this, get me that"—and I'm always trying to encourage him to ask politely. Now he's the getter!

Sarah's Story: Praise Rephrase

I used to believe girls were easy because my oldest has always been exceptionally cooperative. But lately my three-year-old, Mia, has been doing everything she can to annoy or defy me. When we have to go somewhere, she squeezes behind the back seat of the van and refuses to climb into her carseat, making the whole family late. When we have to get out of the car she bolts into the parking lot. She breaks her siblings' crayons, yells when my sister's baby is sleeping, even shoves big kids in the playground. If it's known as bad, you name it, she does it.

I've really tried hard *not* to put her in the role of the "Bad Child." As a matter of fact, I was making a big effort to tell her what a good girl she is. The funny thing is, it seemed to make it even worse. At dinner I was telling my husband what a good girl she was at story hour at the library, and Mia said, "No, I *wasn't* good. I knocked the books down on the floor. I was loud."

She was angry and pouting all evening. It's like she wanted to remind us that her sister is the good girl, and she's the bad one.

After our session on praise, I switched tactics. I told my husband how Mia helped me at the library by carrying all the heavy books down the stairs and checking them out by herself. Mia smiled from ear to ear. You could see how proud she was. She stuck out her chest and said, "I did do that. And I held the door for the stroller, too!"

When I described what she did, she praised *herself*! I have to admit, Mia has not been magically transformed from a tiger to a pussycat. But this new way of praising is changing the way she sees herself.

TOOL #3 Describe Effort

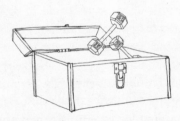

A researcher at Stanford University, Carol Dweck, formally studied the effects of evaluative praise on children. She was interested in exploring the phenomenon of bright children who do very well in elementary school and then seem to lose confidence and stop trying by the time they reach middle school, despite repeated reassurance that they are smart, gifted, talented . . . exceptional![1]

She designed a study in which two groups of children were given a sheet of math questions to solve. When the task was completed, the first group was given evaluative praise. "Wow . . . that's a really good score. You must be smart at this." The message is clear: *You are a bright child, talented at math.*

The second group was also told that they had done well. But they were not labeled or evaluated. Instead their process was described with appreciation. "Wow . . . that's a really good score. You must have worked really hard." A different kind of message: *You stuck with it. You kept trying until you figured out all the problems.*

Now the two groups were asked if they would like to try an even more challenging set of math questions. Guess who said *yes* and who said *no*. If you guessed that the first group said *no*, give yourself some praise! When a child has done well and been told that she's gifted and talented, why would she risk her status by trying something more difficult? She might fail. It may turn out she's not gifted after all. She's just ordinary.

The children in the second group, whose *efforts* had been described, were enthusiastic about taking on a more challenging task.

Both groups were then given a new sheet of math questions. But this time the first group, the children who had been showered with evaluative praise, did *worse*. Their confidence was shot. In contrast, the children whose efforts were appreciated did better.

It's no surprise that children who are told they are smart and talented often fall apart when they encounter their first real challenges. When things are easy for them, their label is confirmed. They are the best and the brightest. But when they find themselves struggling, as eventually they will, their faith in themselves is shaken. *Maybe I'm not so smart after all.* Better to stick to the safety zone and not reveal weakness.

As you can see, praise is indeed powerful. Used the wrong way, it can deter children from activities and behaviors that we mean to encourage. Maybe all of that "overpraising" of children is really just the wrong kind of praise.

Here's how it sounds when you praise effort instead of evaluating the child:

Instead of, "What a smart boy you are!"
You can say, "You kept on working on that puzzle until you figured it out."

Instead of, "You're very talented at gymnastics."
You can say, "I saw you climbing onto that balance beam again and again until you walked the whole beam without falling off."

Instead of, "Good job dressing yourself."
Try, "You kept working on that button until you got it into that little buttonhole."

Sarah's Story: Ready or Not

Every spring I'm required to give my five-year-olds a screening test. The children are supposed to fill out a twenty-page packet of written activities to assess their readiness for kindergarten, from shape recognition, to math puzzles, to cutting and tracing. In all the years I've done this I've never been able to get more than a few kids to complete the whole packet, in spite of my best effort to give positive feedback: "Nice job." "You're doing great." "Keep up the good work." "Just do your best."

This year I used what I learned in our session on praise.

Instead of evaluating, I described their effort, "I see how hard you're working!" "You've been concentrating hard for a long time!" "Looks like you're really using a lot of brainpower to figure this out."

I thought it would help a little, but I was amazed that not a single child gave up. Even when recess came, several insisted on continuing until they completed the packet.

TOOL #4: Describe Progress

One advantage of descriptive praise is that you can use it even when things aren't going particularly well, by pointing out what has been achieved so far.

When a child is making a mess or struggling with a task, it's tempting to point out what she's doing wrong. After all, won't that help her improve?

The problem is, criticism in the midst of a struggle can be discouraging. On the other hand, inauthentic praise ("Don't worry, you're doing *fine*!") can be infuriating ("*No*, I am NOT doing fine!").

With descriptive praise, we can point out *progress* in a way that feels supportive and genuine. Often pointing out one positive thing is more effective than pointing out ten negatives.

Instead of pointing out what's wrong . . .

"This handwriting is so sloppy it's almost impossible to read, honey. It looks like a chicken with muddy feet walked across your paper. You need to at least *try* to get the letters on the line."

. . . you'll have a more motivated child if you point out what's right:

"Look at this letter *B*! It's a real beauty contest winner. It sits so politely on the line. It's not busting through the floor and bothering the downstairs neighbors. It's not flying up in the air and banging on the ceiling."

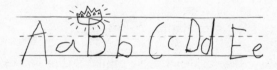

"Look at the big spaces between these four words. This part is very clear and easy to read."

Sometimes we do need to point out what's wrong. Kids don't always notice on their own. In a case like this it's important to appreciate the positive *first*. If you want a criticism to be accepted graciously, a good rule to follow is to notice three positive things before mentioning the negative. And even then it's most useful to put your criticism in positive terms. Talk about what "needs to be done" rather than what is still wrong.

Tools for Praise and Appreciation

Instead of criticizing an unfinished task . . .

"Are you kidding me? You think you're finished? This room isn't even close to being clean. There are blocks all over the floor and your desk is under a pile of trash!"

. . . you'll be more likely to inspire a child to finish cleaning if you notice what he has accomplished so far:

"I can see you got your dirty clothes in the laundry basket, you hung up your wet towel, and there's a clear path from the door to the bed! Now all this room needs to be ready for company is for the blocks to be tossed into their box and the dirty tissues on the desk to be thrown in the garbage can."

Instead of focusing on the mistakes . . .

"I can see you haven't been practicing. You're playing a lot of wrong notes, and your rhythm is wrong, too. Quarter notes aren't the same as half notes!"

. . . you'll give a child the confidence to tackle the hard parts if you start by focusing on what he's accomplished so far:

"Those first two measures make me want to dance. I get a lively feeling when I hear the staccato notes. I can imagine a little frog jumping. The second line has a tricky rhythm. Let's work on that next."

Toni's Story: DIY Disaster

Grandma was visiting and brought a kit to make a gingerbread house. It should have been a lovely opportunity for the generations to bond. Unfortunately the icing was stiff and the gingerbread was crumbly. Thomas was getting frustrated. Grandma tried to encourage him: "Thomas, that's really good!"

Thomas was red-faced and angry. "No it's not! The blue is all smushed on the side and the edge broke off!"

I could see it coming. He was about to stomp off and my mother was going to be very disappointed that her gift didn't work out.

I knew what to say! "Thomas, I see you got half of the window done, even though the icing is so stiff."

Thomas sighed. "Yeah, I'm getting the other half now."

Whew! Good save, right?

Anna's Story: Beginning Reader

Anton sounded out his first few words and actually read a sentence. I was very excited and about to say, "You are a great reader!" but I caught myself and came up with, "You sounded out each of the letters and you put them together. You read a whole sentence!"

Anton grinned. "Let's do another one!"

Are you getting the idea that description is more genuine than the old style of praise? We don't have to be inauthentic and tell a child he is *wonderful* and his work is *great* in order to inflate his ego. We can give him specific descriptive feedback that is realistic and helpful.

Sometimes acknowledging feelings can be more helpful than praise.

Sometimes a kid is not happy with the results of his labor. His picture of a bicycle doesn't look like a bicycle. Our impulse is to offer encouraging words: "No, it's really good, honey. It does look like a bicycle. You did such a nice job!"

This kind of response often produces rage and wailing: "No it doesn't. I HATE it!"

But we don't want to show a lack of faith in his ability, either. "Oh dear, a bicycle is too hard to draw. Why don't you just draw a ball for the letter *B*? Your teacher will be happy and all you have to make is a circle. You can do that!"

Time to switch gears and acknowledge feelings. When kids are unhappy, we don't have to prop them up with frantic praise. It's more helpful to say, "Ugh, you are *not* happy with the way that bicycle came out. It doesn't look like what you see in your head. It's not easy to draw a bike. It's hard to put something from real life onto a flat piece of paper and get it to look right."

Your child may respond with renewed efforts to draw that infernal two-wheeler. Or he may decide on his own to draw a ball instead. Either way, your emotional support helped him through his moment of frustration, and he can think more clearly.

Another situation in which our impulse is to offer reassuring words of praise is when a child compares himself to his peers and finds himself lacking.

"Everybody can climb the monkey bars except me! I can't even get across two. I'm the worst in the whole class."

"Ethan and Jason can already read chapter books. I'm the slowest one at reading."

Our instinct is to jump in with words of praise to bolster our child's flagging self-esteem.

"Oh no, honey, you're really good at climbing."

"You're a really good reader! You're doing an excellent job. I'm sure there are lots of kids who aren't as good as you are."

This kind of response usually does not achieve the intended effect. Kids will protest even more vehemently that they are indeed the worst, the slowest. When a child is feeling down, it's more helpful to acknowledge feelings first, instead of offering empty reassurance:

"It's frustrating to see other kids get across all the monkey bars when you can't do it yet."

"It sounds like you're feeling discouraged about reading. It's annoying to be stuck with a picture book when you want to be reading chapter books."

If you think the mood is right you can try giving wishes in fantasy:

"Wouldn't it be nice if you could just eat three magic raisins and . . . zip across the whole playground hand over hand without getting tired! . . . read a thick chapter book and know all the words?"

But that's not the end of the conversation. When a child is feeling low, you'll want to give him a picture of himself that inspires him to strive.

 **Give a child a new picture of himself.**

It's time to tell your child a story about himself. And this is a story only you can tell. You know your kid like no other!

"I'm pretty sure that if you want to master those monkey bars you will get there. When you want to do something you are a pretty determined kid. I remember when you were just five months old, too young to crawl. But you wanted to get to that dog bowl. You kept trying and trying. I had to go to the bathroom, and I thought it would be okay to leave you alone for just a minute. But when I got back, there you were, munching on Rover's dog kibble. You made it all the way across the kitchen on your own. Nothing was safe from you!"

"It's weird. Each person is different. Some kids, like Ethan, learn to read chapter books before kindergarten, but they can't ride a two-wheeler yet. And some kids, like you, learn to ride a bike without training wheels when they're only three, and they're still working on reading a chapter book. Some kids learn reading faster and some kids learn riding faster, but they all learn to read and they all learn to ride. I've seen you sounding out words and reading sentences, so I know you're learning. And I've seen Ethan working on balancing on his bike, so I know he's learning. I just hope you don't start reading while riding. That could cause a big crash!"

Another way to give a child a new picture of himself is to give him opportunities to demonstrate his competence.

"Rashi, can you help me with this key? It's sticking in the lock again."

"Asher, I have to put away groceries and Shiriel needs someone to read the *Things That Go* book to her. Can you do it? She likes hearing it read by her big brother."

You may find yourself "needing help" a whole lot in the near future, with opening jar lids, filling juice glasses, finding your glasses, tightening screws, buckling the baby into the carseat, feeding the animals, arranging dessert on a plate, handing out art supplies, collecting papers, shutting doors, and turning off lights. Don't forget to enlist your competent child or student to give you a hand. And then be sure to appreciate the help with descriptive praise.

Maria had her hand up in the air. "How about telling your child 'I'm proud of you'? Isn't that one more way of making a child feel good about himself?"

Here's my reservation about that statement. When a parent or teacher says, "I'm proud of you," she's taking credit herself for the child's accomplishment. When she describes what the child has achieved, the child gets the credit. When in doubt, credit the child.

Instead of, "You're riding without training wheels. I'm so proud of you!"

You can say, "You did it! You figured out how to balance on your bike without training wheels. You must be pretty pleased with yourself!"

 **Resist the urge to praise by comparison.**

It can be tempting to parents of more than one child to praise by comparison. We fall into the trap of trying to boost the ego of the "big boy" at the expense of the baby. It seems like a harmless ploy. After all, the baby can't understand what we're saying. "You got your shoes on by yourself. Your little brother can't do that. He's just a baby." "You're such a neat eater. The baby makes a big mess."

Sometimes we want to give a little boost by comparing a child favorably to his peers.

"You can already ride a two-wheeler. None of your friends can do that." "You're the best reader in the class. Not many five-year-olds can read a chapter book!"

So what's wrong with that? Proud parents and teachers, happy kids, right? The problem is, we don't want a child to feel that our pride in his success comes at the expense of others' failures. We don't want him to feel threatened by the accomplishments of his rapidly growing sibling, or the triumphs of his classmates.

Instead you can stick with **describing his actions, his efforts, his progress, and his effect on others**:

"You got your shoes on by yourself. I guess I know who'll be teaching the baby to tie his shoes when he gets a little bigger." (Now he can see himself as a teacher of his little brother instead of as a rival.)

"Thanks for putting the dishes in the sink. I like having a cleanup partner."

"You did it! You figured out how to get that bike to balance without training wheels. That is tricky."

"You finished the whole book. Did you like that funny part where frog and toad hid the cookies?"

In desperate times, you need to be a praise ninja. In this story, Michael uses every tool in the chapter (and some other chapters besides).

Michael's Story: Preschooler on Ice

Jamie was very excited about our first trip to the skating rink. In the car on the way over he told me he knew he'd be good at it. He was so confident, he was setting himself up for a fall . . . literally. He started off wobbly, falling every ten seconds, and by midway around the rink he declared he'd never skate again and he wanted off.

I was glad I had my tools. First, I acknowledged his feelings. "It's frustrating to learn something new, especially balancing your body on something so slippery. It's not easy. In fact, it's really tough! It doesn't feel good to fall down on hard ice."

I didn't argue when he wanted to take a break. I didn't push him to stick with it. I suggested that we get a snack to get our strength up before giving it another try.

After our snack, he was not quite convinced to go back out, so I asked if he'd be willing to try with me again after three or five minutes. (A choice!) He agreed to three minutes. When we got back out I gave him descriptive praise, telling him I could see that he was using his arms to balance himself and pointing out how much farther he'd gone from our last round.

When he got frustrated, I showed him how to take it out on the ice by stomping along, doing "angry skating." We made it three or four more times around, and at the very end, he let go of my hand and made it back to the gate all by himself without falling.

There were so many moments where it was getting bad and it could have been a disaster, but all of the elements we've been talking about in the workshop helped me to keep him in the game. He was so proud of his improvement. It melted my heart!

If you still have doubts about praise that evaluates versus praise that describes, try it on yourself. Here's the scenario: Your partner arrives home from work to find that you've cleaned up the kitchen, gotten the kids bathed and PJ'ed, and prepared a hot meal for the family. Using the language we so often apply to our kids, your partner says enthusiastically, "Wow, you are such a good spouse! What a perfect marriage I have. Great job, honey. I'm proud of you!"

Did you feel patronized? Did you feel a little offended by the assumption that you wish to be judged? Did you wonder, *So what if I'm tired and order pizza, does that make me a bad spouse?* Did you think, *I'd better not bring expectations up like this again!* Did you wonder why your partner is proud when you're the one who did the work?

Okay, new scene.

Your partner comes home to the same setup and says, "Wow, you got the kids ready for bed and you took care of that big mess we left in the kitchen this morning *and* you made dinner for us, all right after work! Sit down, honey. Let me get you a drink."

Now you might think, *Hey, it was worth the effort. My partner appreciates what I do around here. Maybe I'll even do it again sometime.*

By praising descriptively—by looking, listening, and noticing—we hold up a mirror to our children to show them their strengths. That's how children form their image of themselves. These are more than nice individual moments. We're creating a stockpile of memories that cannot be taken away.

"Good boy" can be canceled out the next day by "bad boy." "You're a smart girl" by "What a stupid thing to do!" "Careful" by "Careless" . . . and so on.

But you can't take away the time he shoveled the whole walkway even though his arms were tired and his toes were frozen.

Or the time he made the baby laugh with his goofy faces when the babysitter couldn't get her to stop crying, or found his mom's reading glasses, or figured out how to make the alarm on the cell phone stop going off when no one else could do it.

These are the things he can draw upon to give himself confidence in the face of adversity and discouragement. In the past he did something he was proud of, and he has, within himself, the power to do it again.

Tools for Praise and Appreciation

INSTEAD OF...

DESCRIBE WHAT YOU SEE

INSTEAD OF...

DESCRIBE THE EFFECT ON OTHERS

INSTEAD OF...

DESCRIBE EFFORT

INSTEAD OF...

DESCRIBE PROGRESS

REMINDER: Tools for Praise and Appreciation

1. Describe What You See

"I see green lines that are zooming up and down the page. And look how they connect all these red shapes!"

2. Describe the Effect on Others

"The baby loves it when you make those funny sounds. I see a big smile on her face."

3. Describe Effort

"You kept working on that button until you got it into that little buttonhole."

4. Describe Progress

"You sounded out each of the letters and you put them together. You read a whole sentence!"

- Consider asking questions or starting a conversation instead of praising.

- Sometimes acknowledging feelings can be more helpful than praise.

- Give a child a new picture of himself.

- Resist the urge to praise by comparison.

Chapter Five

Tools for Kids Who Are Differently Wired . . . Will This Work with *My* Kid?

—Modifications for kids with autism and sensory issues

Julie

This chapter is for those of you who are thinking, "This all sounds very nice, but you haven't met *my* kid. This will never work with *him*!"

Some of you have children who are particularly sensitive, rambunctious, or strong-willed. Others have children who have been diagnosed with an autism spectrum disorder or sensory processing disorder. Many of these children have outsized reactions to ordinary, everyday experiences—the ticking of a clock, fluorescent lights, socks with seams, getting bumped by another kid. Others are underresponsive, like the child who seems not to feel pain. Sometimes they talk too loudly, hug other children too tightly, or seem not to have any interest in interacting with people at all. They might insist on talking about only one subject—train schedules or maps. They might fall apart if their rigid routines aren't followed precisely. Many have great difficulty with transitions and cannot bear to be rushed from one activity to another. Much as we try to minimize their distress, we cannot create a world that is comfortable for them.

If you don't have a child who is wired differently, you might be tempted to skip this chapter entirely. But if you have a spare moment, you may discover that the tools in this chapter help with some of the challenges that are still lingering after you've gone through the earlier chapters.

I used to read about what to expect after my first baby was born. The books reassured me that babies vary in how quickly they develop. So I didn't worry that the other babies in my mothers' group were crawling and standing, when all Asher could do was sit. At his one-year checkup, Asher's pediatrician asked me if I was concerned about his progress. I remember telling the doctor that if *he* wasn't worried, I wasn't, either. Two months later the pediatrician suggested I see a specialist, and I was told my baby was "very developmentally delayed." By then I noticed the disparity—the other babies in our group had turned into toddlers, toppling over Asher as they staggered around the room, while Asher shrank from them in fear because he could only do a slow sit-scoot. I still remember the offense I took when another mother suggested I was being overprotective of my son, as if it were somehow my fault that he was not yet mobile. Beneath my anger was the fear that she might be right.

And it wasn't just his physical development that was different. I started to notice that his sensory system was different, too. As a baby Asher couldn't tolerate having his feet touched, and he resisted being held in a standing position. This obviously did not bode well for learning to walk, which would require that he touch his feet to the floor. In his physical therapy sessions I learned a brushing technique to desensitize him to being touched. I was supposed to brush his arms, legs, and back every two waking hours. It added to my guilt that I found this schedule impossible to keep.

When my second baby, Rashi, looked "different," too, I told myself it was no big deal—I can handle this. I didn't bother reviewing the what-to-expect books and took him directly to the child development specialists. I thought it'd be easier to navigate the emotional roller coaster the second time around, but I found myself in unfamiliar, scary territory again. Rashi was unlike Asher in many ways. Asher had been a floppy baby, but Rashi was stiff. Asher cried when his legs or feet were touched; Rashi didn't even cry when he got a vaccination in his thigh. If we took Asher somewhere with lots of new sights, sounds, and people, he would get wound up and cry; Rashi would just shut down and fall asleep wherever he was. For a while I was scheduling them for back-to-back appointments with the pediatric physical therapist.

By the time my third child came along, I figured it was standard procedure to take a baby of mine for a checkup with the developmental pediatrician. I was shocked to find out Shiriel was developing typically. As a toddler she was jealous that her older brother got to go to "O.T." (occupational therapy) and she wondered when she could have a turn, too.

From the time my children were little, I have led "How to Talk . . ." workshops. Even though Asher had sensory processing disorder (SPD) and Rashi was eventually diagnosed with

Asperger's Syndrome (now known as an Autism Spectrum Disorder), the skills I was teaching were just as useful in raising my two boys as they were for the parents whose kids were neurotypical. Over the years, I connected with other parents of children with SPD and autism, and I led workshops specifically for parents and professionals who live or work with children with special needs.

What I learned, both from my participants and from my own experience, is that the core principles of the "How to Talk . . ." approach apply whether children are "typically developing" or different in their various unique ways. All kids want to connect, all kids want to be understood, all kids want a say in what they do and how they do it. The challenge for those of us with differently wired kids is to figure out how to achieve all these noble goals without getting mired in frustration, or blaming our kids, when they are . . . well . . . different.

Imagine you're at home alone, reading an engrossing book and enjoying a cup of tea, when a neighbor you hardly know walks in without knocking. She's standing too close, staring straight into your eyes, and she's chatting loudly as she shakes your chair. "Hello! How are you? What are you reading? Do you wanna play cards? Can you make me a sandwich? *Please?*"

How would you feel? A little scared, perhaps? *How did she get in*? Annoyed by the interruption? Confused by the questions? Disturbed by her loud voice? Wanting to get away from her? I'm guessing you're not likely to throw together a grilled cheese sandwich in that moment.

This exercise helps me relate to some of what makes daily life such a challenge for kids on the spectrum. Kids whose bodies don't process sensory experiences such as sound, light, movement, touch, or taste in a typical way can get overwhelmed by any or all of these. Sometimes even interactions with their own parents can feel like an assault on their senses. It's no wonder they have a harder time feeling close and comfortable with other people. Better to find a place to hide from all those sensory intrusions!

This doesn't mean they can't develop strong connections with people, but we may have to work at it.

Admittedly, this can feel like an impossible task, especially with a child who appears to be in his own world and who wants to stay there by himself, *thank you very much*! It's tempting to try to drag that child out of his world and into ours. After all, he's going to have to learn how to get along in a world where people *do* talk in voices above a whisper, or accidentally bump into each other; where kids yell and run around on the playground; where supermarkets have harsh fluorescent lighting and crowded aisles.

The problem is, our world feels *wrong* to him—too loud or too quiet, too much touching or not enough, too much to look at, and too exhausting to make sense of it all. Before we can hope to acknowledge feelings or engage cooperation or solve problems, we need to connect.

TOOL #1: Join Them in Their World

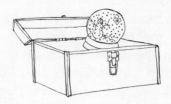

The next time your child seems to be in her own world, un-interested in relating to you or anyone else, and you have a little extra energy to spare, try getting down on the floor (or wherever your child happens to be) and joining her in her world.

For example:

> If Angela is lying on the floor in a quiet room, watching her fingers make shadows on the wall, instead of saying, "Angela, come here! I'll read you a book!" try getting down on her level and adding your own finger shadows.

> If Peter likes to talk about train schedules, talk about train schedules with him.

> If Evan is repeatedly banging his light saber on the floor, grab a wooden spoon and bang along with him.

If your child usually prefers to be alone, you may have already suffered the sting of rejection so often that it's hard to believe you'll have any success with this. People in my groups looked downright skeptical at these suggestions, but they were willing to give them a try. Here are some of their stories:

Head in the Tent

Aiden would spend all his time in his tent playing on the iPad, if we let him. He goes in there and he's in his own little world. He won't look at me, he won't talk or answer a question,

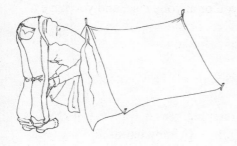

and he certainly won't play with me. This past week, when he went in the tent again, I went over very, very quietly, and I tapped on the tent. It's just fabric, so he could barely hear it. I said very quietly, "I want to watch you play." I just sat outside the tent and watched for a while.

I asked him, "What game are you playing?" And he answered me—which was surprising! He was playing the Bubble Game. I said, "Oh, can I see?" It's a tiny little one-person tent, but he let me stick my head in.

I asked if I could play, too, and at first he shook his head no, but then he said he would show me how. We ended up passing the iPad back and forth and playing this bubble video game. It's the first time he's ever done anything like that. I always thought he didn't want anyone to be near him, but now I think we've been trying too hard to force him to do what we want, without playing the way that he likes.

Train Connections

Henry is very logical. He doesn't respond to silliness or fantasy. He spends a lot of time playing alone with his train set and he doesn't like to be interrupted.

Yesterday, when he went to the train table, I sat down with him and picked up one of the trains. He said, "Mama!"

I said, "I want to be this train!"

"No, you can't be that train! That's not your train."

So I grabbed one of his toy guitars and said, "Is this a train?"

"That's not a train!"

"Well, what do you do with it, then?"

"You play it!"

"With your hands or your toes, or your knees or your nose?"

He thought this was hysterical. "Say it again! Say it again!"

I started playing the guitar with my hands and my toes, and knees and nose, and then he tried to do it, too. And he *loved* it! Normally he would have spent all that time alone.

Cave-Boy Play

Peter was learning about caves at preschool and he became obsessed with the topic. It can get pretty tiresome, talking about caves all the time, so I'm always trying to change the subject and get him interested in something else. But this week I tried "joining him in his world," or in this case, in his cave.

We talked about his new favorite word (spelunking!), the special headlamps that cave explorers wear, and how sometimes they have to slither through tiny cracks in the ground to climb into a cave. I suggested we build a cave in our living room with the couch pillows. At first he was disappointed that we couldn't go to a real cave, but then he got excited about the project. We covered the pillows with blankets to make it dark and then we climbed in. We had a sweet time together, and he was in a really happy mood afterward.

TOOL #2: Take Time to Imagine What Your Child Is Experiencing

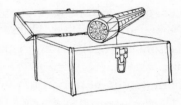

When a child is being difficult, our impulse is to focus on what we want him to do. He has to get those socks on, eat breakfast, take a bath, start therapy. We don't stop to think about how he's feeling. And even if we do, it can be hard to figure out just what the heck those feelings are. Kids on the autism spectrum can be insistent on routines and sameness in a way that completely baffles us. We adults don't fall to pieces when a meeting is rescheduled. We don't refuse to wear socks if our favorite pair is in the laundry.

When my own son's behavior is bewildering, it helps me to try to imagine myself in a situation that would bring up the same emotions that he's feeling.

Here's an example. My son refused to start physical therapy until the chairs in the waiting area were in the same alternating pattern—red, yellow, red, yellow. No amount of logic would convince him to leave the chairs as they were.

What was the big deal? Can I imagine a situation where I, too, would be bothered by the arrangement of chairs? What if I were leading a workshop, and I arrived to discover the chairs were in rows, instead of the usual circular setup. Would I insist that they be returned to the "proper" arrangement? You bet I would! If the room manager explained to me that it was "no big deal," and I should "just be flexible," would that help? Not at all!

I'm not claiming that the arrangement of the chairs in the waiting room was as important for my son's physical therapy as the arrangement of the chairs is for my workshop. But we would both have similar *feelings* that things were not right, and we'd both be similarly upset if we were unable to make things right again.

What we'd both want to hear is, "Oh, you don't like the chairs this way. They're arranged all wrong." Then, of course, we'd want to return the chairs to their proper places!

Understanding that this was how my son felt, I made a point of arriving a few minutes early so we could get the chairs "right." Inevitably, though, the waiting area would be missing a chair, or people would be sitting in the chairs, and we couldn't rearrange them. Tempted as I was to lecture him (*Really? You're going to cry because there's an extra yellow chair? Honey, you can't always have everything exactly as you want it!*) I knew that would only make it worse. Again I imagined myself in a similar situation. What if the chairs at the workshop were bolted down in their rows? What would help me deal with an uncomfortable situation?

This is what I said to Asher: "Oh no! You want a red chair here. That's frustrating."

Asher repeated, "*Fustating!*"

"You wish we had a red chair to put here."

He replied, "Put here."

I said, "Hmph," he said, "Hmph!" And then he took my hand and walked into therapy.

You don't need to run down the hall looking for a red chair, or ask the nursing mother, or the elderly lady, to get up so you can move her chair. There is value to giving a child the experience that he can handle frustration, with your sympathy and support. *When we demonstrate generosity of spirit by accepting feelings, we help our children become more resilient,* and we increase their ability to deal with the inevitable bumps and detours in the road of life.

Scratchy Grass

Last Saturday was a warm day—shorts and T-shirt weather at last, after our brutal winter! I took Ivan to the park. We sat on the grass to eat a snack, but he wouldn't stay put. He kept popping up and running around me in circles. I told him he needed to sit while he was eating, but he yelled, "No!"

This wasn't like him. I wondered what was going on. Did he suddenly have attention deficit disorder? I tried to imagine what he might be feeling, and that's when I realized the grass was probably bothering his exposed legs. Maybe the grass was tickling him, or maybe it felt like sandpaper. I said, "You don't like sitting on the grass!" He said "No!" I laid my sweater out for him to sit on. Suddenly he was happy to sit and eat the rest of his snack. The sensation of grass on his legs had been too much to bear. I remember thinking, "Wow, people are different in ways I didn't even know they could be different."

Seams of Socks

Jack has lots of socks in his drawer, but there are only three pairs that he likes. When I have to get him to school in the morning, it's always a battle if none of his favorites are clean. In the past I always said things like, "Don't make such a big deal about a pair of socks," and "There's nothing wrong with the other socks." Sometimes I figured he was making a fuss because he didn't want to go to school. I wasn't going to stand for that!

When you told me about how sensitive your son's feet were when he was younger, I wondered if maybe my son really *can* tell the difference between these three pairs of socks and all the rest. I bought another package of his favorite socks, and you know what? We didn't have one sock fight all week. That is, until his babysitter came one day and insisted he wear one of the pairs he doesn't like. I snapped at her, "Jack can feel the difference between those socks and the ones he likes! You need to listen to him!" Then I realized that I was mad at her for doing the same thing I'd been doing for months. I had to apologize. Anyway, now I know, my son feels what he feels . . . but he sure didn't get his sensitive feet from me!

Julie's Story: Soccer in the Summer

I signed Asher up for a week of soccer camp, and it turned out to be one of the hottest weeks of the summer. The temperature was expected to hit 90 degrees. Asher has always refused to wear shorts. He can't stand the feeling of air on his legs, and he always insists on wearing thick cargo pants. So of course, he wore his pants to soccer camp.

I foresaw trouble. The woman in charge of signing kids in was going to insist he wear shorts, which would be reasonable if Asher didn't have such sensitive legs. So I taught him to say, "I have hypersensitivity in my lower extremities."

Well, when he told her that, she was drop-jawed. She let him sign in without any protest. I felt good about empowering Asher. Now he could let other people know how he's feeling all by himself, instead of needing his mom to interpret for him and protect him. And those were pretty big words for a little kid!

Gummed Up

My six-year-old son Evan is very sensitive. This is a mixed blessing to say the least! A few weeks ago he had a bad experience during lunch at school. One of the kids at his table had a pack of wintergreen gum and shared it with the other kids. The smell nauseated Evan so much that he couldn't eat. After that he got upset whenever he saw someone chewing gum. Even if he saw their mouth moving *as if* they were chewing gum, he imagined the smell and he couldn't eat.

Last week it got worse. He would eat a few bites and then give up because he was *thinking* about gum. I tried telling him to just not think about it, but that made him cry. I started looking into child psychiatrists.

After the workshop last week I spent some time trying to understand what Evan was experiencing. It's not that strange if you really think about it. We're all taught not to discuss certain topics at the dinner table. Why? Because even the thought of something disgusting, like vomit or feces, makes us lose our appetite. (For some reason my brother-in-law has a hard time with that concept. He works at a hospital and he's infamous for talking about the gross details of his job while we're eating.)

I started writing a list of ideas to help Evan. Could he substitute a different thought? Could he substitute a different smell? Maybe he could test different spices and find one he likes. Then if he started thinking about gum he could take a whiff of cinnamon or oregano.

At dinner that night, it happened again. Evan couldn't eat, he was crying. I said, "Ugh, the smell of wintergreen gum is so disgusting to you that the very thought of it makes you lose your appetite. That's a tough problem. It's not easy to eat when you have those thoughts in your head. And it's really hard to control your thoughts. Even grown-ups have lots of trouble doing that."

He looked at me with relief, and said, "Yeah." He walked away from the table, then came back as we were finishing the meal, took a few bites, and wandered off again. For the next few meals I followed the same script. By the end of the week he was eating normally. Just knowing that I understood what he was going through relieved a lot of his tension. I never even got to try out any of my other ideas.

TOOL #3: Put into Words What Kids Want to Say

It can be hard to figure out what little kids, wired differently or not, want to say. Maybe it's because their brain-to-mouth connection hasn't matured. ("Ungh. Ungh!") Or their tongues and lips aren't yet coordinated. ("Yook, a ef-lent.") Or they just don't have the vocabulary to express themselves. ("Want dat!" "What is it you want, darling?" "Want dat! Dat! DAT!")

Even when we *can* figure out what they're trying to say, we may not want to give them what they want. It can be tempting to ignore them, or act like we don't understand.

How to respond in these situations? Let's do a thought experiment.

Imagine you're learning a language called Kwarben, with difficult pronunciation and complicated grammar, and you're utterly dependent on people who speak only this language. You're very hungry. You try your best to ask for scrambled eggs—kwazikrai—but the only response you get is, "F'wij troyk thwarpel, brigahzee par klafik" (which means, "I don't understand you; speak more clearly"). Feeling frustrated, you try again, shouting "Kwazikrai!" Your host responds in Kwarben, saying, "I can't hear you when you shout." How long will it be before you give up, or cry, or throw a shoe at your host?

Even if my host can't figure out exactly what I want, I would feel better if she said, "You want *something*! You need it right away!" *Ah, I've communicated at least part of my message. She's getting it! I'll keep trying.*

Like us, children who have difficulty communicating still want to express themselves and be understood. We can help by putting into words what they want to say, as best we can.

For early talkers, this may mean picking out the few words we do understand ("Oh, an elephant! You're saying *elephant*!"). For more advanced talkers, we can expand on their words and acknowledge how they're feeling. When the child says, "No Daddy go!" we can say, "You don't want Daddy to go! You miss Daddy. You wish Daddy could stay home."

"blumph mmmph siggle zouzo chi"

"I'M HUNGRY – I WANTA SANDWICH"

INSTANT TRANSLATOR

Parents and teachers in my workshop were surprised to discover that putting children's feelings and desires into words is helpful, even when we can't give them what they want. When kids feel understood they also feel more calm, connected, and able to tolerate frustration.

Trapped in the Kitchen

My older son was playing with a friend in the backyard. Jacob, who is nonverbal, was with me in the kitchen when he noticed his big brother outside. He started banging on the door, and it was clear he wanted to go outside, too. Normally I would've been afraid to acknowledge that he wanted to go out because I knew I couldn't watch him out there at that moment—I was in the middle of making dinner. But this time I tried putting into words what I thought he wanted.

"You see Andy and Max playing outside. You want to go outside, too. I wish I could take you outside, but I'm making macaroni and cheese for dinner. You can help me make dinner, and then after we eat I'll take you outside."

To my amazement, he came back into the kitchen and started playing with the pots and pans! I always thought if you acknowledge what a child wants, you have to give it to him or he'll have a fit. This was a real eye opener for me.

Repeat After Me

Elliot's speech is still pretty hard to understand. We've had a lot of "conversations" where he says something incomprehensible, and I say, "What did you say? Say it again."

He tries again, and I still can't make sense of most of it. "Slow down, Elliot. Say it clearly. I can't understand you."

The next thing you know, he's screaming his head off.

I started trying to let him know the words I *do* understand by repeating everything I could figure out. So if he says, "mumble mumble mumble BALL mumble," I say, "You said something about a BALL."

He'll try again, and I'll catch another word, so I repeat that, too, "Oh, you said a GREEN BALL."

Now whenever he says anything, he waits patiently for me to repeat back his words.

Dinner Disappointment

My son, Will, is four, and he's a screamer. He often has a fit when he doesn't like what's for dinner. Last night we were having chicken, and he pointed at the plate and started screaming. Normally I'd get angry and tell him to be quiet. But this time I said, "Oh *no*! You're upset! You wanted mac and cheese and you got chicken."

"Mac and cheese!"

"You *really* wanted mac and cheese!" I pounded on the table.

He pounded along with me, "Mac and cheese, mac and cheese!"

I sang, "Oh mac and cheese, I wish you grew on trees, I love you more than peas, without you my heart will freeze, I want to smear you on my knees . . ." I was emoting with him, hamming it up.

The freak-out was over. He wasn't screaming anymore. We looked at the food on the table. He decided he'd have some of the potato with cheese on top and some of the carrot sticks. After he polished off those, he ate a little chicken. I didn't say a thing!

Written Record

Sometimes Peter gets so upset he has trouble speaking. It can take him a long time to get the words out. It happened last week after he came home from school. He was crying and gasping for breath between words. I really wanted to scream at him, "WHAT HAPPENED?? JUST TELL ME!!" Of course that would only make him more upset and slow him down even more.

I decided to try writing down everything he was saying—mostly to give myself something to do. But it also helped him calm down faster. I literally wrote down every word he said: "The . . . teacher . . . said . . . the . . . fastest . . . person . . . to . . . clean . . . up . . . would . . . win . . . a . . . prize. . . . But . . . she . . . made . . . me . . . stop . . . to . . . give . . . her . . . the . . . science . . . worksheet. . . . . It's . . . not . . . fair! . . . She . . . made . . . me . . . lose!"

He made me read it back to him several times as he was telling the story, and listened with great satisfaction. Crisis over.

Rain, Rain, Go Away!

I teach kindergarten. We couldn't go outside for recess as usual because it was raining (and if you don't live in California you may not realize what a rare event that was!). Johnny normally has a fit when the schedule changes. He throws himself on the floor or bangs on the window.

He said, "I want outside!"

I said, "I know, you really like to go out for recess. You don't like being inside."

"I want outside!"

"I bet you wish the rain would stop!"

"Outside!"

We were stuck, so I said, "Let's go outside to see if it's still raining."

We went outside and stood in the rain. I shook my fist at the sky and said, "You, rain! You took away Johnny's recess!"

Then I turned to Johnny and said, "It's still raining. Let's go inside and play bowling."

He wasn't happy about it, but he was much calmer than usual. He went inside and he got involved in bowling.

After-hours Agony

When Dustin lies down to go to sleep he can get sensory overload. Without the distraction of being in motion, discomforts crowd in on him. Last night he was having an especially hard time. He complained about the sheet rubbing against his feet. He had an uncomfortable feeling in his throat when he swallowed. His fingertips had an unpleasant tingling because I trimmed his nails earlier in the day. He brushed his teeth five times to get rid of a bad taste in his mouth. We did our regular routine of me karate chopping his back, scratching his back, lightly tickling his back. He was screaming and agitated. I was at a loss for how to help him feel better.

Dustin asked me, "Can I say a bad word?"

I said, "Sure, you say as many bad words as you want."

He started yelling. I asked, "Can I yell with you?"

He looked surprised but he nodded. I yelled with him, cursed the awful feelings he was feeling in his body, yelled that it isn't fair, IT JUST ISN'T FAIR!! (These are things he has said to me in the past.) And then the magic happened. I saw it in his face. He sobbed with relief, hugged me as hard as he could, and said, "I love you *so* much, Mommy!" We held each other and cried. That was the turning point. A few minutes later he was able to drift off to sleep.

TOOL #4: Adjust Expectations:
Manage the Environment Instead of the Child

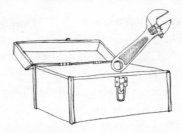

One of the (many) challenges of raising children who are wired differently is figuring out what we can reasonably expect of them, and what is *too much*. Even those of us who aren't child development experts have a sense that three-year-olds should be able to eat without throwing food, at least most of the time; that four-year-olds should be able to pee in the toilet instead of in their pants; that five-year-olds should be able to play nicely with a friend; that six-year-olds should be able to get themselves dressed independently. It's hard not to worry when our kids don't fit the norm. Are they being intentionally oppositional? Is their demand for help a sign that we've spoiled them? Are they more impaired than we realize?

It's disheartening when seemingly normal, enjoyable activities are irritating or overwhelming to our kids: a friend's birthday party that results in a show-stopping tantrum; a family dinner celebration that ends in an embarrassing meltdown. It can be hard not to feel resentful when our own social lives are affected by our children's sensitivities. And even if we're willing to avoid situations that might feel intolerable to our kids, it's impossible to anticipate all the challenges we'll encounter at home or out in the world with our differently wired children.

What to do? People in my workshops were quick to share what doesn't help:

> Commands: "You need to get yourself dressed, now!"

> Shaming: "You're too old to be peeing in your pants."

> Denial of feelings: "Come on, this is fun. I don't want to hear any more complaining."

> Lectures: "We can't leave, honey. Your relatives came a long way so they can see you and visit with everybody. It's going to be over in a couple of hours. You need to be polite to your cousins. They just want to play with you."

> Questions: "Why did you do that? Didn't I tell you not to stuff bread in the heating grate?"

> Threats: "I'm counting to three! One . . . two . . . two and a half . . ."

Kids might not be developmentally ready to meet our expectations. We may be better off skipping the loud, crowded party at the indoor playground and instead arranging a short playdate to celebrate a friend's birthday. As cute as those new Mary Jane shoes are, we may decide to let our sensory girl wear her old, worn-out comfy shoes to Grandma's dinner party.

Once people made the shift from trying to change the kids to changing their expectations, they found many ways to make life more pleasant for their children and themselves.

Julie's Story: Shorter School Days

Rashi never had a particularly hard time separating from me in preschool, but after a week in kindergarten he started clinging and crying. It was awful. I tried acknowledging his feelings. "You don't want me to go!" I tried telling him when I'd be back. "I'll see you at the end of afternoon circle time." I tried getting him interested in an activity. "Look, blocks!" and having a teacher talk with him. "Ms. Jones, Rashi brought a magic trick to show you." Nothing helped.

One day I had to take Rashi out of school early for a doctor's appointment. I told him, "I'm going to pick you up right after story time." That day he didn't cry at all when I dropped him off. But the next day, when he was staying the whole day, he cried again.

I wondered if the full day was just too long for him. I decided to experiment. I made up an excuse to pick him up early, and again that day he didn't cry when I dropped him off. I talked to the teachers, and we all agreed I would start taking Rashi home right after lunch. Not only did he stop crying at morning drop-off, but the teachers said he also started talking and participating in class. They didn't realize he could talk!

Julie's Story: Info Relay Delay

One of the lessons I learned about communicating with my son was to adjust my expectations of how long it should take him to respond. Here's a typical interchange before I learned my lesson:

Me: Hey, Rashi, do you want a peanut butter and jelly sandwich or a turkey sandwich? (Three-second pause.)

Rashi . . . ? Okay fine, if you're not going to answer me
you're getting peanut butter.

Rashi: Waaaah! I want turkey!

I finally learned.

Me: Hey, Rashi, I have a question for you. Tell me when
you're ready for it.

I wait 10 seconds.

Rashi (looks up): What?

Me: Do you want a peanut butter and jelly sandwich or a
turkey sandwich?

(I wait twenty long seconds. I'm so impatient I actually
count the seconds in my head to distract myself from shouting *just tell me!*)

Rashi (finally!): Turkey.

Me: Okay. Thanks for telling me.

Playdate Pusher

I invited my friend Alice to bring her daughter, Charlotte, over
for a playdate with my son, Marcos. They're both in a special
class for kids with autism. They seemed to be having a good
time, and Alice and I were enjoying our chance to chat. After
about an hour and a half Marcos started getting cranky, but I
guess I didn't want *my* playdate to end, so I kept encouraging
him to "play nice." All of a sudden he shoved Charlotte hard
enough to knock her over.

I was so embarrassed. My first impulse was to punish Marcos even though Charlotte wasn't really hurt. But part of me realized I had pushed *him* past *his* breaking point. So I told Marcos, "Charlotte doesn't like to be pushed. It looks like you need a break from playing together." Alice was understanding and took Charlotte home. We're going to limit the next playdate to an hour.

Julie's Story: Potty for a Printer

It was taking forever to potty train Rashi. All the other kids in his class had it down. When he seemed to have some control I put him in underpants, but then he peed and didn't even notice that his pants were soaked. I didn't like the idea of using a reward system, but everyone—the pediatrician, his teacher, even the occupational therapist—told me I should try rewards. They wore me down. Rashi was fixated on getting a color printer. We had an ancient black and white one that we'd been thinking of replacing, so I told him that if he stayed dry for three days in a row, we'd get a new printer.

The first day he did pretty well. He had just one tiny accident, and he was trying so hard I told him it didn't count. But he couldn't make it through three days in a row. It was heartbreaking. He'd mostly make it through a day or even two, but then he'd have a major accident and he'd cry his eyes out, he was so upset with himself. It became crystal clear to me that the problem wasn't that he lacked motivation. He really could not stay focused on his body signals and feel when his bladder was about to burst. He had low sensitivity in his legs, so I shouldn't have been surprised that this was especially hard for him.

I finally decided to end the torture. I told him, "Your body isn't ready to always tell you when your bladder is full. We can try again when you're a little older, but in the meantime I think we need to replace our printer now." He was so relieved.

The hardest part was admitting to myself that he wasn't ready to get rid of the pull-ups.

Dinner Isn't Served

We have a regular dinner with extended family, but it's too loud for our son, Cameron. He just cannot sit there. He gets overwhelmed by all the cross-conversations. So now we feed him ahead of time, and while we eat dinner he gets to hang out in the playroom. It causes some friction with the family. They say, "Why can't he sit and eat with us?" "Why can't he behave?" "When I was a child, I was expected to sit at the table and visit with the family."

Well, they didn't have autism! We're not going to put our son in a stressful situation just to satisfy their definition of "normal." It's better for us to take the heat from the family than to make our son (and ourselves) miserable at dinner.

 **Don't expect new skills to be used consistently.**

"He *knows* how to sit still . . . tie his own shoes . . . use the potty . . . behave in the grocery store. . . . He's just being contrary!"

Just because your kid did something yesterday doesn't mean he can do it today. Just because he can do something in the morning when he's fresh, doesn't mean he can do it in the afternoon when he's tired. Kids aren't consistent in their use of new skills. It makes having realistic expectations even harder for parents and teachers. But who ever said it was going to be easy?

Diaper Vacation

Every time Emily peed in her pants I got upset with her. "Why didn't you go to the bathroom when I asked you?" "I'm not taking you out if you're going to keep peeing all over yourself!" I made her feel really bad for having accidents. I knew she could use the potty if she put her mind to it. She's done it before.

After our session on developmental readiness, I finally got it through my head that she doesn't have the ability to control her bladder *all the time*. It depends on how tired she is and how engrossed she is in an activity. I started saying, "Your body sure can be tricky, not telling you when your bladder is full and then giving you a big surprise."

She was so grateful when I showed her I understood, I decided to take off the pressure altogether. "Would you like to have a break from having to go to the bathroom all the time? We could have a 'diaper vacation.'"

Well, she *loved* that idea. She was so excited, I was a little nervous she'd never wear underpants again. On Saturday morning, she put on a diaper. I have to admit, it was a nice break for me, too, not worrying about finding a puddle of pee somewhere, or trying to keep track of how long it'd been since she'd used the potty. I was surprised that after three hours she said she was ready to wear underpants again.

We have a long way to go with potty training, but now our relationship is not so antagonistic. I still have to constantly remind myself that she isn't doing this to spite me or because she's lazy or unmotivated. It's easy to jump to conclusions like that, even now. Most kids her age have had control for years. I have to accept that when it comes to potty training, she isn't like most kids.

TOOL #5: Use Alternatives to the Spoken Word: Write a Note, Use a Gesture, Draw a Picture, Sing

Kids who are wired differently often have more difficulty making sense of what we say to them. They benefit from multiple ways to process information. Parents and teachers got creative designing charts, singing directions, and making colorful checklists. Here are a few examples:

Wardrobe Checklist

Rudy is six. It used to be that if we didn't help him get dressed he wouldn't do it. It's not that he was resisting. It's just that he's easily distracted. If I'd tell him, "Go get dressed," I'd find him in his room thirty minutes later, half naked, stuffing cars into his pillowcase. Honestly, that kid can be distracted by a speck of dust. So I made a checklist and I put it at his spot on the kitchen table.

He ran to his room to get his T-shirt on, and then ran back to the table to see what was next on the list. After a few weeks, I taped the list to the wall in his room, and he got himself completely changed without supervision or help. I made sure to notice, "You did everything! Shirt, pants, socks. And secret undies we can't see." He looked pretty pleased with himself.

Missing Mom Blues

I teach preschool. I had a little girl who was waiting for her mom to come pick her up, and she was distraught that she had to wait. So I made up a song for her:

(To the tune of "Clementine":)

I want my mommy, I want my mommy, I want my mommy, *right now!*
I want my mommy, I want my mommy, I want my mommy, *right now!*

Where IS she? Where *is* she, Where *is* she, right now!
Where *is* she? Where *is* she, Where *is* she, right now!

The song helped her calm down. She actually seemed to enjoy it. She gave a little smile every time I yelled *right now*.

Plan in a Pocket

Jeremy gets upset if he arrives at school and discovers his teacher is out for the day. Sometimes he refuses to go in. So now she lets us know ahead of time when she's going to be absent. I drew a picture of the substitute teacher, Mrs. Kay, on a little card. Jeremy knows if he has the card in his pocket,

Mrs. Kay will be his teacher for the day. I don't know if he ever takes the card out, but it reassures him to have it there.

Your Table Is Ready

Nick is six and can be very rigid about routines. His little brother Charlie is four. They fight us over where they're going to eat dinner. They don't want to eat at the table with us, ever! They want to eat at their own little table. We allow it on the weekends, but they want to eat at the little table every night. They're always asking, "Why can't we?" We tell them we need to eat as a family. They don't like that reason.

Finally I put a chart on the wall. It has all the days of the week, with "LT" and "BT," for Little Table and Big Table. They looked at it and Nick said, "Really? This is what it is?"

"Yup, this is what it is."

I explained the chart to Charlie and he said, "Well, what about tonight?"

I said, "Let's look it up. Let's see, it's Tuesday. Nope, not tonight. It's not going to happen tonight."

They said, "Aww . . ." And they sat down at the big table without any more fuss.

Joanna's Story: Silent Cynthia

In my job as a resource room teacher in West Harlem, I had to give children screening tests to see if they needed extra help in reading and language development. When Cynthia was brought to me for testing, the counselor shrugged and said, "Do what you can."

Cynthia was a five-year-old Haitian girl who did not speak. At the beginning of the year many of the teachers and classroom aides made an effort. They'd crouch down to her level and say, "Cynthia, what's your name? Tell me your name!" I guess they were trying to give her an easy question. But Cynthia would just stand and stare, expressionless, arms limp at her sides. Eventually she was left alone to sit at the back of the classroom where she bothered nobody. Finally she had been flagged for screening, and now it was my turn to try.

I sat down with her and opened my book. I was uneasy; I didn't want to be one more adult harassing this sad little girl with tests and questions. But I had to do my job. "Hey Cynthia," I whispered. "I'm Ms. Faber. I need your help. I want you to make a special sign. It's the wiggly finger sign." I wiggled to demonstrate. "I'm going to say a color and you wiggle your finger over the color that I say."

Cynthia wiggled her finger and identified all the colors correctly. For "same and different" we did thumbs-up and thumbs-down. She didn't smile, but she was very intent. She didn't miss a single one. Finally I needed her to name pictures of animals and common objects. I said, "This time I'm going to *try* to read your thoughts. I don't know if I can do it! Just move your lips but don't say the word out loud. I'm going to concentrate as hard as I can to see if I can do this."

I pointed to the tiger. Cynthia mouthed the word *tiger*.

I leaned my head toward her. She leaned into me. Our foreheads touched. "Did you just think *tiger*?" I asked.

Cynthia nodded.

"I did it, I did it! I read your thought!" I was truly pretty thrilled. Cynthia's mouth twitched into a tiny, swift smile.

"Do you want to try another one?"

Cynthia nodded. We finished all the questions. According to the test she was a very bright little girl. After that, whenever I saw her in the hall or at recess, she would run over to me and mouth words. Eventually she started gently pulling my head down and whispering in my ear. I never had her as a student and I don't know if she ever talked to anyone else at the school.

TOOL #6: Tell Them What They _Can_ Do, Instead of What They _Can't_

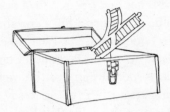

I remember waiting to cross the street with my mother when I was about six years old. I was just learning to read, and I figured out that the sign said DON'T WALK. I was proud to have read the sign, but I was confused. _I'm not supposed to_ run _in the street. But the sign says not to walk. How will I get across?_ I would have understood better if the sign had said WAIT.

Even when children understand our individual words, they may fail to grasp what we're trying to say. This is especially true of children who are on the autism spectrum or have other developmental delays. They tend to interpret words literally, which can lead to misunderstandings. When you tell a child what _not_ to do, you may be confusing him. You can't assume that he'll automatically know what _to_ do.

The next time you need to stop your child, try redirecting him instead. Think of a runaway train heading for a precipice. It's better to switch tracks to avert catastrophe than to try to stop all that momentum cold.

As a bonus, by offering an acceptable activity, you'll encounter less resistance than you would have with warnings and reprimands.

Our group worked on a "track-switcher" for adults.

Adult wants to say:	Tell them what they *can* do:
"Don't chase the kitty."	"You can wiggle this yarn for the kitty."
"Don't wake the baby."	"Let's use our whisper voices."
"Don't run in the parking lot."	"Hand-holding time."
"Don't throw sand."	"Sand is for pouring and digging."
"Don't be so bossy."	"I like to be asked, 'Can you please help me?'"
"Don't wiggle while I'm trying to tie your shoelaces."	"Time to freeze like a statue!"
"Don't throw laundry."	"You can throw your stuffed animals."
"Don't jump on the couch."	"You can jump from the bottom step to the beanbag chair."

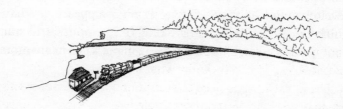

TOOL #7: Be Playful!

Kids on the autism spectrum take longer than neurotypical kids to move from the stage of literal thinking to imaginative play. It can be a challenge to figure out how to appeal to their sense of fun. Here are some examples of parents who discovered ways to encourage cooperation and connection with a bit of silliness:

Food Magician

Mornings during the week are hard. Jason gets distracted when he's supposed to be eating, even when he's clearly hungry. We have very little time for breakfast because school starts so early. I'm always saying, "You're not eating. Why aren't you eating?" This week I tried being more playful. Anytime he takes a bite of something I say, "Oh my, the apple is disappearing from your plate." When he gets distracted, I try to catch myself and say, "The food isn't disappearing. What's going on?" Then he'll put the food in his mouth and start eating it. It's great. He's eating, and I'm not a tyrant anymore.

Underwear Options

Justin is six. He has high-functioning autism. He still sleeps in a pull-up at night. Every morning I remind him to go to the bathroom and change out of his pull-up. And he says, "I don't want to."

This week, instead of telling him what to do, I pulled out two pairs of his underpants. I said, "Do you want Thomas, or Thomas?" He thought that was hysterical. That's our new morning routine. He likes choosing his underwear, and then he goes to the bathroom, and it's not a big deal.

Cleanup Crawl

My son hates to cleanup. I've tried telling him, "It's cleanup time." "You have to put back what you took out." "You have to put the blocks away before you take out the train set." Nothing works.

It occurred to me that he loves to play a game he learned in physical therapy. I put him on his stomach on the big therapy ball. I hold on to his ankles and he crawls out on his hands to reach a little stuffed animal I've thrown for him to retrieve. So this time I said, "Let's do wheelbarrow cleanup." I got out the therapy ball, grabbed his ankles, and steered him to the block pile. He grabbed one, I pulled him back, he put it in the block bag, and then went out for another. It took longer than doing it myself, but this way I don't get mad at him. And it has the added bonus of giving him a workout!

Kids who are wired differently may be delayed in their developmental milestones. They may be ever-so-much-more-so in their sensitivities. But they have a commonality with all children. They want to be understood, to act autonomously, and to feel competent. They need adults in their lives who can connect with them and support them in their quest. We hope these tools will make it easier for you to do just that.

INSTEAD OF...

USE ALTERNATIVES TO THE SPOKEN WORD

INSTEAD OF...

TELL THEM WHAT THEY CAN DO INSTEAD OF WHAT THEY CAN'T

REMINDER: Tools for Kids Who Are Differently Wired

1. Join Them in Their World

> "Can I play the Bubble Game with you? Will you show me how?"

2. Take Time to Imagine What Your Child Is Experiencing

> "So to you, the seams of the socks are very irritating!"

3. Put into Words What Kids Want to Say

> "You bad old rain! You took away Johnny's recess!"

4. Adjust Expectations: Manage the Environment Instead of the Child

> "Let's take a diaper vacation. We need some time to relax and not worry about peeing in the potty."

5. Use Alternatives to the Spoken Word: Notes, Checklists, Pictures, Songs, Gestures

6. Tell Them What They _Can_ Do, Instead of What They _Can't_

"You can throw your stuffed animals."

7. Be Playful!

"It's time to put away the blocks. I need help from the human wheelbarrow!"

- **Don't expect new skills to be used consistently.**

Chapter Five and a Quarter

The Basics ... You Can't Talk Your Way Out of *These*

—Conditions under which the tools won't work

Julie

Before we move on to part two, I'm going to take a fraction of a chapter to state the obvious, because the obvious can be easily overlooked by a weary parent: We need to meet basic needs before any communication tools will work for us. For example, if there's a carrot stuck in your throat you need air before you need empathy. If your leg is broken you need a cast before you need encouragement to walk.

The first two basics of everyday parenting are **food** and **sleep**. If your child is overtired or hungry, it's likely that none of the communication tools in the previous chapters will work for you.

Remember the first rule of chapter one? *Kids can't act right when they don't feel right.* Little kids aren't always aware that they're feeling bad because they're tired or hungry. It's up to us to keep those possibilities in mind and to offer sustenance and slumber when those two vital ingredients might be lacking.

Cheese to the Rescue

I had an appointment in the afternoon, so I left Rashi with our familiar, longtime babysitter. I came home several hours later, and he walked down the hall to greet me but stopped halfway. "What's wrong?" I asked.

He started to cry. "Oh no! What is it? You're crying." He couldn't talk. I asked the sitter if she knew what the matter was. She had no idea.

"What time did you give him lunch?"

"I thought you fed him lunch before you left . . ."

Realizing that Rashi hadn't eaten a thing since breakfast and it was now late afternoon, I ran to the kitchen, grabbed a stick of cheese, and put it in his mouth as he stood in the hallway. He chewed and swallowed. I gave him some more. He calmed down and was able to walk to the kitchen table for a very late lunch. No amount of talking would have helped as much as that stick of cheese.

Sleepless in San Francisco

I got a distressed call from a couple I'd been working with for a year. Their normally cooperative son, Gavin, had suddenly become obstinate and difficult. For the past two days he refused to get ready for school on time, he was whiny and uncooperative, and he was making his little brother miserable as well. They had tried the How to Talk tools without success.

When I asked for details, I learned that Gavin had gone camping with his father over the weekend. They'd slept out Friday night, staying up late to set up the tent, and then gotten up with the sun for an adventure-filled day of hiking and fishing. Saturday they were up late making s'mores over the campfire. Sunday they were up late again unpacking gear from the trip. By Monday, Gavin was dragging, and by Tuesday, he had become a little terror, which is when his parents contacted me.

Rather than giving them tools to try, I suggested they get him to bed early. They had not made the connection between lack of sleep and challenging behavior. As soon as Gavin started getting more sleep, the difficult "phase" disappeared.

Since this chapter is far from a quarter full at this point, I'm going to throw in a few more basics that may be a little less obvious than food and sleep. One of these is the biological need for **recovery time**. When we get angry, our bodies are flooded with hormones. Our heart rate increases and our blood pressure rises, making us more likely to withdraw or react with aggression. Most people have heard of the flight-or-fight response. You learned about it in your high school biology class, but you probably haven't given much thought to it since. One of the best things we can do for children in times of stress is to give them time to recover from the physical changes of anger, fear, and frustration. Don't expect a child to be able to "snap out of it" immediately.

And don't forget that adults need recovery time, too. Give it to yourself if you can. Instead of trying to force yourself to act calm when you're feeling anything but, let children know, "I'm still very upset! I need some time to feel better. I'll be able to help you in a few minutes."

Joanna's Story: The Terrible Bus Ride

I got distracted and didn't make it to the top of the driveway in time to get Zach off the kindergarten bus. I called the school to let them know I was home, and 30 minutes later the bus returned. The big yellow doors opened to reveal a hysterically sobbing five-year-old. The driver informed me that my son had kicked him.

Zach tumbled into my arms, barely able to breathe from crying. "I hate him, I hate him!"

This was not the time for a lecture on violence. I hugged him tight, saying, "That was scary, being stuck on the bus."

"He didn't let me off. I *told* him you were home. He didn't believe me!"

I repeated, "You knew it would be okay for you to get off, but he didn't let you. You *knew* that I was home."

Zach was shaking. "He grabbed me! He wouldn't let me go!"

"You didn't like that!"

Zach finally calmed down enough to go inside and get a snack. I let the topic drop.

A full hour later, when Zach was completely calm, I sat down next to him and said, "I know you hated what the bus driver did. The problem is, the driver is actually *supposed* to keep kids on the bus so they won't go home to an empty house. He was actually doing his job. He could actually get fired if he lets kids off without an adult there." (Note that "actually" was one of Zach's favorite words at this point in his life, hence my overuse of it.)

Zach started sniffling again. "I know!"

I doubted that he knew much about the job requirements of a bus driver, but I wasn't going to argue.

"I think we need to say sorry to the driver for kicking him and for me being late."

Together we wrote an apology letter and we both signed it. Zach filled a carton of eggs from our chickens to add to the apology.

The next morning the driver accepted the note and the eggs graciously. Zach and I decided that if I was late again Zach would know to stay on the bus, and I would get in my car and follow the bus to the next stop so he wouldn't have to wait so long to get home.

A five-year-old made the transition from physical assault to socially acceptable grace. He and his mother solved a problem and made amends. It could not have happened without first waiting for the panic and fury to subside.

The next basic need I want to address in this fractional chapter is **the need not to be overwhelmed**. If too many demands are made and too many frustrations have piled up, even a simple, respectful request can be the proverbial straw that breaks the camel's back. We need to be aware of when a child is nearing his breaking point so we don't add that last seemingly harmless straw.

Let's see what this final straw might look like.

Unenchanted Evening

My son, Eli, is four years old. We recently moved to a different state and we no longer have the au pair who lived with us since Eli was two. After the move, we enrolled him in full-day preschool since both my husband and I are now working full-time.

Last night I picked Eli up from after-school care at 5 o'clock. When we got to the house, Eli said, "Mommy, let's play."

"I can't do that. It's late. I need to start cooking so we can eat."

"No, Mommy! Don't make dinner. Play with me. Play the tickle game."

I told him I have to cook right now. He looked like he was going to start crying so I told him he could be my assistant chef.

He went to get his apron. I told him he needed to wash his hands first. He made an angry grunt and threw the apron down.

I took him into the bathroom to wash his hands and noticed he needed to poop. I could see him dancing around in that way. While he was sitting on the potty I noticed his ragged fingernails, so I got the scissors and started cutting them. He started to cry and said he wanted his video game. I reminded him that we don't play video games on school nights.

At that point he jumped off the potty and began to scream. "NO! NO! NO! I'm playing. You can't stop me." He was running around with no pants on. It was a bad scene and it didn't get any better. I could go on, but suffice it to say that he cried himself to sleep.

Such simple requests. Such a difficult child! Take another look with eyes on those straws piling up.

A long day at school and after-school care, the loss of a familiar au pair, a new school, a new house, new teachers, a new schedule, a distracted mom, an unpleasant chore of cutting nails—Eli might have been able to handle any one of these things, but all together, it was too much!

The moral of the story is: watch out for all those "straws," both hidden and obvious, that may be overwhelming your child. When the load is getting heavy, spend more time relaxing and reconnecting and less time making demands—of yourself or your child.

Finally, we need to **match our expectations to the child's stage of development and level of experience**. This is not the book to turn to for an exhaustive discussion of developmental stages,[1] but we can't get away without mentioning it. When things are going badly it may be helpful to ask yourself, *Am I expecting my child to behave in a way that is beyond his current level of ability?*

Here are a few stories of parents with unrealistic expectations.

Downhill Ride

It seemed like a great idea at the time. We hadn't had a vacation since the twins were born. Now that they were three, we planned to take them skiing at this fantastic place that provides all-day classes for the little ones while their parents ski. Heaven! We live in California and the girls have never seen snow. They also love physical challenges. We were pretty sure they'd be thrilled.

When we got to the resort, the girls refused to go with the instructor. We left them anyway, only to be called back 20 minutes later and told that we had to pick them up because they wouldn't stop crying. We were not able to ski and we lost a very large deposit for the lessons. It was a huge disappointment. What could we have done differently to make this work?

• • •

What, indeed, could these optimistic parent have done differently? Well, for one thing, they could've been less optimistic. Three-year-olds are not generally amenable to so many new experiences at once. The idea that children of this age will go off with a complete stranger, in an unfamiliar setting, wearing strange bulky clothing in freezing cold temperatures they have never experienced before, to engage in a completely unfamiliar and difficult activity for hours on end . . . That scenario may exist in a fantasy novel, but it was too much to ask of the real world. For three-year-olds, an exciting vacation would be a trip to a new playground for an hour, another thirty minutes to muck about in a muddy stream, then a nice snack, and home to sleep in their own bed. Keep your plans simple and humble when your kids are small, and you will have simple (and less expensive) disappointments.

Puppy Promises

It was Saturday morning. My husband was asleep, as was our new puppy. My seven-year-old son, Theo, was awake and playing computer games. I realized we were out of milk, so I told Theo that I was going on a quick shop, and he needed to be sure to let the puppy out *as soon as she woke up*. I told him it was very important. He nodded and went back to his game.

When I got back, the first thing I noticed was my sandaled foot in a puddle of urine right by the door. There was a bad smell, and then I saw dog poop had been tracked all over the kitchen floor. Where was Theo? Still in front of his computer, completely oblivious.

I was furious. I yelled at him so loudly the puppy ran under the table and peed again. I reminded him that he had promised to take care of the puppy when he begged us for a dog. We even had him sign a contract agreeing to feed and walk the dog. I threatened to give her back because he was behaving so irresponsibly. My son was sobbing his eyes out. Is it too much to expect a seven-year-old to clip a leash on a puppy and take him out into the backyard?

Not necessarily. But just because a child has the physical ability to walk a dog doesn't mean that he's ready to suddenly take full responsibility for a living creature. Kids aren't good at splitting their attention and tend to become absorbed in the moment, especially when the moment involves computer games. You can't rely on the fact that he "*promised!*" Devising a plan for the future and giving your child plenty of opportunity to practice will get you where you want to go more effectively than a signature on a contract.

So there you have it, folks. When you're feeling frustrated by a child's miserable behavior, do a quick check to see if addressing any of these "deal breakers" will save the day.

<u>**REMINDER: The Basics—Conditions Under**</u>
<u>**Which the Tools Won't Work**</u>

- **Lack of food**
- **Lack of sleep**
- **Need for recovery time**
- **Feeling overwhelmed (the last straw syndrome)**
- **Lack of developmental or experiential readiness**

PART II

THE TOOLS IN ACTION

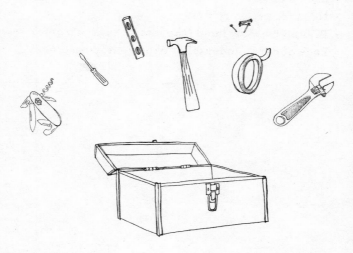

Welcome to part two of our survival guide.

Here we invite you to listen in on some of our "special topic" workshop sessions about common conflicts that crop up in life with little kids. You can read stories from workshop participants who have tried the strategies in this book with real-life, nontheoretical children. At the end of each chapter you'll find a summary page of ideas you can see at a glance.

This section of our book is not intended to be read sequentially. You can dip into whichever topic you like, in any order you like, without reproach!

1

Food Fights—The Battle at the Kitchen Table

Joanna

When food is a source of conflict, we're fighting with our kids every day . . . many times a day. Parents in the workshop had no problem compiling a list of flashpoints:

The Battleground

- Getting kids to eat their vegetables instead of just pasta and dessert.
- Getting them to eat what's served without a mountain of complaints. ("Eww, that's disgusting!")
- Getting them to try new foods. (Why are they so suspicious? Do they think their parents are trying to poison them?)
- Getting them to eat *enough*. (How are they going to grow if they're determined to survive on air and potato chips?)

Toni was the first to weigh in. "Every night is a festival of bargaining and bribery in my house. I'll say, 'Come on, you can't have your ice cream until you take three more bites of broccoli.' Thomas will say, 'One bite.' I'll say, 'Okay, how about two?' It's ridiculous."

Maria was nodding in agreement. "Benjamin is on the white-food diet. All he wants to eat is pasta, bread, and vanilla ice cream. When I grew up you ate what your mother put in front of you."

I wondered out loud if the good old days were as good as we remember them. My mother used to tell me stories about how she dreaded mealtimes. One of her earliest memories was of her mother poking more and more food into her mouth and then patting her cheeks to force her to swallow. My father had his own battles at the kitchen table. His mother demanded that the children "clean their plates." He has vivid memories of being unable to choke down gluey hot cereal, and being served the same unfinished bowl for lunch, and again for dinner. He stuck to his fast until he fainted from hunger.

"Well, that is sad," snapped Toni. "But what are we supposed to do? Let the lunatics run the asylum? We'll have candy for breakfast, pasta for lunch, and potato chips with soda for dinner. I think in this case it's more important to make sure your child has good nutrition than to be his best friend."

"Let's look at this from a different angle," I suggested. "We know a lot of kids are naturally suspicious of new tastes and textures, foods with strong or bitter tastes, and even foods touching other foods on their plate. There's actually a scientific explanation for picky eat-ing. Little babies put everything in their mouths, but around age two they become cautious about new tastes. That caution protects the freely moving toddler from the danger of eating poisonous things. In fact, we're a species of picky eaters, since historically the pickiest of toddlers survive to reproduce. Picky eating is in our DNA!"[1]

"It can be worse for kids on the autism spectrum," Anna

added. "Anton will only eat foods with certain textures, or very bland food. Even though he likes the taste of apples, he can't stand the texture, so he won't eat them."

Toni looked frustrated. "Fine, so they're naturally picky. We still need to get them to eat."

I wasn't done with my science lecture. I told the group about a study in which very young children were offered a variety of healthy foods and were allowed to make their own choices. The children *did* actually choose a balanced diet on their own. It wasn't necessarily balanced for that particular meal, but it was balanced if you looked over the course of a day or a week. None of them came down with any kind of vitamin or protein deficiency, and they all gained a healthy amount of weight.[2]

Toni wasn't convinced. "Well, if that were true, we wouldn't have to worry about anything. So why do I read in the news about kids eating too much junk food and drinking too much soda?"

It was a good point. The researchers had only offered healthy food to the children. Our craving for sweets and fat would ruin the experiment if soda and chips were included.

"If you think about it, evolutionarily speaking we haven't been around refined sugar and a limitless supply of fat for very long. Kids can't handle that."

"Heck, *I* can't even handle that!" said Sarah. "If I see chocolate, I'll eat it! The only way I can control my diet is to have certain things out of sight or out of the house."

I dove back into my lecture. "Here's what we have so far. Many children are naturally picky eaters. It may even be genetic, or developmental. But given a range of healthy choices, children will choose a balanced diet—so long as junk food isn't included in the mix. Children are tempted by sweets and fried food just as much as we are.

"It seems to me we have two important goals here. The first is to provide kids with a healthy diet, but that's not enough. We also want to help them form a healthy *attitude* toward food, so they can tune in to their own bodies—eat when they're hungry and stop eating when they're full, be open to trying new things, and enjoy eating food that nourishes them. The big question is, how do we get there?

"There's one thing I'm sure of. We're not going to get there by demanding that children eat a certain number of bites of broccoli in order to get to the dessert. That only teaches them that if they choke down the 'bad stuff' they get to eat the 'good stuff.' The lesson becomes, 'What I really love is bad for me and what I really hate is good for me.' It's extremely difficult to enjoy a food that you are being forced to eat."

I asked the group to imagine that they were invited to a dinner party where the host made up a plate for them with a mound of mashed potatoes, a large pile of spinach, a quarter of a chicken . . .

"Oh, I wouldn't eat that. I'm a vegetarian," Sarah said.

I continued the role play. "Sorry, I'm deciding what you eat. Your job is to clean your plate or you won't get cherry pie for dessert."

"I wouldn't go back to that person's house for another dinner party!" Sarah said.

That brings me to the most important recommendation I can offer: **Serve your child an empty plate!**

Pretend he's an adult at a dinner party. He didn't get to choose the menu, but he does get to fill his own plate. Let him spoon out his own pasta, put his own sauce on or not, sprinkle his own cheese on top, and grab some carrots and string beans on the side for crunch. Or if he's too young to handle the serving spoon, at least he can ask you for what he wants and guide the amounts he gets. It's a great opportunity for a kid to practice autonomy.

Toni still looked skeptical. "That's a lot of extra dishes to wash, to put everything in a separate serving bowl."

"Oh my gosh, no!" I agreed. "I just put the pots right on the table. Serving bowls only when we have to impress company!"

"But what if he just wants to eat the dessert?" Toni asked.

Anna raised her hand. "I don't know if everyone would be comfortable with this idea, but for me it works better to take dessert out of the equation. It's too hard to get Anton to eat a healthy meal when he's focused on dessert. We have cookies in the house, but we don't serve them after dinner. We have them as an afternoon snack. And I make sure to call sweet things 'treats' rather than junk food. I don't want to teach him that what tastes good to him is junk or garbage. Anton knows he can have two cookies at snack time, and after that if he's still hungry he has to choose some 'growing food,' like nuts or fruit."

That brings up another important point. Using dessert, or any reward, as a bargaining chip does not help children learn to enjoy healthy food. One study investigated the effect of rewards on attitudes toward food.[3] Researchers offered two groups of preschoolers the chance to try an unfamiliar food, kefir, a yogurt-based drink. In the first group they offered the kids a reward to try the kefir. Most of the students enthusiastically agreed. In the second group the researchers offered no bribe. They simply asked if the kids wanted to try a new, interesting drink from the Middle East. Many kids in both groups tried the drink. A few weeks later the researchers returned. They offered the kefir again. In the first group the children asked, "What will you give us if we drink it?" "Nothing" was the reply. Nobody wanted to drink kefir for nothing! In the second group the children were enthusiastic. "Oh, kefir! Sure, I love that stuff!"

Michael raised an eyebrow. "Don't you think children should be required to at least *try* new things? How will they know if they like it if they refuse to try it?"

"I don't think they'll know if they like it if they're forced to try it. More likely they'll be choking it down to get it over with. I prefer to say, 'Sam, here's something I think you might like if you give it a try,' and leave it at that.

"You can even say, 'This is grown-up food, and you might not like it.' My family once went to a New Year's party where the host served stuffed mushrooms 'only for the adults.' My children were so offended! I explained that this was not the kind of food children usually like, and the host didn't want her fancy hors d'oeuvres bitten once and tossed in the garbage. But sure, if they wanted they could have a little bite of mine to see if they liked it. You've never seen such enthusiasm!"

"One thing I do that makes the kids excited about eating healthy food is to have them help prepare it," offered Sarah. "When they help to make the salad by ripping up the lettuce, or pour the rice and water from the measuring cup into the pot, or stir the beans and sprinkle in the spices, they're always more excited about eating."

"And what about shopping?" Maria added. "When I take Benjamin to the grocery store, I let him pick which peaches and plums we should buy for our fruit salad. He loves eating 'his' fruit."

"So getting kids involved in the planning and preparations can make a big difference in their interest in the meal," I said.

"Here's something else that might help. I make a big deal about how tastes change. My husband and I tell the kids about foods we thought were disgusting when we were kids but that we now love—mushy stuff like mushrooms and avocado. I remember one dinner when Sam was chewing on a piece of cooked zucchini with a very unhappy look on his face. 'Sam!' I said, 'I thought you didn't like zucchini. I cut the pieces big enough for you to pick out.' Sam said, 'I'm seeing if my tastes have changed.'

"'Did they?' I asked him.

"'Not yet.'"

Even though Sam still didn't like zucchini, he was willing to give it a try.

"But what if he tries something and says it's disgusting?" asked Toni.

"I'd say, 'Hey, that's not nice to the people who are eating it!'"

"Not to mention the person who made it!" Toni said heatedly.

"Right!" I agreed. "But I've noticed that kids are less inclined to insult our food if we're not forcing them to eat it. Respect is a two-way street."

Toni frowned. "It seems like what you're suggesting is that parents become short-order cooks. If I have to respect each of my children's likes and dislikes I'll end up preparing five meals a night. That's just not happening! In the old days you put the food on the table and your family ate it."

"I'm with you, Toni," I said. "One meal a night is my limit! It's a bad idea to drive yourself crazy making different meals for everyone. I'd be resentful.

"What I'm suggesting is that we serve some of the food as separates so our kids can make choices about how to combine them. And if a kid is truly horrified by what's in the family pot, he can have a very simple substitute—a peanut butter sandwich and a carrot, for example."

I thought about my own family. My younger brother was the classic picky eater. He couldn't eat anything with sauce on it. The different foods on his plate were not allowed to touch, and gelatinous substances such as tomatoes disgusted him. My mom never made a big deal about it. Since she and my dad were raised by parents who forced them to clean their plates, they were determined not to do that to their own kids. I remember many dinners where my brother had his cheese sandwich with a carrot and bell pepper on the side, while the rest of the family ate whatever my mom had prepared. That brother grew up to be the gourmet of the family.

We had come to the end of the session. I sent the group home to experiment on their children. Here are the stories they brought back.

THE STORIES

Michael's Story: The Empty Plate

We really didn't think it would work to let Jamie serve himself, but he loved it! He was so interested in the whole process of choosing what would be on his plate. He kept saying things like, "Hmmm, maybe the potatoes would taste good with some string beans stuck in them." "Hmmm, maybe I'll have some more chicken. I still have some room in my stomach."

At one point he scooped half the bowl of mashed potatoes onto his plate and we had to remind him to divide it up with his eyes, because Daddy and Mommy and his sister needed some, too. He had never thought about that. He started asking us if *we* wanted more of things, too. Usually we spend the whole meal bargaining with him—two more bites of broccoli if you want your ice cream. And then he'll make the counteroffer, "How about just one?" And we end up giving in because we don't want the crying when he doesn't get dessert.

The most amazing thing was that at the end of the meal *he didn't even ask for dessert*. He was full! And then he made a big announcement: "This was the *best* meal I've ever had!"

It was just a regular meal we'd served many times before.

Maria's Story: Grapes of Wrath

A few days ago I got into one of those food fights with Benjamin. I wanted him to have something in his stomach before school. I had some grapes for him and he wouldn't eat them. He said they tasted rotten, and I told him they weren't. I was actually trying to stuff the grapes into his mouth, and he was keeping his teeth tightly closed. Then I just stopped. I said, "Oh, you don't like these grapes. You don't like them when they're even a little bit brown on top."

He said, "No," and that was it. It was a relief. So what if he was a little hungry that morning at school? I get so crazy thinking that I have to make him eat! It's making him crazy, too. The next day I just put a few things out for him and walked away to load the dishwasher. He ate a banana. A much better result.

Toni's Story: A Different Shape of Pasta

The twins always find something to complain about at dinner. This time it was the pasta. "We don't like the spirals. Why didn't you get shells?" I reminded them that spirals are their favorite. Jenna said, "No, they are my most *un*-favorite!" I told them that it's all the same taste, just a different shape, and it all gets mushed up in your stomach anyway. Ella started to cry. And then I had that *oh yeah* moment, so I started saying, "Oh boy, you used to really like spirals but now you really like shells. You're tired of stupid old boring spirals. Shells can be filled up with sauce; spirals can't."

They both said, "*Yeah!*" And then I asked if they would come with me to the grocery store next time to help choose some different shapes to try. They liked that idea. After dinner they drew all kinds of scribbly shapes for pasta on their "grocery list." Oh, and by the way, they ate the spirals. I told them I was too tired to start cooking pasta all over again, plus I didn't want to waste food. At that point it didn't matter anymore. They were excited about their new plan.

Sarah's Story: Eating Emergency

Sophia has hypoglycemia. When she goes without food for too long, her mood crashes, along with her blood sugar. The problem is, if we don't catch it in time she gets into such a state that she'll refuse to eat. Even though she's seven, she throws a tantrum like a two-year-old.

Last night we went out to a restaurant. Sophia hadn't eaten in hours, and she was getting teary. She couldn't find anything on the menu she liked. In the past my husband or I have always been very stern with her. "You have to get food into your body. You're just upset because you're hungry."

Then she screams that she is *not* upset and does *not* need to eat. I never thought of this as an opportunity to accept feelings. It's a health issue, not a feelings issue.

But this time instead of insisting that she put some bread in her mouth, I stuck with accepting feelings. "You really don't feel well! And a restaurant with strange food on the menu is probably the last place you want to be." (It was also the last place I wanted to be with a screaming kid!)

She immediately replied, "*Yes!* I feel sick! This always happens when I'm hungry! I need to eat something to feel better."

She grabbed a roll and started chewing.

I was amazed. She usually fights me when she gets into that state. This time she showed self-knowledge and was able to move right on to a solution. It's really hard to resist telling her what to do when the solution is so obvious, but this is clearly the better way.

Sarah's Story: Something Fishy

In our preschool we do a unit on food every spring. We talk to the kids about healthy foods, and we plant a vegetable garden in the courtyard. By June kids are making their own salads out of the vegetables they grew themselves—lettuce, peas, and radishes for the brave. So it's ironic that I can't get my own son to eat healthy food at home. I tell him he can't have dessert if he doesn't clean his plate, but he doesn't care. He just shrugs and says, "So I won't eat dessert."

I tried the empty plate idea this week. I made fish, and it came out really good. I seared it just a minute on each side in a hot pan. Jake refused to eat it. Everyone else said it was delicious. My husband urged Jake to taste it, but I told him, "It's okay, you don't have to eat it if you don't want to." He asked, "But what about dessert?" I said, "No problem. You can have dessert."

About halfway through the meal I saw Jake's hand sneak out and grab some fish off the serving plate. I never would have thought he'd try something without me insisting. For the rest of the week mealtime has been very relaxed. There's less fidgeting and arguing at the table. Once Jake asked how many bites of salad he needed to eat, and I told him, "Ask your stomach."

Toni's Story: Juiced Up

When my twins were three years old they were juice fiends. At mealtime they ignored the solid food and just drank juice. I tried to regulate it—making them dilute the juice with water; insisting that they take three bites of chicken or broccoli before they could have their cup refilled; telling them they won't grow up strong if they only drink juice. It was always a battle. They begged, I argued, they cried, I gave in a little bit, they pushed for more. The bottom line is that they filled up on juice, and then a half hour later they were having sugar meltdowns.

I finally decided to manage the environment. After all, they don't do the shopping! I stopped buying juice entirely. All there was to drink in the house for that year was water, or as we like to call it, "earth juice." You could have it on the rocks, or with a squirt of lemon if you wanted to get fancy. They screamed about it the first day, but then, no more juice battles. It was a relief!

Of course they still had their quirks. They ate mounds of frozen berries with yogurt for lunch, and they rejected spoons. They insisted on using their plastic frogs as utensils. They would plow the frog through the yogurt and then lick it off the frog's head.

One day we had their friend Emma over for lunch. Emma is this very sweet, cooperative, inside-the-box kind of kid. She looked at me with her big blue eyes and asked, "Why are the girls eating with frogs?"

I said I didn't know. "Ask them." Emma asked, and my girls just shrugged. I never thought being a parent would be this weird.

<u>REMINDER: Food Fights</u>

Resist the urge to . . .

- . . . insist that your child clean his or her plate, eat a specific food, or eat a predetermined amount.
- . . . offer dessert as a reward for eating healthy food, or withhold it as a punishment for not eating.
- . . . be a short-order cook.
- . . . label your child a *picky eater.*
- . . . make food a battleground!

Instead you can . . .

1. Acknowledge Feelings

"Even though you usually like chicken, you're not in the mood for it tonight."

2. Offer Choices

- Put an empty plate in front of your child and let him serve himself, or ask for what he wants if he's too young to serve himself.

- Serve some of the meal as simple separates so kids can make choices about what they put on their plates.

- Offer a simple alternative if kids don't want the "grown-up" food—peanut butter sandwich, bread and cheese, hard-boiled egg, raw carrots, red pepper.

3. Manage the Environment

Keep sweets and sugary drinks out of sight. Make it easy to avoid temptation!

4. Put the Child in Charge

Let kids have as much involvement as possible in planning, shopping, as well as preparing the meal, if you can tolerate some food landing on the floor. (Your dog will thank you!)

5. Give Information

Let kids know that "tastes change," so they don't feel stuck with their limited palate. Tell them, "You might want to give this a try when you're ready."

2

Morning Madness—Escaping the Intense Gravitational Pull of Your Home

Julie

Anna took the floor. "These tools are working really well with Anton. I wish I could relax and enjoy that. But Luke is driving me crazy. Do you think he's still too young to get it? He just turned two and he is definitely living out the dream of being a terrible two-year-old."

I sat back. "Give us the gory details."

"Okay, you asked for it." Anna took a long sip of her coffee and started in. "Luke is suddenly into power struggles. The worst is in the morning. He flails around on the floor and fights me when I need to dress him. None of the techniques I use with Anton work with Luke. I offer choices. He yells, 'NO CLOTHES!' I tell him that's not an option, and he throws them across the room. I try to put him in charge and let him do it himself, but he couldn't care less.

"Sometimes I try counting down. I tell him, 'If you don't start getting dressed I'm going to dress you on three. One . . . two . . .' I know, I know, we're not supposed to threaten. Anyway it doesn't even work. He runs away and hides . . . in small hard-to-reach places, let me tell you.

"I've even tried bribes, offering him ice cream for breakfast if he gets dressed. But he holds out and then he has *another* tantrum when he doesn't get the ice cream. And that's not

231

all of it. Yesterday I spent ten minutes wrestling him into his carseat.

"The actual activities aren't the problem. Sometimes he loves to get dressed and is excited to get into his carseat. The problem is, when I need him to do it *now*, he automatically resists.

"I've thought about natural consequences, but the only consequence that's happening naturally is that I'm late for work. I suppose I could take him to school naked, but I don't think he would mind. Honestly, I can ignore the screaming, but he's only getting bigger and stronger. Soon I won't be able to force him anymore."

The group heaved a collective sigh. There are few things more stressful than trying to rush a two-year-old in the morning. We are in an impossible bind. Grown-up time demands that we move efficiently, with purpose, toward a goal. Toddler time meanders with no particular direction, enjoying the moment, purpose unnecessary.

"I'm guessing you're in no mood for whimsy when you're trying to get out of the house in the morning," I said, "but being playful is your best bet for avoiding a power struggle with a two-year-old. The good news is that the older kids get, the more reasonable they become. Then you can start to use problem-solving and put them in charge of themselves. But for now, it's all about changing the mood."

Anna looked annoyed. "What about *my* mood?"

Michael leaned forward. "Hey, your mood will get better if it works, right?"

Anna folded her arms. "Okay, let's hear it. What works?"

Sarah raised her hand. "It works for me to make the clothing talk. I make the socks and shoes say, 'I'm hungry! I want to eat these sweet little toes.' Or sometimes I make them protest, 'No, no, no! Don't put that smelly foot in me. I want to be free!' Then I scold them. 'Bad little sock, it's your *job* to cover Mia's foot and keep it warm.' The sock keeps arguing, 'I don't care, it's a stupid job.' Then I say very sternly, 'You must *cooperate*! You will make poor Mia late for school.' Mia laughs and forgets to fight me."

Maria chimed in. "Ben likes it when I give him silly choices. 'Do you want your shirt on regular, or backward? Or inside out? Do you want to put your right leg in the pants first, or your left leg? Whatever you do, don't jump in with both at the same time. That would be too dangerous!' Of course he tries to jump in. Sometimes I ask if he wants to walk to the car forward or backward, or pretend he's on skates, or jump like a frog. He also likes it when I make it into a race. 'How many seconds will it take to get to the car and get buckled in? Ready, set, *go*!' I got a little kitchen timer he can run with. I say things like, 'Ben *wins* the race! The crowd goes wild!'"

Michael offered, "Jamie never gets tired of the robot voice. I pretend I'm a droid when I dress him. 'Must . . . put . . . arm . . . in . . . sleeve. . . . Malfunction. . . . Shirt . . . stuck . . . on . . . nose.'"

Toni looked a little impatient. "I'd rather have my kids doing a little more for themselves. They're old enough for that. I'd go crazy if I had to do robot voices and games with all three of them every morning.

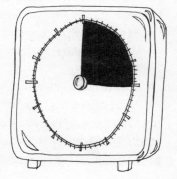

"What I did was to have a problem-solving session about the morning routine. I told them I hated yelling at them every morning, and I know they hated being yelled at and being rushed. We bought that special timer for kids, where the red part of the circle gets smaller as the time runs out, so they can see for themselves how much time is left. Then we made a chart with all the tasks they need to do in the morning. I stapled a strip of cardboard on the bottom of the chart to make a long pocket. Each kid has a Popsicle stick with a face on it, and they move their stick to the next task when they're finished."

I was intrigued. "Can you show us what it looks like?"

Toni quickly sketched it out on a piece of paper. "There are six steps—shirt and pants, shoes and socks, eat breakfast, brush teeth, get coat and backpack, and then the last step is FREE PLAY. They all like moving their little Popsicle people from step to step, and if they finish all the tasks they get to play whatever they want. If all three of them get ready with time to spare, we play Touch the Couch."

"What?" Michael looked confused.

"I can't believe you don't know the greatest game on earth. The parent has to stop the kids from touching the couch. You can block with your body but you can't use your hands. The kids have to run around the parent and touch the couch to win. It's like football, except with no ball, and the goal is a couch."

"Ahh, I understand now. Sounds like fun in your house in the morning."

Toni rolled her eyes. "You should come visit!"

We had compiled a lot of good strategies in a short session. But there was one more important aspect of the morning conflict we hadn't discussed yet—the transition from sleep to the demanding world of "get up and get ready!"

Nobody likes to be dragged out of that cocoon to face immediate demands and pressure to hurry. One sure way to sabotage the morning mood is to start with, "Time to wake up! You have five minutes to get yourself downstairs. Let's not miss the bus today!"

For a kid, that can set the tone for a morning of resistance. Here are some more gentle approaches that parents have used to start the day.

"I give a little back massage to help wake up my son. He loves it. I used to shake him. He hated that!"

"I get into bed with her and snuggle for ten minutes. She used to get up angry, but now she gets up calm. I didn't think I had the time for this, but it makes the rest of the morning go so much better that it's worth it."

"I say, 'Do you want to get up now or do you want another five minutes to snooze? Wiggle one finger for now and two fingers for five more minutes.' She always wiggles two."

"I say 'It's morning time, my sleepy submarine. Poke up your periscope (finger) if you can hear me. You're invited to breakfast in ten minutes, so start coming up to the surface . . . not too fast, though. You don't want to scare the fish.'"

THE STORIES

Anna's Story: Ready for Action

I have to tell you how great my week was. I know you said that Luke is too young to do problem-solving, but I tried it anyway. I started by saying, "You don't like to be rushed in the morning. You are not in the mood to get dressed right after you wake up. It's no fun at all." Luke nodded.

Then I said, "I have an idea. Do you want to get dressed at night, after your bath, and sleep in your next-day clothes? Then you could wake up ready to go, with more time to play."

Luke agreed. His daytime clothes are soft pull-up pants and T-shirts so they're comfortable to sleep in. This has transformed my life! Now my day starts without a huge battle.

Michael's Story: Lego Lament

Jamie likes to play with Legos in the morning before school. The problem is that he doesn't like to *stop* playing when we have to leave. It's always, "Just one more piece! I'm almost finished." I get in huge fights with him about it.

In the past I'd give him the consequence of not being allowed to play with Legos in the afternoon if he refused to listen to me in the morning. That didn't help. It just made him grumpy in the afternoon.

Last week I tried problem-solving. Here's my worksheet.

The problem	*Ideas*
It's fun to play with Legos in the morning, but it's very hard to stop in the middle. It's frustrating not to get to finish what you're building! Dad gets mad when he is late for work.	- Set a timer and stop playing when the timer goes off. - Take the Legos in the car with you. - Use only ten pieces of Legos in the morning. - Let the Lego guy sit next to your plate and watch you eat. - Don't play with Legos in the morning at all. Do something else that's not as frustrating to stop.

To tell you the truth we never even got around to picking solutions. Jamie was happy to talk about it for a while, then he lost interest and wandered away. I figured we'd pick it up another time. I was going to object to Legos in the car. I can just imagine the tantrums when pieces fall under the seats. And I was ready to take action to protect myself—not punish!—by saying, "Look, this just isn't working. Legos aren't a morning toy. Let's keep them for the afternoon when you have lots of time."

But it never came to that. After the unfinished problem-solving session Jamie didn't play with Legos in the morning anymore. Somehow just talking about it seems to have solved it. At least for now, and that's good enough for me!

Maria's Story: Another Benjamin on the Floor

Benjamin *can* dress himself, but some mornings he just refuses. Last Monday he took off his pajamas and then went running around the house naked. I took his clothes—shirt, underpants, pants, and socks—and I laid them out on the floor, like a little person on the floor, and I said, "Look, Benjamin, there's a little Benjamin on the floor!"

Benjamin ran over and lay down on top of the clothes. Then he put the underpants on, put the pants on, put his arms through and put the shirt on. It was so easy—at least that time.

REMINDER: Morning Madness

1. Be Playful

(Shoe talking.) "I don't want that foot in me. Nooooo!" (Parent talking.) "You'd better get on Luke's foot right now. You're making him late!"

2. Offer a Choice

"Do you want to walk to the car the regular way or backward?"

3. Put the Child in Charge

"Can you set the timer? I need you to let me know when it's time to go out the door."

4. Try Problem-Solving

"It's not easy to remember all the things we have to do in the morning. What do you think about making a chart?"

5. Acknowledge Feelings

"It isn't easy to get out of a warm, cozy bed. It's nice to snuggle for a few more minutes!"

3

Sibling Rivalry—Give the Baby Back!

Joanna

Michael opened the session. He looked somber, without his usual happy grin.

"We thought we were done with sibling rivalry. Jamie was pretty happy to be a big brother, once he got over the shock of having a new baby. But now that Kara's two, she's demanding a lot more of our attention and getting into his things, and he's beginning to resent it. He shuts his door in her face, grabs things from her, tells her what to do, says 'no' to her a lot, and talks down about her.

"I know part of the problem is that he's getting less of our attention. Jan started working full-time. I take the morning shift with the kids and catch up on my work after dinner. So when Jan reads to Jamie at bedtime, Kara's on the floor playing with his toys. It's not the relaxed cozy bedtime it used to be."

Maria was nodding. "Well, at least you had a couple of good years! Benjamin has never accepted Isabel. He gets angry at the sight of her. He's always telling us to give the baby back because her diaper smells and she yells too much. I've tried telling him that we all had smelly diapers when we started out, and as for yelling, well, Benjamin is the prince of yelling. But it never helps. What's driving me crazy lately is that he wakes her up from naps. He says he doesn't want her to sleep. It makes him mad that I shush him and that we can't go out while she's napping. But still, you'd think he'd appreciate having his mom to himself for that time. It's so frustrating. And upsetting! I'm afraid to even admit this, but he says things like, 'Why don't you chop her up?'"

The group gave a collective groan. "Those are painful words to hear," I said.

"They sure are," said Maria. "We're supposed to be family. Family is the most important thing! They need to love and support each other. I tell them that every day."

"Okay, that's what we want," I agreed. "Now we have to think about how to get there. And you know what I'm going to say. We have to start with accepting feelings. This is one of those times when you have to bite the bullet and accept some truly awful feelings. Big brotherhood is a burden. The first message he needs to hear from you is that you understand. It isn't easy having to share your parents with a smelly baby or a two-year-old pest! The more we try to convince our kids that it's not so bad, the harder they'll work to convince us that it is indeed that bad."

"So what am I supposed to do?" asked Maria. "Talk to him about killing the baby? I can't stomach that."

You don't have to use a child's violent language to let him know you understand how he feels. You can model a different way to express strong feelings.

"Boy, it's not always easy having a little sister around. It can be really frustrating!"

"I'll bet sometimes you wish you could be the only child."

"It's annoying to have to be quiet when the baby is napping. You'll be happy when she's old enough not to need a nap anymore!"

"Two-year-olds can be hard on your things. They just don't understand how to be gentle. It can make you mad."

If the mood is right, he might enjoy hearing your fond memories of some of his own notorious exploits as a baby.

"When *you* were two, you used to get into the cabinets and pull out every single pot and pan and bang on them with the serving spoons . . ."

"When I tried to stop you from climbing onto the roof of the car, you screamed and cried because you loved climbing so much . . ."

"I remember when you poured an entire box of Cheerios all over the floor and then crunched around in them like they were fall leaves . . ."

The second message he needs is that he hasn't been displaced. He may want some babying himself. We're always telling our older children what big boys or girls they are. But they need to know they can still be your baby, too; they haven't been pushed aside. You can say something like:

"Come here and sit on my lap and be my baby. Oh my gosh, look at you—you are the strongest baby in the world. A super baby who can run and jump and climb a tree."

The third message is to help him see himself as the kind, helpful older brother you have glimpsed in the past. Go out of your way to appreciate positive interactions with his younger sibling.

"Yeah, sometimes it is a pain in the neck to have a baby sister, but sometimes it's not so bad. I remember when the two of you were running around the kitchen table and you got Kara so excited she couldn't stop laughing and she peed on the floor. "

"Isabel sure is lucky to have you as a big brother. You really know how to cheer her up when she's sad. She loves it when you blow soap bubbles for her to pop . . . make block towers for her to crash down . . . read picture books to her . . . play peekaboo under the table . . . push her stroller over bumps . . . help her get her socks on . . ."

You can also put him in a position where he sees himself in a new light, as a helper rather than a rival.

"Jamie, I need to put away the groceries right now. Can you read a board book to Kara to keep her out of the refrigerator?"

"Benjamin, I need Isabel to wake up. Can you do it for me? She likes it when you wake her up by patting gently on her stomach."

Sibling Rivalry

"Kara is in a wrecking mood. I need someone who can build a good block tower for her to knock over."

"We have some cookies for snack time. Benjamin, can you pick two good ones for Isabel?"

Even in the middle of an episode where he's tormenting his sister, instead of criticizing him for being a beast . . .

"Benjamin, there you go again teasing your sister; this has to stop!"

you can state the positive . . .

"Uh oh, Isabel is starting to melt down. Benjamin, you know how to make your sister feel better when she's upset. What do you think we should do?"

But what if your older child is still feeling displaced by the little invader? When you have a hankering to coo and fuss over the baby in front of her brother, you can use the opportunity to "coo" about all the marvelous things big brother did today. The baby won't mind, and your older child will enjoy hearing stories about himself instead of feeling resentful of the attention the little one is getting. In your best lilting baby talk, you'll say . . .

"My little boo boo! Do you know what your big brother Benjamin did today? He made us peanut butter and jelly sandwiches all by himself. Yes he did, my little pumpkin. He climbed up on the counter to get the plates from the cabinet, and he smeared the peanut butter with a knife, and he put lots and lots of grape jelly on top. It was so tasty! He will teach *you* to do that one day. Yes, he will!"

While you're doing this rather intricate dance, you may feel tempted to throw in a little comparison to make the older child feel better about not being babied. It can *seem* like a good idea to reassure the older sibling of his superiority. ("You're a big boy. You can climb the stairs and the baby can't. You can get in the carseat all by yourself. You know how to bake cookies with me. The baby can't do that!")

This kind of talk is risky! The baby won't stay helpless forever. We don't want an older child to feel threatened by a younger sibling's progress. His self-esteem shouldn't rest on the shaky foundation of the baby's ineptitude.

Instead, tell him how lucky that baby is to have a big brother who is such a skilled seatbelt buckler, and that soon he will be teaching his little sister how to buckle herself in, or climb the stairs, or bake a cookie. We want him to feel proud of his competence *and* of his position as a benevolent helper.

And finally, I hate to say it, but kids don't care about our work schedule, bills, and emails. They want our undivided time and attention. If it's at all possible to carve out, say, a half hour just to be with a child who's feeling deprived, it can make a big difference. You can talk to your child about what he wants to do with that "fatherly sonly" time, as my little brother used to call it. Part of the pleasure is in the planning.

"What should we do for our special time? Do you want to cook something together, make play dough, read *The Way Things Work,* or wrestle on the bed?"

Be sure to make a specific time that your child can look forward to. Six o'clock means very little to a three-year-old. It works better to say "after dinner," or "as soon as the baby takes her morning nap."

When angry feelings do boil over and you have to protect a sibling from physical attack, it's important to take action without reinforcing negative feelings. While grabbing up the aggressor, resist the temptation to say, "There you go again. You're too rough! Now you made the baby cry. That's mean!" Instead, snatch him away without insulting his character:

"I can see you're angry! I can't let anyone get hurt. We need to separate!"

I have one last pitfall to warn you against. One of my own biggest problems with keeping harmony between the siblings was that I tended to take the younger one's side. "Oh, Dan, just give it to him. He's only two years old. You need to be patient. Don't be so rough, you're hurting him. Be nice." Without fail this would incite mutual hatred and resentment. Dan would angrily defend himself, "But I had it first . . . I barely touched him . . . It's not fair . . . You always take his side!" And Sam, the little one, would get even more worked up. He'd hide behind my leg while I was defending him and then lunge out and try to kick his older brother in a fit of righteous rage.

It helps to hold back that first "protect the baby" remark. Resist the urge to demonize the older or stronger child. If you can describe the problem from both points of view it will make a big difference in the mood.

"Dan wants to build something with his blocks without the

loose pieces being moved around, and Sam wants to touch the blocks, too. This is a tough problem. What can we do?"

Notice that I also resisted the temptation to be dismissive of the problem itself. I wanted to say, "Oh, gee whiz, it's only a few blocks! Can't you just get along?" But it's more helpful to be respectful of the problem. Building that block tower is just as important to a four-year-old as your work is to you!

No matter how brilliantly and consistently you carry out these suggestions, you can't expect to eliminate sibling rivalry completely. There will still be conflict! But you can help change the mood and make it easier for kids to return more quickly to fond feelings about their siblings after the conflicts are over.

THE STORIES

Michael's Stories: A Trilogy

Pros and Cons

This new approach is already making a difference. I've been spending more time acknowledging Jamie's feelings about being a big brother. It works best to talk to him when he's not already frustrated. We had a good conversation about the pros and cons of having a little sister. A few hours later he said, "I love you, Dad," out of the blue, something that doesn't happen that often. I think it's a sign he felt heard.

Jamie Reflects on the Past

Jamie: Dad, my life used to be totally different before Kara came.

Me (thinking I'm about to hear a list of complaints): Oh, how is it different?

Jamie (sounding surprised): Well, it's so much better, of course!!

Color Wars

Jamie wanted each of them to color on their own side of the paper. Kara wanted to color on Jamie's side, of course.

Me: Oh, this is a tough problem. Jamie wants Kara to color on her own side, and Kara wants to color on both sides.

Jamie: Oh well, she's two. She doesn't understand yet.

(He lets her color on his side.)

Maria's Story: The Baby Whisperer

I have to tell you, I really went all out with the idea of accepting the negative feelings this week. I told Benjamin some of the things you said in the group about how it's a big pain in the neck to have a little sister. He loved it. He had a long list of suggestions for what to do about it, too. Instead of scolding him I offered to write them down. Here are some of them: "Screech her away! Make her spin out and whip her away. Grunk her away! Whip her away in a fast jet plane."

He was very satisfied with his list. Later on, when it was time to wake Isabel up from her nap, Benjamin insisted that he be the one to do it, because he does it gently. That is one thing he likes to do, and she really does wake up smiling when he pats her stomach, so I had been mentioning that a lot. Now he's the only one who is allowed to wake the baby since, according to him, he's the expert.

I still get tired of hearing all the negative things he has to say. I can only stand so much. So I tell him my ears are tired, and he can draw me a picture so that I can see how mad he is. He did this once. It was a lot of crazy scribble. I put it on the refrigerator and said, "Thank you for showing me these mad feelings."

Joanna's Story: Down for the Count

I threw my back out when Dan was three-and-a-half and Sam was only one-and-a-half. I was flat on my back on the couch praying that nothing would go terribly wrong. I did my most desperately brilliant parenting that week. When I heard crying from another room I didn't allow myself to ask the obvious question, "Dan, what did you do to your brother?"

Instead I called out, in my best neutral tone, "I hear crying. Do you need help in there?"

"No, it's okay. I'm fixing it!"

The crying stopped. Whew!

All day long, instead of physically intervening in their conflicts (which I was helpless to do) I stayed neutral and put Dan in charge. It was the smoothest day ever. Every conflict was resolved peacefully and I didn't have to call the fire department to hose anybody down as I had feared.

They say that necessity is the mother of invention, but I claim that desperation is the mother of great parenting.

Anna's Story: Breaking News

When I was pregnant with Luke I really worried about telling Anton. The one time we'd talked about having a little brother or sister for him, he was completely against the idea. "No baby!"

When we finally told him, we did two things that helped a lot. One was that we said we wanted him to be the first to know about the news. He took great pride that he was so important! He actually asked us not to tell anyone else yet. I could see he wanted to enjoy feeling special.

The other was that we asked him for ideas about how to handle the big changes in our family. He came up with a good one. Buy bunk beds! He would sleep on the top and the new baby could have the bottom. He'd asked for bunk beds before, but we always told him this kind of bed was for two siblings. We thanked him for his "helpful idea."

I didn't think of it this way at the time, but I guess we made Anton feel like he was in charge and solving problems even before Luke was born.

Toni's Story: Good Guy Gripe

This was amazing. All I did was accept one little feeling. Easiest fix ever!

Jenna: So I will be the good guy and you will be the bad guy.
Ella (starting to cry): I don't want to be the bad guy.
Me: This is a tough problem. Both of you want to play Ghostbusters but no one wants to be the bad guy.
Jenna: Okay, I'll be the bad guy.

Joanna's Story: Selfish Son

At age five and a half, Dan got a shiny new bike. The whole family went to the bike store to buy it. The day was all about Dan. The plan was for three-year-old Sam to inherit Dan's old bike. When we got home with Dan's gleaming prize, Sam went to touch Dan's old bike. Dan yelled, "That's not your bike, it's *my* bike!"

I felt a flash of rage at him. *What kind of selfish brat have I raised?* I started to explain to him that he couldn't have two bikes and leave his brother with none. Sam wasn't even getting a new bike. Just Dan's old secondhand one. Dan covered his ears with his hands. "I'm not going to listen to you no matter what you say!"

A phrase from my mother's book popped into my head. "Ears can hear only what emotions will allow." My anger drained away and I took Dan on my lap. "I have a sad boy. That bike was really special to you."

Dan began to sob. "Grandma and Grandpa gave me that bike when I was three. It's like my turtle shirt. It's too small for me but it's still mine! Remember they tied the happy birthday note to a string, and I had to follow the string to find the bike in the carpet room? And I learned to ride without training wheels on that bike."

Sam was crying too at this point. A combination of having been yelled at by his brother and seeing his brother in tears had sent him over the edge. "I have two sad boys," I said.

Dan jumped off my lap and started making up a song, "I'm the magic man," and dancing in a goofy way in front of Sam, to cheer him up.

I wanted to explain to Dan that he still needed to give his bike to Sam. But the two boys were both happy now. It was a moment of grace and I was reluctant to bring up the conflict again. Sam did it for me. He said, "Well, you can still touch the bike, Dan."

I asked Dan if he wanted to call his grandparents to tell them about the new bike. He liked that idea. I listened in on his side of the conversation: "Well, I already finished riding on my tiger bike and now Sam has the tiger bike, which is hard to give up, you know. But my new bike has twenty-inch wheels . . ."

After the phone call Dan asked me, "Can I have the tiger bike back after Zach (who was six months old) uses it, so that I can give it to *my* children?"

Only a half hour before, I was disgusted with my son's selfish, greedy behavior. Once his feelings were acknowledged his heart was full of generosity. He'd felt sentimental about his grandparents' loving gift. And now he was contemplating passing it on, not only to his younger brothers, but to his own future child.

REMINDER: Sibling Rivalry

1. Accept Feelings

"It can be frustrating to have a baby sister!"

2. Give Wishes in Fantasy: Let the older child pretend to be a baby

"Come sit on my lap and be my super baby."

3. Describe What You See: Notice and appreciate the positive interactions between siblings

"You figured out how to cheer up your sister when she was crying."

4. Put the Child in Charge so that he has an opportunity to see himself differently

"Can you pick a board book for the baby? She likes it when you read to her."

5. Reconnect With Your Child

- **Plan for Special One-on-One Time**

  "Would you like to make cookies when the baby takes her nap? Or snuggle up and read your pop-up truck book?"

- **Tell the Older Child Stories About his Baby Days**

  "I remember when you . . ."

6. **Take Action Without Insult:** Avoid casting a child in the role of aggressor

> "We need to separate. I don't want anyone getting hurt!"

7. **Try Problem-Solving:** Resist the urge to take sides and don't minimize the problem!

> "Jamie wants to build by himself and Kara wants to touch the blocks. This is a tough problem. We need ideas."

4

Shopping with Children—
Mayhem at the Market

Julie

Maria opened up today's session. "It seems like I spend a major part of my life telling Benjamin he can't have something he's begging for. Every time we go to the grocery store. Every time we have to buy a birthday present for another kid. I used to like shopping. Now I wish I could avoid it altogether."

"It's hard for kids," I said. "We're constantly taking them to stores where they see all this *stuff* laid out in front of them. And they see us buying that stuff. They don't understand about working for money and paying bills. They want to do what we're doing—take stuff off shelves and bring it home!

"I get it," sighed Toni, "but does that mean we should just let them do what we're doing, but with the brain of a four-year-old? Let's see, I would end up broke and homeless, deeply in debt to the dentist because of all the candy Jenna bought, and living out of a battery-operated Barbie car."

"We can give them *some* choices, though," Michael said.

"Yeah, but do you really think that'll stop them from begging for junk food?" challenged Maria. "If they think they have the right to make their own decisions, every aisle will be torture."

"We can always put limits on the choices," I said. "We could ask them to pick out two different kinds of pasta. They could put their energy into choosing the different shapes. And how about produce? They could pick out three of the best-looking apples. But it's nice to have some open-ended decisions to make too. I used to tell my kids they could have one free choice out of the whole produce section. That was a very engrossing challenge for them. I remember one time Asher settled on an orange bell pepper. It was more expensive than the green ones, but it was worth it."

"I give my kids a small allowance," said Sarah. "I got tired of agonizing over each little request. On the one hand, it would make shopping easier to give them everything they want, but on the other hand I didn't want them to get in the habit of getting everything they want. This way *they* have to agonize over what to spend their precious dollar on. Much better!"

"You can also give kids a job," said Toni. "That's what works for me. I have my kids help me make the shopping list, and they each have certain things to look for."

Maria grumbled. "I don't always have time to make grocery shopping an exciting activity. Sometimes I just need the food."

"Yeah, well . . ." I had no great remedy for this complaint. "Let's face it, it's never going to be efficient shopping with children. Children don't really make *any* part of life more efficient. But if you can get them involved at least some of the time, they'll be more cooperative most of the time."

"Okay, but how would you do that at a toy store?" Anna

asked. "I'm not going to buy my kids a new toy every time I buy a birthday present for one of their friends."

"Well, that is one of the harder challenges of being a kid," I said. "Being dragged through a toy store and getting to look at all the marvelous toys and choose one for another child, but being scolded if you want one for yourself. Think about it. If you had to devise a kid torture, that might be it."

I reminded the group about the wish list. When a kid pines for something, you can write it down. Instead of saying, "Don't be so spoiled, you just *got* a Lego set last week. You're never satisfied!" Try, "Wow, that looks pretty cool. You really like the spaceships." Take out the pen and add to his list: "Star Wars jumbo Lego set." Keep the list stuck to your refrigerator where he can check on it and keep it updated. Some items will get crossed off and others will be keepers. By the time a birthday rolls around you'll have a useful reference sheet. If there are things on the list that are beyond the scope of birthdays—my sister always wanted a horse—you can still talk about them and plan for the future, which may include barns full of horses.

THOMAS' WISH LIST:
1. JUMBO LEGO SET
2. MARBLES
3. AIRPLANE KIT

It also helps to tell your kids ahead of time, "We're only shopping for Elena's birthday present today. Nothing for us! Be sure to let me know if you see something you want to put on your wish list."

THE STORIES

Toni's Story: To Buy or Not to Buy

My kids love the hands-on science museum in the city, but I dread the exit. To leave the museum, you're forced to walk through the gift shop. It's an effective and cruel design! You've got overstimulated children, expensive toys at a kid's eye level, and worn-out parents. My kids always beg me to buy them some overpriced gadget. I don't usually cave in, but it can get ugly. I don't feel great about myself or my kids by the time we get out of there.

I didn't have much hope that the write-it-down tool would do much good, but I figured it couldn't hurt to give it a try. So on our last visit, right before we walked into the shop, I told them, "We're not going to buy anything in the gift shop today, but if you see something you like, let me know so I can write it on your Wish List." I pulled out a piece of paper and a pen, and they ran around admiring everything and telling me what they wanted on their lists. It was the first time I've gotten out of there without the usual whining and misery.

Anna's Story: The Lovely List

When Anton wants something he wants it *now*. That's typical of kids on the spectrum. This time it was chicken nuggets and ice cream. I didn't have those items in the house and there was no way I was going shopping the day before Thanksgiving and facing the crowds. He was winding up into a tantrum so I decided to try writing down what he wanted. Anton said *he* wanted to do it. I was amazed because he's never volunteered to write before; it's such a struggle for him. He began to construct his list, consulting me frequently about spelling: ice cream, chicken nuggets, French fries, sausages, and samosa! It took him half an hour to write those words but he stuck with it. It's beautiful, and it's still hanging on my fridge.

In the past, when we'd go shopping, Anton would insist on running away from me to the frozen food aisle, taking ice pops out of the freezer, opening them, and eating them . . . and I would run behind him like a monster mother screaming, "No, no, no, NO!"

This time I gave Anton his list and told him to put all of the items in the cart. Well, lo and behold, he did. I was busy trying to find an unbruised avocado and a jar of curry while Anton, to my great surprise, was busy running up and down the aisles gathering all of the things on *his* list. Unbelievable! When I looked into the grocery cart there were a few extra bags of French fries and a few extra cartons of ice cream, but he very agreeably returned the extras. This has become our new shopping routine.

Sarah's Story: The Very Long Ride

We had a five-hour drive to get home from a weekend visiting my parents. When we were almost home, I stopped at a supermarket because I realized I was coming back to an empty refrigerator. The kids were out of control in the store, running up and down the aisles and yelling. They didn't respond to any of my attempts to get them to calm down.

Finally it occurred to me that they needed to move! I don't know why it took me so long to figure it out. I think the road vibration numbed my brain. I took them outside and told them to run up and down the sidewalk in front of the store three times, then hop, jump, skip, then go backward, and then zigzag around the poles. I only went back in after they were semi-exhausted.

<u>REMINDER: Shopping with Children</u>

1. Put the Child in Charge

Have him help make a shopping list and gather groceries to put in the cart.

Give her an allowance: "You can bring your dollar to the grocery store in case you see something you want to buy for yourself."

2. Offer a Choice

"Should we get the spiral pasta or the elbow pasta? You pick!"

3. Acknowledge Feelings with a Wish List

Thomas's Wish List:
Star Wars jumbo Lego set

4. Give Information—Let Children Know What to Expect

"We're going shopping for Elena's birthday present today. Let's bring the wish list in case you see something you'd like for yourself."

5

Lies—Kids and the Creative Interpretation of Reality

Joanna

"Can we talk about lying?" asked Toni. "Last week I caught Jenna with chocolate all over her face. When I asked her if she'd eaten the cake, she completely denied it. She knew she wasn't allowed to touch it. I bought it because we were having guests for dinner. I told her she'd better tell the truth or she'd be in even bigger trouble, but she stuck to her story and got all teary. I made her go up to her room after dinner and miss dessert. I know you don't believe in punishment, but if there's one rule I consider sacred, it's telling the truth. The sooner my kids learn that, the better."

CAKE? WHAT CAKE?

Toni's question got me thinking about why lying pushes our buttons. After all, kids misbehave in all sorts of ways. They kick, they bite, they yell in the library, they crayon the wall, they resist bedtime like their lives depend on it. We understand that these are things kids do. We don't really worry that they'll grow up to be violent, loud insomniacs with a penchant for vandalism. But when kids lie to us, often we do worry. We see it as a moral offense. Somehow we've failed to teach good character to our children.

When a child tells a lie, it may help to remember that it is both common and normal. In fact, the latest research shows that learning to lie is an important milestone in a child's cognitive development.[1]

Children lie for a variety of reasons. Sometimes they lie out of embarrassment. "I'm not the one who pooped in the playhouse!" Sometimes they lie to get their own way. "I didn't have a turn!" Often they lie to avoid the unpleasant consequence of facing an angry parent. "I did *not* throw a ball in the living room and break the lamp." In many instances the lie represents a wish.

Although it's normal for children to "experiment with the truth," we still want them to learn the difference between the truth and a lie and why they should stick to the former most of the time. The challenge for the adult is to resist the temptation to shame the child or to label him a liar.

I turned to Toni. "Look at it this way. If you see your son with a bat in his hand standing next to a freshly broken window, there's no need to ask, 'Did you break that window? Did you use the bat in the house even though I just told you not to?' That road leads to a traffic jam of denial. 'No, I didn't.' 'Yes, you did, now you're lying!' 'Am not!' 'I'm going to have to punish you more if you don't tell the truth!' 'But I didn't! The dog did it!' 'Stop it, that's not even a good lie. Dogs don't break windows!'"

So what *is* helpful?

Instead of accusing and interrogating, **state the obvious**. In the case of the purloined dessert, you can simply say, "I see you ate the cake." If she protests, don't call her a liar. Instead, you can **accept the feeling** behind the protest. "It's not easy to resist eating chocolate cake when it's sitting right in front of you. I bet you *wish* you hadn't eaten it!"

Let her know how you feel: "I'm very upset that the cake was eaten! I was going to serve it for dessert when our friends come for dinner tonight!"

Make a plan for the future: "Next time you're tempted, let me know. I'm sure we can find a way to help you wait." And you might also do some planning of your own. *The next time I buy chocolate cake, I'll put it out of sight until it's time for dessert.* Make it easier for your child to practice honesty— **adjust your expectations and manage the environment**.

If possible, **help her make amends**: "We're going to need something for dessert when our friends come over. Can you get out some cookies and arrange them nicely on a plate?"

"It still seems like something's missing here," said Toni. "I get that you're guiding kids toward being truthful rather than labeling them as liars. But meanwhile, in your scenario, the kid told a lie and there was no consequence. What's to discourage her from lying next time? How is she going to learn that lying is wrong?"

"Toni," I said, "you summed it up beautifully. I don't think I can improve on your words. We're 'guiding kids toward being truthful rather than labeling them as liars.' Lying is a natural stage of development. To punish them for it is counterproductive. It would be like punishing a baby for pooping in her diaper. It's natural, but we want to help them move on to the next stage."

"Let me give you a few snapshots of my son learning about telling an 'inconvenient truth.'"

Dan at Age Two: The Mysterious Stranger

Dan was playing with his little friend Ian while his mother and I chatted, not paying close attention. Suddenly Ian was on the floor wailing. "Danny pushed me!"

I hustled Dan away and asked him what happened. Dan replied somberly, "A bad man pushed Ian down." Clearly he needed some distancing from this awful deed.

Dan at Age Three: Pocket Trouble

Dan came in from playing in the backyard with a torn front pocket dangling from his pants. I asked, "What happened?" indicating the pocket. Dan gave it some thought and then carefully stated, "Let's just say a boy ripped it."

I couldn't help laughing. He was getting a little closer to putting himself on the spot, but he wasn't quite there yet.

Here's his next step.

Dan at Age Four: Lesson from a Mouse

I was reading *The Mouse and the Motorcycle* to the kids. We had just finished the chapter in which Ralph (the mouse) "borrows" the boy's motorcycle and crashes it. He tries to hide his misdeed from the boy, but eventually confesses. The boy is angry, but ultimately forgives the dejected mouse.

Dan looked at me very solemnly and said, "I'm just like Ralph."

"How are you like Ralph?" I asked. "Because you both love motorcycles?"

"No. Because we both wrecked something and we were afraid to tell."

"Oh?"

"I pulled the sheet off the pull-out couch and it ripped."

He looked so upset, I tried for a soothing tone. "Oh. Well that doesn't sound so bad."

"It *is* bad! It's the special sheet!" he moaned.

The "special sheet" was the one that the kids had picked out for the sofa bed, for when Grandma and Grandpa came to visit. It was very cheap and almost frighteningly colorful, with a wild geometric pattern of pink, green, and yellow on a black background. The kids all loved it.

"Well, let's look at it," I said. "Maybe we can fix it."

Dan led me to his dresser and pulled the crumpled sheet out of the bottom drawer. It had a ripped corner where the sheet had caught on the metal frame of the sofa bed. I asked Dan if he wanted to sew it up. It was as if a great weight had fallen from his shoulders. He gave an enthusiastic, "Yes!"

I showed him how to thread a needle and he proceeded to make careful stitches until the sheet was "almost as good as new."

Thanks to Ralph the Mouse for his moral guidance!

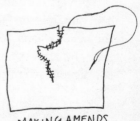

MAKING AMENDS

Dan continued in this path of full disclosure with confidence that he could fix almost anything. The burden of secrecy and lies was not for him. He much preferred the relief of laying it all bare.

I saved one note from him as an older child . . .

Dan at Age Twelve: Broken Wings

We had a few whimsical magnets attached to the refrigerator—birds and bugs with moving wings that we had purchased at an outdoor fair. I went into the kitchen one morning to see a broken bird taped to a piece of paper on the refrigerator with these words:

> Apology from Dan
>
> I'm so sorry I crushed the wings of this poor little guy when I reached up to get the vitamin C out of the cabinet over the fridge. I realize he is special and I mourn his death. I hope to find more of these little "fridge friends" so I can bring them home and acquaint them with our family.
>
> Sorrowfully, Dan

It's very hard to learn to tell an uncomfortable truth. We help our children face up to this challenge when we minimize the accusations, let them know we understand how they feel, and show them how to make amends. It's easier to be courageous when there's hope of redemption!

THE STORIES

Toni's Story: Sugar Between the Sheets

Jenna lies at the drop of a hat. And it's not fanciful lying, it's very deliberate. She does it when she wants to get away with something. Last week I found empty candy wrappers in her bed. She knows she's not allowed to eat in her room. We have trouble with ants. I'm sorry to say I started out with the wrong question, "Did you eat candy in bed?"

"NO!" She denied it vigorously, as usual.

I was tempted to call her a liar, but I remembered just in time and shut my mouth and breathed for a minute. Then I said, "Look, I can see that there are candy wrappers in your bed, and I don't think a little bunny put them there. I know that a candy-loving girl ate some chocolate in bed. I don't like that. I don't want ants in the bed. My rule is, 'Food stays in the kitchen.'"

She came right back at me, saying, "*My* rule is, food *doesn't* stay in the kitchen! There are no ants in my bed!"

You would be proud of me. I accepted her feelings, when I really felt like slapping her and banning candy for a month. "I can see that you really like getting all cozy in bed with your books and stuffed animals and a snack. The problem is, sugar attracts ants. We get them in the kitchen and I certainly don't want them in your bed. It may take the ants a little time, but they can find those sugar crumbs, even the crumbs that are too tiny to see."

She remained defiant. My daughter is tough. "I don't care if an ant gets in my bed."

"Well I do care!" I said. "And I am not going to allow candy in the bedrooms. Maybe we can make a cozy nest in the kitchen for you."

Jenna looked interested. "Can I use the beanbag chair?"

"Hmm," I said. "That's easy to wipe off if anything spills on it."

"Can I put it under the table? That will be cozy."

I nodded—*hey, why not?*—and she dragged her beanbag chair under the kitchen table. She ran to her room and came back with a few stuffed animals and crawled under the table. I handed her some pretzel sticks as a housewarming for her new nest. This is the first time a situation like this ended with anything other than punishment and resentment. I have a feeling she'll be less likely to lie to me next time.

Julie's Story: Paying It Forward

Out of the blue, our Internet service was shut down. When we called the company they explained that we'd violated the terms of service agreement because our son, Asher, had used a curse word in a chat room. But when we asked Asher about it, he said he didn't do it. He seemed so genuine in his denial, we figured someone must've gotten his password and used his account. We had to jump through a lot of hoops to get our Internet service back.

About five months later, Asher confessed that he had lied—he *had* used the bad word. He was crying as he told us. He'd been carrying around this secret for a long time, and it had been weighing on him. My husband wanted to punish him by taking away his computer privileges for a week, but I talked him out of it. Instead, we talked to Asher about that feeling you get when you do something that a part of you knows is wrong. I said, "It can be scary to tell the truth when you feel bad about what you did. But you did tell the truth, even though it wasn't easy."

I wasn't sure this was the best way to handle it. I was worried we may have let him off too easy. Here's what convinced me otherwise. A few days after Halloween, long after the chat room confession, Shiriel sneaked into Asher's room, stole some of his Halloween candy, and stuffed it under her bookshelf. When Asher noticed his candy was missing, he asked Shiriel if she knew what happened to it. Shiriel played innocent, but Asher went in her room and immediately noticed the candy under the bookshelf. And you know what he said? "Shiriel, maybe you *wish* you hadn't taken my candy. But if you don't listen to the part of yourself that knows you should tell the truth, you just end up feeling really, really bad about yourself, so it's not worth lying."

Then he gave Shiriel a hug and collected his candy. He was so kind to his little sister I almost wanted to cry.

<u>REMINDER: Lies</u>

1. **Describe What You See:** Instead of asking or accusing, state the obvious.

   "I see chocolate on your face."

2. **Describe How You Feel**

   "I'm upset that the cake was eaten! I was going to serve it for dessert when our friends come for dinner tonight!"

3. **Acknowledge Feelings**

   "It's not easy to resist cake. I bet you wish you hadn't eaten it."

4. **Try Problem-Solving:** Make a plan for the future

   "Next time you're tempted, let me know. I'm sure we can find a way to help you wait."

5. **Adjust Expectations:** Manage the environment instead of the child

   Think to yourself, *The next time I buy chocolate cake, I'll put it out of sight until it's time for dessert so it's not so tempting.*

6. Help the Child Make Amends

"We're going to need something for dessert when our friends come over. Can you get out some cookies and arrange them nicely on a plate?"

6

Parents Have Feelings, Too

Julie

"What about *my* feelings?" Sarah's voice had an uncharacteristic edge. "When do those start to count? I'm feeling kind of low in the sympathy department lately."

"What, Sarah, you?" asked Toni. "You're endlessly patient and sympathetic. All those little preschoolers wish they could go home with you. I know Jenna and Ella do. They always tell me, 'Sarah never yells at us.'"

"Well, it's easier with other people's kids. I don't know, maybe I'm using up my patience at work. Last week I wouldn't let Sophia go to a sleepover on a school night and she started up with, 'You're mean. You never let me do anything fun. You're always so strict.' *You never, you always* . . . I hate those words.

"I know what I'm *supposed to* say. 'Oh gosh, Sophia, it's so disappointing. You were looking forward to a sleepover. It seems like you never get to do fun stuff.'

"I just couldn't do it. I gave her a lecture about how privileged she was and reminded her of the *long* list of fun things I've been doing for her. She stomped out and everyone was grumpy for the rest of the night. I knew the lecture wasn't going to fly, but I couldn't help myself. I'd have had to bite my tongue so hard it would bleed. Part of me thinks all this accepting feelings is making her self-centered and spoiled. I wouldn't have dared talk to my parents that way."

"Well, what about *your* feelings?" said Anna. "What if you told her your feelings instead of lecturing? I'll bet she could take it. After all, she's seven, not three. What if you said, 'Sophia! When I hear *you never* and *you always* it makes me mad! It doesn't make me feel like being helpful to you at all!'"

"That would have worked better than the lecture," Sarah admitted. "I'd probably give advice like that to my students' parents. It's harder to think straight when your own kid is pushing your buttons."

Anna was encouraged. "Maybe you could say, 'If you're disappointed, you can tell me, "Mom, I'm disappointed! I *really, really* wanted to go to the sleepover!"'"

"Sure, if she put it that way, I'd be more in the mood to figure out a solution," Sarah said. "Maybe she could go for a while and I could pick her up at bedtime, so she could sleep at home and not be exhausted for school. Her friend's school has a different spring break, so her mother doesn't care if they stay up all night giggling and act like sleep-deprived zombies the next day."

"I like your two-part approach, Anna," I said. "First you let her know how you feel, and then you give her the words she can use to express herself without irritating you. It can be tricky, because you really *do* have to bite your tongue to some extent. Kids can't take *too* much disapproval, even when you're gentle about it. The younger they are, the less they can handle.

"But they do need to know when the words they use result in a resentful parent. That's valuable information! If we take abuse with a sympathetic smile, we're teaching them the wrong lesson."

"So what you're saying is there's a complex equation where we balance tongue biting and feeling sharing," complained Toni. "And we're supposed to be able to do this calculation when we're really irritated."

"Yeah, basically," I admitted. "Except that you can always go ahead and say the unhelpful thing, and then come back later when you're not so upset and give it another try. That's what I often end up doing. When I'm feeling attacked I don't usually come up with the perfectly crafted response. But even while I'm yelling, there's a little voice in the back of my head saying, 'I'm going to fix this later.' Kids can be pretty forgiving as long as you don't say anything truly damaging.

"And don't forget, it takes time to calm down when you're all riled up. You can't just flip a switch. One thing you can do for yourself is to *give yourself that time*. Tell your kid, 'I'm too upset to talk right now! We'll talk about this later.' Or roar it. 'Ahhhhhhhh!' Then take a break if you can. Go for a walk if there's another adult around, or to your room, or the bathroom, or wherever you can find refuge. Do whatever it is you do that makes you feel better. Run around the block, do push-ups, put on music, curl up with an understanding dog. You'll come back refreshed and ready to use some tools."

You can have a truly miserable interaction with a kid and still come back with a triumphant finish. Here's the bad start: You accuse your kid of acting like a spoiled brat. She counter-attacks with, "You're mean! I hate you!" You both stomp off in a huff.

Here's the good finish: You go to your kid's room later that evening when your anger has subsided and say, "Hey, Sophia, I was really annoyed with you for saying I never let you do anything fun. And you were really annoyed with me for saying no to your sleepover. I'm not annoyed anymore and I'm ready to talk about different possibilities for a sleepover. Come to the kitchen when you're ready and we'll figure out a plan that's good for both of us." Then you can sit down and do some problem-solving together.

What has the child learned? That when an adult gets angry it's not the end of the world. It's a temporary condition. Problems that cannot be solved in the heat of the moment can be solved later, when calmer, cooler moods prevail.

THE STORIES

Maria's Story: Bagel Bite

I was at the supermarket with Benjamin. He was sitting in the cart eating a bagel while we shopped. When we got to the cereal aisle he wanted to get down and check out the options. He put his last bit of bagel in my hand and went off on his mission. I popped it in my mouth. Big mistake. When Benjamin got back and realized his terrible loss he started screaming, "You ate my bagel!" at the top of his lungs and whacking my leg. Other shoppers were giving me horrified looks. It was awful. I yelled back at him, "I don't want to be screamed at and hit! Tell me, 'Mom, I didn't want you to eat my bagel. Next time please *ask* before you eat!'"

He repeated those exact words back to me, in a pretty

loud mad voice, but at least it sounded civilized and there was no more whacking. So I said back to him, still in a loud voice, "Thank you for telling me! Next time I will *not* eat a bite of your bagel without asking, even if you put it in my hand. I thought you didn't want it anymore, but now I know you did."

Then we looked at each other. What now? I asked him if he wanted to go choose another roll or bagel to eat. We went back to the bread aisle and he picked out an onion roll. I warned him, "If you don't want me to take a bite, don't put it in my hand! Just put it in the cart."

"You can have some, Mom." He tore off a piece for me. It was just a small piece, but hey, it felt like a giant leap for mankind.

Sarah's Story: Let Them Eat Cake (Without Milk)

We had ten five-year-olds in our backyard tie-dying T-shirts at Jake's birthday party. After we hung up the shirts to dry we had cake and ice cream. As I was serving, one of the kids started banging his fist on the table and chanting, "I want milk! I want milk!" The other kids joined in. I was almost mad enough to dump the milk on their heads. Why am I running myself ragged to entertain these rude little brats? Luckily I couldn't let loose because some of their parents were there, too. I said in a loud voice, "I don't like to be yelled at while I'm serving people! If you want milk, you can say, 'May I please have some milk when you're finished cutting the cake?'"

Nine of the kids stopped banging. They politely repeated my words. I said, "Sure! And thank you for asking so nicely." They said, "You're welcome." It was magical.

The tenth kid, the one who had started it in the first place, kept on banging and chanting. I didn't serve him any milk. I guess he wasn't so thirsty. A ninety percent success rate is good enough for me!

I think it was important that I stood by my words. If I had told them how I felt but still served them while they were banging, they wouldn't have taken me seriously.

Toni's Story: Flour Power

I let the twins talk me into baking cookies. What a mess. Can I tell you how easy it is to spill flour? And how instantly it turns into glue as soon as it hits a wet spot on the counter . . . and the floor . . . and the stove. . . . Well, anyway, the girls were being pretty obnoxious. They kept shoving each other and saying, "Me first!" "No, *me* first!" for every task—adding ingredients, stirring, spooning out the batter. Finally I kind of roared at them, "Hey, when I let you make cookies I don't want to hear *me first* and see shoving. I want to hear, 'Thank you, Mom,' and, 'Let's take turns going first.'"

Well, they parroted my words right back to me and started taking turns without a fuss. I can't believe it was so easy! All this time I've wasted telling them not to be rude when I should have just told them what I expect.

Michael's Story: Wasted Day

Jamie and I decided to have a special father and son day. We had his favorite breakfast (pancakes), I took him shopping for craft supplies and seeds for his garden, and then to one of those fast-food restaurants with a play area for kids. That was a sacrifice! I hate those places. To top it off I took him to the movies. When we went into the movie it was still daylight, but when we came out it was dark. Jamie started this angry crying that he does. He kept saying, "You wasted the whole day!"

I was so mad. But I still used my tools. I said, "Hey, when I take you shopping and out to eat and then to the movies, it makes me mad to hear, 'You wasted the day.' I want to hear, 'Thank you, Dad!'"

Do you want to guess how well that went over? Like a lead balloon. He cried all the way home, and I fumed all the way.

After I handed him, still sobbing, to my wife for bedtime I had some time to calm down. I went into his room and sat on his bed. "Jamie, I had a really nice day with you. I think you didn't want this day to end."

He said, "Yeah," and snuggled up to me.

At the movie theater, he was too upset to hear about my feelings. But I was upset, too! I really like the idea that I can come back later with a better response when I feel more sympathetic. We turned a bad ending into a good one.

<u>REMINDER: Parents Have Feelings, Too!</u>

1. Express Your Feelings . . . *Strongly*

Instead of, "You're being rude!"
Try, "I don't like being told I'm mean. It makes me mad."

2. Tell Them What They *Can* Do, Instead of What They *Can't*

"You can tell me, 'Mommy, I'm disappointed! I wanted to go!'"

3. Don't Forget the Basics—Give Yourself and Your Child Time to Recover

"I'll talk to you about it after dinner. Right now I'm too upset."

7

Tattling—Snitches and Whistle-Blowers

Joanna

"I've about had it with my twins," Toni exploded. "They are in some kind of a phase—at least I pray that it's a phase—where every little tiff gets dumped on me.

"'Mommeee, Jenna ate a cookie before lunch. What are you going to do to her?'

"'Ella didn't take her shoes off inside. She broke the rule!'

"'Jenna touched the stove dial and you told us not to.'

"'Ella poked me and you said no poking!'

"I've tried punishing the rule-breaker, but that only makes them more vigilant to point out every misdeed. It's like they're vying to see who can get more dirt on the other. I've tried telling them that they shouldn't tattle and I'm not interested, but that doesn't seem to help either. They just get louder and accuse me of being unfair. They'll actually hurt each other if I leave them to their own devices."

"That's been a dilemma for me, too," said Sarah. "On the one hand, I don't want my kids to tattle. I want them to feel like they're on the same side. On the other hand, I feel a bit hypocritical if I'm making rules and then not enforcing them. And I certainly don't want to discourage them from telling on their siblings if there's something dangerous going on.

"It happens at the preschool, too. A few girls have appointed themselves the teacher's little helpers. They come running to me every playtime with tales of who pushed who on the playground, or who ate half the green crayon. Sometimes it's useful, but mostly it's annoying."

"Why not just make a rule that you can only tell on your sibling or classmate if someone is going to get hurt?" offered Michael.

"I don't know if I'd be comfortable with that," said Maria. "When I was a kid, we didn't tell our parents anything. I want my kids to trust that they can tell me about whatever bothers them, even if it's trivial. Besides, can we really depend on kids to have good judgment about what's dangerous enough to tell? If they think I'll disapprove of them for tattling, they might not tell me something important."

"Well, I know that I do *not* want to know every little thing," declared Toni. "Sisters, especially twins, should be loyal to each other. I always tell them that."

"I'm wondering, what's behind the impulse to tattle?" I asked the group.

"Power!" shot back Michael. "You can get your sibling in trouble. I know that's why I used to tattle on my older brother when I was a kid. He was so much stronger and smarter than me, and he'd lord it over me. It was the only way I could get even. I had the power to get him punished."

"I think for the kids at school it may be that they're just trying to please," ventured Sarah. "I mean, we're always emphasizing how important rules are, and then we get annoyed when they try to help enforce them. It's got to be a little confusing."

I had to admit that my sympathies were with Maria. When my son was in a mixed first- and second-grade program, the teachers told the students that they should only interrupt a teacher during independent activity time if someone was bleeding. There was a recurring problem with older children bullying the younger ones. Dan complained to me about it, but he never asked a teacher for help because he took their words literally. "No one was bleeding," he explained to me very seriously, "so I'm not allowed to tell."

SHOULD I TELL?

I'm uncomfortable with the idea of teaching children that it's not okay to tell us things that bother them. Sometimes it takes bravery to tell on somebody. Don't we all wish someone had tattled about the corner-cutting that led to the oil spill that killed a dozen people and dumped almost five million barrels of oil into the Gulf of Mexico? Or to keep it closer to home (unless you live on the Gulf Coast, in which case you're already close to home), what if some adult is inappropriate with your child and then warns her not to tell? Do we want our kids even to consider that we might disapprove of them in that situation?

"But I don't want to hear about every little poke!" protested Toni. "Is that the only way to protect the ocean? I don't know if I can take it."

"I feel your pain." I laughed. "Here's what I can offer you. Michael made a key point. One of the main impulses that drives the urge to tattle is the satisfaction of getting the other kid in trouble. I'd like to remove punishment from the equation and see what happens. What if we responded by accepting feelings, addressing the problem, and offering support if needed—without punishing anyone? We can help our kids resolve conflicts when they need our help, or encourage them to work it out between themselves when it seems like they are capable."

Toni looked skeptical.

"Here's what I mean," I said. "When a kid says, 'She poked me!' instead of focusing on the perpetrator, we can focus on the victim. We can respond, 'Oh, you didn't like that! Show me where you got poked. Does it need a kiss or a rub?'"

"I don't think that would satisfy my girls," said Toni. "They would want to know what you're going to do to the poker."

"I'd say, 'Hey, Ella, that poke hurt Jenna's arm. She doesn't want to be poked, even a little bit!' and then I'd wait and see what happens. Maybe Ella will say she's sorry and they'll go back to playing without any more pokes. Maybe there will be more poking and they'll decide to play separately for a while. I don't know what the outcome will be, but I do know that I won't be inspiring them to greater animosity by punishing one or dismissing the other.

"If one child tells on another for breaking a rule, you can restate the rule and express confidence that they'll respect the rule in the future. Or help the little rule breaker fix her mistake."

"Oh, I can see why you'd be worried about Jenna touching the stove controls. If that gets turned on by accident it can start a fire or let out dangerous gas. Do the two of you want to make some signs for a reminder? They could say DANGER or DO NOT TOUCH. Or maybe you could draw a picture of fire. What would work best?"

"Oh dear, muddy shoes on the carpet. Let's go bang them outside to get the dirt off. And here's a broom to sweep up the dirt inside. . . . Ah, you got it all!"

If we ignore the tattler she'll be confused and frustrated. Why is this rule suddenly not a rule? When we accept her feelings and address the problem, she's going to calm down. By not punishing the perpetrator, we remove the incentive to tattle purely for the pleasure of power.

THE STORIES

Toni's Story: Flattened Fingers

I hate to admit it, but when you're right, you're right. I followed your script. Jenna came in and said that Ella stepped on her fingers. I didn't say a thing to Ella. I just took Jenna's hand and said, "Oh, poor little squashed fingers!" and I kissed each one. They both stood and looked at me for a few seconds, like *what now?* I didn't say anything. They went back to playing together. In the past when I've told them, "I don't want to hear it," or scolded the one who did it, they always stayed angry with each other for a long time.

Sarah's Story: Swing Wars

I had one of my little "teacher's helpers" come running to me this week to tell me that Jared was hogging the swing. In the past I might have told her to mind her own business because she was playing hopscotch and nobody was complaining about the swing. I mean, poor Jared gets in enough trouble during class time. And this little girl knows it! But instead I asked her if she thought the kids needed help taking turns. She said, "Yes," so I went over and did a little problem-solving. All I said was, "It looks like a lot of children want to swing. What should we do?"

Jared said, "I want ten more swings!"

The other kids started counting out loud while Jared pumped like a maniac. "One . . . two . . . three . . ." and on ten he jumped off at the highest arc. I heard them counting for each kid after that. They were very pleased with themselves. They created a new game, but they also have a method for taking turns now. And this little Goody Two-Shoes girl made it happen by asking for help.

Joanna's Story: Prison Play

One afternoon I broke my own rule against punishment. But it was all in good fun, and it changed the mood from hostile to happy.

Six-year-old Dan was pestering four-year-old Sam one afternoon. It had started as play, but then Sam got fed up and Dan didn't want to stop. They had made a game of pulling blankets off each other's beds, laughing uproariously. At one point Sam realized he was losing all of the tug-of-war battles to his stronger, older brother and started to complain vociferously. Dan kept on slyly returning to snatch yet another item of bedding, until Sam was in tears. Sam came running into the kitchen to tell on his brother.

"Dan," I roared. "Sam is not enjoying this game!"

"But he was laughing!"

"Yes, he *was* laughing, but he's not laughing anymore. It's time to stop."

Sam gave his brother a venomous look and cried, "You should punish him!"

I was taken aback. Where had my darling innocent developed such a thirst for vengeance in this nonpunishing family? Where did he even get the idea? But I decided to go with it. "Should we put him in jail?"

Sam was delighted. "Yes!"

Dan looked intrigued. "Off to jail with you," I cried.

I pointed to the space under the desk. Dan grinned happily and crawled in. I put a milk crate in front of him for bars. I turned to Sam. "Should he stay in jail for one year or ten years?"

Do I even have to tell you the answer? "*Ten!*"

I waited a minute and then said, "I think ten years have passed. Should we let poor Dan out of jail?"

Sam agreed that Dan had paid for his crimes with our pretend punishment. Dan was just thrilled to participate in the drama. Play had saved the day.

<u>REMINDER</u>: Tattling

1. Acknowledge Feelings

   "Jenna didn't like being poked. That hurt!"

2. Help the Child Make Amends (without scolding)

   "Let's get a broom and sweep up the mess."

3. Try Problem-Solving

   "How will we remember not to touch the stove dials? We need ideas."

8

Cleanup—The Dirtiest Word

Julie

Anna came in looking frazzled. "So how do you get them to clean up after themselves? I'm starting to get resentful. Last night I spent half an hour haranguing Anton to clean up his blocks before bedtime, and then I finally did it for him. About ten minutes later he dumped the whole bag out on the floor again. I was ready to throttle him!"

"I can relate," said Michael. "As soon as you walk in the door of my house, you're wading through toys. I think I have a few Lego spears permanently embedded in my foot. Sometimes I just try to shove stuff aside. But if I really want the place to look civilized, it's much easier to put the kids in front of the television and do the cleanup myself."

"But that's just not right!" Toni protested. "I mean, yeah, I do that, too, put them in front of the TV when I need them out of my hair, but I'm not proud of it. How are they going to learn not to be lazy bums if they're not expected to pitch in?"

Little kids have different priorities from their parents. Let's face it, they don't care about disorder the way we do. Preschoolers aren't going to sigh in pleasure at the sight of a cleanly swept floor and a well-made bed. They'd just as soon pick through the dog hair for stray Cheerios and leap on a rumpled bed to worm under the covers and wrestle with the pillows.

The first thing to do is **adjust your expectations**. We can't expect kids to naturally want to clean up. Like it or not, it's our job to make the task appealing. The payoff comes later, when they're a little bit older and can understand the joys of orderly living.

"So why should we even bother?" asked Michael. "Why not just wait?"

"How long?" moaned Anna.

Let's face it, sometimes it's a hopeless battle. If you're trying to leave a playdate with a recalcitrant toddler and you insist that he clean up his mess before getting in the car, you're setting yourself up for failure. You're asking him to do something unpleasant (cleaning) so that he can do something even more unpleasant (leaving). Chances are he's tired and cranky to boot. Go easy on yourself and don't take a moral stance. Just sweep up the toys, say your good-byes, and tuck that toddler in the carseat with a stuffed monkey for consolation.

On the other hand, there are certainly going to be times when we don't need to wait until the kids are older. Helping out with cleanup is a good opportunity for them to develop new skills and contribute to the family. Even a child too young to care about order and organization can feel a sense of purpose and pride that comes from helping out. The challenge is to manage it with a sense of fun and warm feelings—or at least without blame and frustration.

If everyone is in a reasonably good frame of mind, you have a lot of options.

You can **offer a choice** and at the same time make the task feel less overwhelming: "Do you want to start by picking up all the books, or by tossing all the dirty clothes in the basket?" "Do you want to pick up red Legos or blue?" "Cars or crayons and markers?"

You can **be playful,** and make the block bag talk: "I'm hungry, feed me blocks. Mmmm, I like these crunchy rectangles! Give me more! Yuck, I hate the triangles. They stick in my throat. Ooh, these green ones are extra tasty."

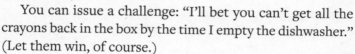

You can **make it a game:** "How many blocks can we get into the bag in two minutes? Johnny, you set the timer. Ready . . . set . . . GO!"

You can issue a challenge: "I'll bet you can't get all the crayons back in the box by the time I empty the dishwasher." (Let them win, of course.)

You can get them counting: "Each citizen must deposit five pieces of trash in the garbage pail before leaving this room."

You can **write a note:** *Jackets away before play.* Even children who can't read enjoy getting a note. You can include a picture or read it to them.

Describe what you see with appreciation. "Wow, look at this big cleanup you did. You guys are quite a team. This floor was covered with dirty laundry and train tracks, and now it's a pleasure to walk on!"

It's important to **point out progress** instead of criticizing an incomplete job. I've derailed many a cleanup effort by saying, "This is nowhere near finished. It still looks like a disaster area!" You'll get better results with a statement like, "I can see you've tossed all the dirty laundry in the basket. Now all that's left to make it totally spectacular is to pick up the books and blocks."

When children have left you an unpleasant surprise, resist

the urge to threaten and accuse: "Who made this big mess? No TV tonight if this doesn't get cleaned up." Instead, **stick with describing what you see and giving information**. "I see crumbs all over the floor. That will attract ants. This room needs a good sweeping. Here's the broom!"

After the cleanup is finished you can say, "I see a clean floor. The ants will have to go outside and find their snacks in the yard."

If you feel the urge to lecture, try to **limit yourself to a word**. You'll get more traction with "Crumbs!" than you will if you launch into a lengthy diatribe: "I just spent an hour cleaning this kitchen and you kids messed it up again in two minutes. When are you going to learn to clean up after yourselves?"

Again, keep in mind that your child *does not care about cleanup* any more than you care about putting together a Lego dump truck (unless of course you *do*, in which case, provide your own alternative example). The main point is to keep the interaction (and the relationship) pleasant. Later your child will understand more about why cleaning up after yourself is the right thing to do, but for a preschooler it's not helpful to think of it as a moral issue. What's important at this stage is developing a positive feeling about being helpful and working together.

And remember, there will be many times when you have to *cut your losses*. You can apply some leverage when your child is feeling energetic, "We can go to the park as soon as these blocks are put away." But when a toddler is tired or hungry, avoid a losing battle. Do it yourself for now. There will be plenty of other opportunities for your child to participate. Don't worry, this is not the last mess!!

THE STORIES

Toni's Story: The Missing Bookbag

Every day, Thomas comes home from school and sheds his bookbag and coat onto the floor as soon as he gets in the door. Every day I lecture him. It goes something like this: "Thomas, you need to hang up your coat and bookbag. That's why we have hooks. When you leave them on the floor they get stepped on and dirty. And covered in dog hair, which you know you don't like. Come on, just do it."

"I'm tired. I'll do it later."

"No, do it NOW."

"I can't. I'm starving!"

This time I wrote a note on a piece of paper and hung it from a string in the doorway so that he would walk right into it when he came inside. It said, *Hang up bag and coat and come in kitchen for special snacks.* Thomas ran to hang up his coat and bag. I gave him a small lump of peanut butter with carrot sticks poking out of it so it looked like a porcupine. He was pleased and added raisins for eyes.

The next morning there was panic. It was time for the bus and Thomas couldn't find his bookbag anywhere. I asked him, "Did you look on the floor of your room? Did you look on the couch in the living room? How about the bench in the kitchen?" It was nowhere to be found. Finally I had a lightbulb moment. It was on the hook! We made it to the bus with thirty seconds to spare.

Sarah's Story: Don't Cry Over Spilled Chocolate Milk

My three kids decided to have a sleepover in the playroom. They dragged in a bunch of comforters and pillows. They came to the kitchen for hot chocolate, and Sophia snuck hers into the playroom. Of course they all started horsing around, and they knocked over the mug and splashed hot chocolate all over the *white* comforters. It got into the foam tiles on the floor, too. It was a huge mess. I felt like canceling the sleepover and taking away their TV time.

But I stuck to description and making amends. I told them, "I see chocolate all over the place. It needs to be cleaned up." I showed them how to scrub the comforters and take apart the foam tiles to get the floor clean.

They actually cleaned it all up. I didn't have to do anything, and it was amazing. Nobody complained, even though by the time they were finished there was no time to watch TV. I'm pretty sure they won't be bringing drinks into the playroom again anytime soon.

Michael's Story: Sibling Sorrow

My kids love making a game out of cleanup. Jamie's four, so he's used to helping out a little, but for Kara this is a totally new behavior, mainly involving her new passion—throwing. She's been cleaning up all week, throwing her dirty clothes in the laundry basket and throwing her crayons in a box. It's not long distance or anything. She aims from about two inches away and slams 'em in. The other day I told her she was an amazing "cleaner upper" and Jamie burst into tears. He's used to being my helper, while Kara is just the little pest. I'm going to have to be careful to praise them as a cleanup team from now on, instead of singling out one kid.

Anna's Story: Monopoly Extortion

This week I tried something new with cleanup. I told Anton I wanted to hire him for a job. I got a wad of Monopoly money out and told him I'd pay him ten dollars to pick up the yellow blocks. He was intrigued. He tossed all the yellow blocks in the bin and I gave him the Monopoly bill. Then I said, "How about another ten dollars for the blue blocks?"

He said, "No . . . twenty!"

"Uhhhh, that's a lot. Oh, okay."

He picked up the blue blocks. Then he said, "I'll pick up the red blocks for a hundred dollars!"

I acted outraged. "What? That's too much! I can't afford that! Oh well, I guess I have no choice. You drive a hard bargain."

He cleaned up the red blocks and I handed over the hundred-dollar bill with a big sigh. Anton was giggling the whole time, and I got to sit on the couch . . . the whole time!

Joanna's Story: A Glimpse Into the Future

My three boys generated an astonishing amount of mess when they were small, a lot of it in the kitchen. As teenagers, all three enjoy cooking—for themselves and others. They are enthusiastic, inventive chefs who wipe down counters, put away perishables, and wash the pots and pans when they're done! As for cleaning their rooms . . . well, that happens when a girlfriend is coming over.

REMINDER: Cleanup

1. Be Playful

(Shoes talking.) "Pretty please, put me in the closet with my friends."

"How many minutes will it take to toss all the Legos into the bucket? You can set the timer. Ready . . . set . . . GO!"

2. Offer a Choice

"Do you want to be in charge of putting away the books or the cars?"

3. Write a Note

"Please hang me on the hook. Love, Your Coat."

4. Describe What You See

"I see orange peels on the floor."

5. Give Information

"Peels belong in the compost."

6. Say It with a Word

"Coat!" "Peels!" "Shoes!"

7. Describe Progress

"You got that whole pile of dirty laundry in the basket! All that's left to put away are the cars and books."

8. Describe What You See with Appreciation

"Wow, look at this big cleanup you did. The floor was covered with dirty laundry and train tracks, and now it's a pleasure to walk on!"

9

Doctor's Orders—Medicine, Shots, Blood Draws, and Other Horrors

Joanna

"Ever since Thomas had his five-year checkup, I've been dreading the day the twins have theirs," Toni sighed. "It was horrible. Two injections. After the first one Thomas was screaming and pulling away from the nurse. She kept yelling at me, 'Hold him still!' I wrapped my arms around him while she gave him the second shot. He was so angry afterward he wouldn't talk to me for hours. I felt like I betrayed him. But what was I supposed to do?"

Maria looked distressed. "I don't see how we can say anything that's going to help in a situation like this. The shots hurt. There's no way around that."

It's true. We can't protect our kids from the pain of injections, not to mention all the other uncomfortable experiences that life has to offer. They're going to feel what they're going to feel. But this isn't to say our trusty tools won't help. And we need a lot of tools for this one. After all, we're talking about needles here.

When I had to take all three kids for shots, I made sure

to start with **acknowledging feelings**. "Just the thought of getting a needle in the arm can be pretty scary."

Then I went on to **giving in fantasy**, "I wish they could put the medicine inside a lollipop. You'd eat one a day for a week, and then you'd never get sick."

Then I nimbly threw in some **information**. "The shots put tiny little fighters in your blood, called antibodies. They fight against tiny germs so you don't get sick." I added a comforting tip that I had heard from a nurse on the last visit, "The good news is that shots are quick. They're over in the time it takes to clap twice. Like this (*Clap! Clap!*)."

Then on to **choices**. "Do you want me to clap for you, or do you want your brother to do it? I know if you did it for yourself the nurse probably wouldn't be too happy. It would be hard to give a shot to a clapping kid."

Dan liked the idea of clapping. But I wasn't done. No tool left behind! **Problem-solving** was next. "Would it help to have something to look forward to after the shot is over?" We decided to stop at the corner store to find a post-shot treat. Dan chose a pack of peanut M&Ms. He decided that he would get one out ahead of time and hold it in his hand, ready to pop into his mouth as soon as the shot was over.

By this time we were actually getting kind of excited about the whole event. It had become a challenge. Once we arrived at the office it turned out Dan needed *two* shots, not just one as I had envisioned. The nurse gave him the choice of having one at a time, or having them both at the same time, one in each arm. Dan chose to get it over with all at once. Two nurses readied their needles. Dan squeezed a green peanut M&M in his fist. I raised my hands to clap. *Stab!* It was over. Dan popped his peanut M&M into his mouth and grinned. Not so bad.

Toni groaned. "I can't imagine both of my girls going for that. Maybe Jenna, but not Ella. She wouldn't give in so easily."

We always have the fallback of **taking action without insult.** If you need to restrain her, you can do it with understanding and sympathy. "I'm going to hold you on my lap while the doctor gives you the injection. I know you don't like this. I wish there were a less painful way to protect you from diseases."

"What about medicine?" asked Anna. "Shots are only once a year at most. But that disgusting pink goop they put the antibiotics in, you might be facing that at any time. And by facing it, I mean you might have it spit into your face! That just happened to me. The doctor said Anton had strep and couldn't go back to school until he was on antibiotics for twenty-four hours. I tried to give him a choice about how to take it, but he ran into his room and slammed the door. I went and sat him down and forced the syringe into his mouth, and he spit it back out at me. What was I supposed to do when offering a choice didn't work? He definitely wasn't in the mood to be playful."

"This is a good example of why offering a choice may fail," I said. "When a child has strong emotions about something, he's probably not ready for a choice. He needs to have his feelings acknowledged first. What could we say to this poor kid who is being ordered to swallow this nauseating liquid?"

The group responded:

"Yuck, this medicine is really disgusting to you."

"It's your least favorite taste in the world."

"Why can't they make it taste like pizza?"

"The doctors should have to drink this before they make kids drink it! They would spit it out, too!"

"Okaaay," said Anna, "but you do realize I still have to get him to drink it, right? This might make him feel better, but I don't see how it helps."

"You're right, this is just a first step," I said. "But it's essential. It helps put him in the mood to work with you. Now you can say something like, 'Ugh, this is a really difficult situation. How can we get this disgusting medicine inside your body in the least disgusting way possible? We need ideas!'"

Anna looked dubious. "I'll try it," she said. "And if it doesn't work I'm calling you so you can come over to my house and get him to take it."

"Oh, I may have to screen my calls this week. But I'm eager to hear how it works out for you."

Sarah was waving her hand in the air. "I have a suggestion. Jake can't tolerate that liquid antibiotic. When he had Lyme disease, he understood why he had to take the medicine, but sometimes he would actually throw up within a few seconds of swallowing. I ended up asking the doctor to change the prescription to pills. They said they didn't usually do that for young children, but they were willing to give it a try. I put a pill in a spoonful of chocolate ice cream, with another few spoonfuls to chase it down, and he was able to swallow it that way."

"Don't forget **playfulness**," said Michael. "My friend's son had a bad stomach bug and he had to drink a cup of this electrolyte stuff every day for a week. At first he liked it, but after the first few days he got very tired of it and refused to take it. The parents were using the sports coach approach, 'Come on, buddy, let's do this! Take one for the team!' That wasn't working too well.

"I wanted to help out, you know, with my superb skills from being in this group. I picked up the bottle of medicine and said, 'Oh, look, a new bottle of medicine for Tommy and it's *magic* medicine. Tommy, will you take a tiny little sip, so I can see what it does?'

"He took a tiny sip, and I pretended I could see the drop of medicine inside his body: 'Look at that! I can see it going down your throat. Take another sip!'

"He took a bigger sip this time, and I pointed and said, 'Wow, I can see that sip going down your throat, and through your chest, and into your stomach. Do it again!' He thought this was funny, and he took a big gulp.

"'Now it's down to your knees! I wonder if you can drink enough to get it all the way down to your toes.'

"His parents wanted to hire me to come over every night and do my routine."

THE STORIES

Anna's Story: Super Mario Meds

I tried problem-solving and it didn't work out exactly as I expected. I did what you said and talked to Anton about how much he hated the medicine. I let him tell me all of the disgusting things it tasted like, and I even wrote them down. Vomit, rotten cheese, dirty socks. Then I said I didn't know what to do because he really needed the medicine or he'd get sicker. I needed his help with ideas. I suggested ice cream, but his favorite idea was one he came up with. He wanted me to pour the medicine down his throat while he played Super

Mario Kart on his Wii. We did it and it worked perfectly. He just tipped back his head and kept on playing. I got him to school an hour late, but it was worth it.

The problem was that the next morning he refused the medicine again. I was so furious with him. After all that work! I just lost it. I was screaming at him, "We had a deal! You can't go back on it!" and he was sobbing hysterically. He finally choked it down, and we were late again. So much for problem-solving.

When I had some time to think about it, I figured out why it fell apart. Anton really loved sitting with me, having me write down his feelings, and doing the problem-solving. He must have thought we were going to do that every morning! I talked to him when he came home from school and explained that we needed a solution that would last the whole week because I couldn't be late every day. He agreed (whew!) and the rest of the week went smoothly.

Joanna's Story: Medical Mauling

When Dan was an infant, visits to the doctor went pretty smoothly. But around age two he became extremely averse to being touched by strangers. Or anyone he didn't know that well. He stiffened if our next-door neighbor, a lovely woman, tried to hug him. He pulled away when his uncle tried to give him a handshake. So of course he became hysterical when the doctor poked at his stomach and tried to listen to his heart and look in his ears. Forget about needles. Just a stethoscope was sending him around the bend. The doctor acted like he had never dealt with such an unreasonable child. He ordered me, "Hold him tight, keep his arms down!" while Dan screamed and twisted to get away. It was pretty awful.

That was our last visit to *that* doctor. I asked around for a more child-friendly pediatrician, and we eventually got an appointment with Dr. B. It was a revelation. Dr. B had my son in stitches for the entire examination. He made funny noises whenever he had to touch him. He had a little toy fish stuck onto the light he used for the ear exam, and he had some silly patter about what the fish saw inside Dan's head. Dan was so full of giggles it was like I had taken him to see a show instead of to a doctor. I am such a fan of this man for going all the way through medical school while still taking the time to cultivate his inner clown. Playfulness wins the day!

Julie's Story: Vaccination Torture

We were at Asher's pediatrician's office on a Friday for his five-year-old checkup. He was due to get two vaccinations. He was terrified, but he cooperated when the nurse came to give him the first one. After that, though, he lost it. He was crying and screaming, refusing to let the nurse give him the second shot. He was so mad, she had to leave the room.

I said, "That really hurt!"

He screamed, "Yeah!"

"You don't like shots!"

"Yeah!"

"You don't want another one!"

He said, "No more shots! I won't let her!" He was distraught and sobbing.

I held him for a while, and then I said, "I wish you didn't have to get any shots ever again. This is so hard. The problem is, the nurse has to give you one more. What should we do?"

Asher said, "No more shots today. Let's come back tomorrow."

"Tomorrow the office is closed. We'd have to wait until Monday."

"Okay, Monday."

I was worried he would stew in dread all weekend and then refuse again on Monday. Should I agree to this plan? He promised me he'd cooperate on Monday, but he's only five; I can't exactly hold him to a contractual agreement.

The nurse thought it was a bad idea. Better to get it over with, even if we have to hold him down. But Asher insisted that he would let her give him the shot on Monday. I made an appointment for Monday and took him home.

We didn't talk about the shot over the weekend. On Monday, I told him we were going to the pediatrician's office. He knew why, but he didn't object. When the nurse came into the exam room and asked him if he was ready, he said, "Yes." He stuck out his arm and he took the shot without any drama. She and I were both impressed.

I admit I was nervous when I agreed to his plan on Friday. But seeing how much better he coped on Monday, well, I hope you won't mind my saying that he definitely was better off calling the shots on this one!

Julie's Story: The Little Flick

After the experience with Asher and his five-year-old shots, I figured I knew how to handle kids and needles. Live and learn.

Rashi had to get a blood draw—his first of what has turned out to be many. He never made a big fuss when he got his vaccinations, so I figured this would be easy as pie. But no! He was terrified.

I employed all my tried-and-true strategies, starting with acknowledging his feelings: "You don't want this blood draw.

You don't feel ready. . . . This is scary. . . . You're afraid it will hurt."

I gave him information: "They take just a small amount of blood. You'll have plenty left."

I offered to problem-solve: "The doctor needs a little bit of your blood. What should we do? Which arm would be better?" He had no ideas. He didn't want to come back later, he just wanted to skip it altogether.

The nurse was very patient, but after an hour of pleading (her) and crying (Rashi) she gave up. She sent in another nurse—a tall man with big, strong arms. He didn't beat around the bush. "Rashi, this isn't going to hurt a lot. It's going to feel like a little flick of my finger on your arm." And he flicked Rashi's arm before Rashi could object.

Rashi looked surprised, and he stopped squirming. The man whipped out his alcohol wipe as he told Rashi, "That's all you're going to feel, just a little flick," and then he quickly jabbed the needle into Rashi's arm. Rashi watched wordlessly and moments later it was all over. He was so relieved!

So what have I learned? That kids are different. That some tools will work for one kid and not another. That sometimes it helps to put the child in the driver's seat and let him control the action. That other times it's best to take action—take the child *out* of the driver's seat and not burden him with that responsibility. That parenting is an art, not a science. And that I'd better not get too smug.

REMINDER: Doctor's Orders

1. Acknowledge Feelings

Instead of, "Come on, it's not *that* bad. Just let her do it, and it'll be over."
Try, "It can be scary to think about someone sticking a needle in your arm."

Instead of, "Don't cry. You're a big boy."
Try, "That hurt! You didn't like that!"

2. Offer in Fantasy What You Can't Give in Reality

"I wish they could put the medicine inside a lollipop. You'd eat one a day for a week and then you'd never get sick."

3. Offer a Choice

"Do you want the shot in your left arm or your right?"
"Do you want to sit next to me, or on my lap?"

4. Give Information

"The shots are quick. They're over in the time it takes to clap twice. Like this (*Clap! Clap!*)."

"The shots put tiny little fighters in your blood, called antibodies. They fight against tiny germs so you don't get sick."

5. Try Problem-Solving

Parent: What would make it easier to get through these injections? Would it help to have something to look forward to when you're done?
Kid: Can we get peanut M&M's? I could eat a green one as soon as the shot is over.
Parent: Let's do that!

6. Be Playful

"I can see the medicine going down your throat into your stomach. And now it's heading down your leg to your toes!"

7. Take Action Without Insult

"I'm going to hold you on my lap while the doctor gives you the injection. I know you don't like this."

10

Shy Kids—Fear of Friendly Folks

Julie

"Is there a prize for worst weekend?" asked Michael. "We spent Sunday with my cousins, and Jamie was clinging to me the whole time. I couldn't even leave the room without him, never mind the house. I've always assumed he'd grow out of this shy phase, but Jan says he's shy by nature. Every time my aunt tried to talk to him he hid behind my legs. She kept asking him what was wrong. I'd like to know how to get him to be more confident, at least around my own family."

"My sister was shy when she was little," Anna said. "My parents were always trying to get her to talk to people. It didn't work, though. You can't force a kid to talk."

"I was very shy as a little girl, too," said Maria. "My mother protected me. She'd tell people I was too shy to talk. On the one hand, that was a relief—people would usually leave me alone. On the other hand, I was pretty lonely a lot of the time. I didn't really want to feel so shy. To this day I have a hard time talking with people I don't know. Even speaking up here makes me a little nervous."

Michael looked exasperated. "So a kid who's labeled 'shy' ends up living up to expectations, but forcing him to say 'hello' doesn't work either. Is there some third way?"

"Has anybody tried something that worked with a shy

kid?" I asked. "Something that respected their feelings and at the same time freed them to get past those feelings?"

Sarah raised her hand. "My nephew is very shy. I only get to see him a couple of times a year because he lives far away, so every time he comes he has to warm up to me again. Last year I had the idea to put a sock on my hand, and I had the sock puppet talk to him. He really liked that. The next time he came, I pulled that puppet out again. This time I was prepared; I'm no artist, but I made eyes and a nose ahead of time with a Magic Marker. He definitely remembered it, and he warmed up to me much faster."

"What about preparing kids ahead of time for the visit," asked Maria. "Do you think that would help? On the drive over you could acknowledge feelings. 'It can be hard to walk into a new house filled with relatives. Lots of people want to say hello to you. That can feel scary. I remember when I was your age, I was especially afraid of my aunt Sonia. She always gave me horrible, lipsticky kisses.'"

"I like it!" I said. "And then you can plan a strategy for those first awkward moments. Direct greetings for my kids were hard at that age. They always did better when they had a job to do. Like carrying the chips and dip inside and finding a place to put them on the counter. Or being in charge of hanging the coats. You can ask them to choose a job."

Michael looked unconvinced. "You can't plan for everything. What about when Aunt Vivacious asks you, 'What's wrong with Jamie? Why won't he play?' You don't want us to deny our kid's feelings and tell him to go play, but you don't want us to cast him in the role of the shy kid, either."

"It's tempting to announce that your child is shy. It comes from the best of impulses," I said. "We want to protect our kids. But they also need to know we have faith in them if they're going to be brave enough to make the leap into sociability. I have the magic words for you. Are you ready to receive them?"

Vigorous nods all around.

"Jamie will join you *when he's ready*."

The group looked underwhelmed. "What's so special about that?"

It may not sound like much, but those three little words do a lot of work. They tell a child that you respect his feelings and his need to go slowly. They also let him know that he's in charge. He's not being pushed. But the most important part is what you're not saying. You're not keeping him stuck in a role. *Dad said I'm shy. I must be shy. I'd better stay behind his legs where it's safe.*

Instead you're issuing an invitation. You're protecting him while he's feeling uncomfortable. But the door is left wide open. He can ease into the activities without fanfare, as soon as he's ready. The readiness often comes quickly as soon as the pressure is removed.

If the relatives continue to push, you can run interference. When Cousin Lively tries to pull Jamie over to the train tracks you can say, "Don't worry, Jamie will join you *when he's ready*. He likes trains." And to Jamie you can offer a choice, "Do you want to hang out here with the parents and have a snack first, or do you want to sit on the couch in the playroom and watch the kids and the trains?"

In short, it's normal for little kids to feel shy around people they don't know well. We may need to adjust our expectations. Instead of pressuring kids to interact with unfamiliar people right away, we can help them by giving them something to do, or giving them permission to observe until they're ready to join in. And if you're the stranger, it can help to talk to the child in a playful way, using a stuffed animal or puppet.

HE'LL JOIN YOU WHEN HE'S READY.

THE STORIES

Sarah's Story: Put Her in a Pumpkin Shell

Yesenia joined the class in mid-October, a month and a half after all the other kids started. Her family had just moved from Puerto Rico. She was terribly shy and wouldn't speak to me or to the other students. I wasn't actually sure if she understood enough English to know what was going on.

I tried to be as unthreatening as possible—never confronting her with a direct question, always offering her little tasks to do like handing out crayons, and sprinkling fish food into our class fish tank. She cooperated with my requests, but continued to keep her eyes on the floor and maintained her silence.

On Halloween I brought in a small pumpkin for each child. I gave them spoons to scoop out the innards and collect the seeds. We planned to toast some for eating and sprout the rest.

Some of the kids didn't want to touch the gooey mess with

their fingers, but Yesenia dug right in with her bare hands. She scooped and scooped, and as she scooped she began to talk. She talked about her brothers and sisters, and the cat she had in Puerto Rico. She talked about the plane ride and her new apartment. She talked about her mother and father and a TV show she saw about ghosts. It was a river of speech flowing steadily over a broken dam. And all the while she was running her fingers through the slimy wet strings of pumpkin with great satisfaction.

From that day on, Yesenia was a fully participating member of the class. You often had to bend your head down to hear her because her voice was soft, but she answered questions and offered observations and very definite opinions of her own. Something in that pumpkin pulp freed her. If I get a student like that again, I'll be sure to bring out the clay and finger paints, in case it's the wrong time of year for pumpkins.

I'm glad I was patient and resisted the impulse to pressure her to talk. She needed time, and lots of different ways to be involved without talking.

Anna's Story: The Little Flip

No matter how much I try to explain to Anton that he has to look up and say hello when people greet him, he just can't bear to do it. But I hate how rude it looks when he refuses to acknowledge people. And it's not just that. I want him to think about how other people feel, too.

We finally figured out a solution. I suggested that he look up for a second and give a little wave of his hand instead of talking. He just flips his fingers up a tiny bit from his side. It makes him seem sweet and shy instead of sullen and unfriendly.

Joanna's Story: Olden Days

When Dan was three years old I was continually surprised by his shyness. He was such a bold little guy. He'd climb any woodpile in his roller skates, rocket down any hillside on his bike. The word *afraid* was quite literally not in his vocabulary (as my mom discovered when Dan was up in a tree and she nervously asked, "Aren't you afraid to go so high?" and he answered, "What do you mean, afraid?").

But when it came to people, Dan moved forward with excessive caution. He had known my next-door neighbor, Donna, almost all his life. She was a relaxed, experienced mom of three, wonderful with children. We had spent many happy hours with our kids playing together at my house or her house. But Dan still refused to stay at Donna's house without me.

One day Dan begged to go play with the girls next door, but I was swamped with chores to do at home. I told him my problem. We decided that I would go with him for a very short playdate. If he felt comfortable, I could leave him there on his own to play longer. If not, he would come home with me. I figured that if I put him in charge of the decision, he would feel braver.

It worked! He wasn't ready to go there all by himself and commit to a solo run, but once he started playing he decided he *would* stay on his own. The next day Dan asked me if he could ride over to Donna's house on his bike. (We shared the same driveway, so while it would be an adventure, it was a pretty safe one.) I said, "Sure!"

Dan was excited with his new boldness. But he also felt nostalgic. He looked at me thoughtfully and mused, "Hey, Mom, remember the olden days, when I was scared to go by myself?"

Joanna's Story: Too Shy for School?

Dan, at five, was at the brink of a new stage of life—kindergarten! We had gone to the screening and the orientation. We had gotten the class assignment in the mail. School was starting in just a week when Dan announced that he would not be going on the bus unless his whole family came with him. Mom, Dad, Sammy, and baby Zach, and oh yes, the cat and the dogs as well. Not for him the solo trek into the great unknown!

I was worried. What if my child was the only five-year-old in town who failed to launch? What was I going to do?

Well, I started with acknowledging feelings. "It can be scary to go to a new place without your family."

Dan agreed. He was not going to stay with that teacher because he was not "used to her." I knew that teachers had the week to set up, so I suggested we visit the classroom in order to "get used to" Mrs. G. I called the school and Mrs. G welcomed us warmly. Dan and I made three trips to the classroom that week, talking to Mrs. G and playing with some of the toys each time.

The night before the first day of school, we made a project of cutting out little pictures of each member of the family (including the cat and dogs, of course) and putting them into a little zippered pouch, shaped like a friendly lion, purchased especially for the occasion. Dan *would* bring his family with him, and he'd be able to unzip his lion and look at their faces if he needed to.

The next morning my little boy bravely stepped into the big yellow school bus, and I breathed a sigh of relief!

<u>REMINDER: Shy Kids</u>

1. Acknowledge Feelings

"It can be hard to walk into a new house filled with relatives. Lots of people want to say hello to you. That can feel scary."

2. Adjust Expectations: Give a child something to do instead of pressuring him to be social.

"You can carry in the chips and put them in the bowl for people to eat."

3. Offer a Choice

"Do you want to sit on the couch and watch the kids set up the trains? Or do you want to have a snack with the grown-ups first?"

4. Be Playful

(Sock puppet talking.) "Hi there! Would you like a corn chip?"

5. Put the Child in Charge

"Jamie will join you when he's ready."

11

Little Runaways—Kids Who Take Off in the Parking Lot and Other Public Places

Joanna

"I need help!" Michael proclaimed. "If I lose one of these kids my wife is going to have my head on a plate. I was doing pretty well keeping track of Jamie, but now Kara's getting speedy, too. Sometimes they dart off in two different directions in the parking lot. I need a clone of myself to keep track of them both. Or maybe a drone to track them from overhead."

"Oh," laughed Toni. "Let's not miss an opportunity to practice giving in fantasy. Michael, I wish you had a clone to run after Kara while you watch Jamie. Or two clones so you could have a coffee while the clones do all the work."

Michael grinned. "I'll be first in line when they come out. But meanwhile, what do I do? What do you do, Toni? You've got twins. That would be my nightmare."

"Umm, thanks a lot, I guess." Toni made a face. "It isn't easy. I've considered that leash contraption, but I'm afraid of all the dirty looks I'd get for hooking my kids up like dogs. Really, I'm all ears for this discussion."

"Me, too," Maria said. "Benjamin doesn't bolt in parking lots, but sometimes he does go conveniently deaf when I call him. It's not malicious. It's just that he walks away to explore and gets distracted."

I thought about my oldest son, Dan. When he was three

years old he was a runner. He hated more than anything in the world to have his hand held. In parking lots, in crowded public places, on the street—anywhere danger lurked, he felt the urge to be unfettered. He would try to wrench away from me, and the tighter I held, the more desperately he would struggle.

I told the group about the time I made the mistake of taking him to see the holiday displays at a crowded mall on a Sunday afternoon. Dan and I got into a ferocious struggle. He wanted to roam unencumbered by my sweaty grip, and I was petrified of losing him in the crowd. I finally had to pick him up and carry him to the car as he kicked and yelled at the top of his lungs. He was screaming so loudly, I was afraid I'd be accused of kidnapping. I threw him in the back seat and locked the doors while he raged. When he was worn out enough to be handled, I belted him in and drove home. A complete holiday outing failure.

All this is to say that sometimes, in my experience, you just have to cut your losses and slink home with your tail between your legs. Not everything can be solved in the moment. When safety is at stake, you gotta do what you gotta do. But there's always a next time, and that's where the outlook gets brighter. We have a sack full of tools for this problem. The first is to manage the environment instead of the child.

I swore off trips to the mall for a long time after "the incident." I took the simple way out. Stay away from malls— environment managed, problem solved. I also restricted myself to playgrounds that were fully fenced. But I couldn't stay away from the grocery store. We still had to eat! This is where problem-solving came in handy. Here's how our conversation went on the topic of supermarket parking lots.

Me (acknowledging feelings): You don't like having your hand held in the parking lot.

Dan: Yeah!

Me: You like to be free to run.

Dan: Yeah! You squeeze my hand! And you don't talk to me in a friendly way.

Me (describing the problem): Oh, so you don't like having your hand squeezed. That can hurt. I worry about the cars hurting you. The drivers can't see children. It's dangerous. That's why I yelled. (I show him how his head is below the window of the car, so the driver can't see him.)

Me (asking for ideas): What should we do so you're safe but your hand isn't squeezed? Do you want to hold my shirt? Or my belt? Do you want to hold the cart and help push?

Dan: I can help push. But you have to talk to me in a friendly way.

Me: Okay, that'll be great. The cart is heavy. I can use that help. And I'll make sure to remind you with a friendly voice.

Notice that I resisted saying that I didn't use a "friendly" voice because he was being horrible and trying to get himself killed, and that if he behaved I wouldn't be forced to yell at him. That would've undermined the positive mood and endangered the peace talks.

Other parents have come up with different ideas. One mom offered her son the dog leash. He would hook it to her belt loop so that he could pretend she was his puppy and "walk her" to the car, making sure his "puppy" didn't run into traf-

fic. Another suggested that the family walk like elephants, holding each other's "tails" (shirttails that is). One parent of four young children had them pretend to be a choo-choo train and chug from the store to the car, taking turns being the engine and the caboose. That's an age-old favorite of schoolteachers who have to move their group down the hallway without disturbing the other classes.

The main idea is to come up with some kind of fun plan for how to get from point A to point B safely, instead of engaging in a battle of wills. Of course, if your kid breaks and runs you'll have to grab him and hold fast, in spite of the kicking and crying. And that will happen. But then you'll have a fresh chance to talk about it and make a new plan for the next time. It's back to the drawing board. "You didn't like being grabbed, and I didn't like being scared I would lose you. What should we do next time?"

Your little runner will learn quickly, with a combination of your firm refusal to compromise on safety and your good-natured offer to engage him in the solution.

As for the child who wanders off to explore and doesn't respond when called, that's a slightly different problem. First of all, let's get into this kid's head. He's completely engrossed in a fascinating exploration. He's following his drive to discover new territories. There's nothing naughty or defiant here, just human nature at work—the desire to learn. So how can we modify this positive activity to keep him safe?

Little Runaways

One approach is to have a problem-solving discussion ahead of time:

"You like to look around when we go to the park. Sometimes you like to go far away. The problem is, I get worried when you don't answer me. I get scared that I'll lose you. What can we do? We need ideas."

If your child is in on the planning, it's likely that he'll be more cooperative. He may enjoy a playful recall, rather than the plain old "fun's over" announcement. Perhaps he can come up with a secret signal—a whistle or a special word. *Kangaroo* means wave at Mom and keep on hopping around, *tiger* means come running back. A whistle might be earsplitting enough to get his attention if words or gestures fail.

If he still ignores you, you'll have to take action. "We'll try again another time. I have to take you home now because I don't want to lose you." Or, "I have to put you in the cart for now because I don't want to lose you in the store." If he is a truly determined explorer, he may need to have this experience to see that you mean what you say.

THE STORIES

Michael's Story: Handicapping the Race

I solved the parking lot problem. I gave Kara the choice of riding on my shoulders like a monkey, or sitting in the stroller. As for Jamie, I put him in charge of the whole expedition. I pretend I don't know which way to go and he's in charge of leading me to the store. Then I pretend I can't remember where I parked the car. He knows I'm faking it, but he doesn't care. He has a ball telling me which way to go, and it keeps him close.

Toni's Story: Lions and Tigers and Bears

My kids are fascinated with animals, so I tell them, "It's a jungle out there in the parking lot. We have to watch out for lions." We sneak to the car, huddling close together. I call out things like, "Possible lion behind the red car!" The kids love it. So far they've wanted to play it every time. They're making up more predators— dinosaurs, spiders, pythons,  crocodiles, and tigers. It's strangely more effective to give them imaginary threats than real ones.

Maria's Story: Happy Feet

We made up a game called Frozen Feet. We practiced at home. I tell Benjamin to run around as fast as he can, and when I yell, "Frozen feet!" he has to stop right away. It's his new favorite game. Now whenever we're out and I need him to stop, I say, "Frozen feet!" and he stops immediately—most of the time. If he doesn't stop, I put him in the stroller.

I also talk a lot about *the plan* before we go somewhere. For example, I took both kids to the apple festival by myself last week. I talked with Benjamin a few times before we left. I reminded him that we were going to a crowded place, and he would have to hold the stroller handle so I'd know where he was. I reassured him that he'd still be able to see the animals and play on the hay. After all that planning, he knew just what to do when we got there.

Overall, I'm trying to put myself in his shoes more. I'm getting better at combining his need to have fun with my need to keep him safe. Now I can leave my house without worrying, too much, that he's going to run and never stop. This is making a huge difference in my life as a mother!

<u>REMINDER: Little Runaways</u>

1. **Adjust Expectations: Manage the Environment Instead of the Child**

   Avoid outings that seem like fun but will be more stress than pleasure with a small child. There will be plenty of opportunities to see holiday decorations at the mall or enjoy an outdoor concert by the river when your child is a little bit older.

2. **Acknowledge Your Child's Feelings**

   "You don't like it when your hand is squeezed. You want to be free to look around."

3. **Describe Your Own Feelings**

   "I worry that drivers backing out of parking spaces can't see children."

4. **Offer a Choice**

   "You can ride in the cart or you can help push."

5. **Be Playful**

   "We need to stick close together. It's a jungle out there. I think I just saw the tail of a lion behind that car!"

6. Try Problem-Solving

"Let's think of a secret signal we can use that means we have to get to each other as fast as possible."

7. Take Action Without Insult

Grab your kid and go home. "We can't stay here. I have to watch the baby and I'm too worried about losing sight of you by the river."

12

Hitting, Pinching, Poking, Punching, Pushing—I Barely Touched Him!

Julie

> *Imagine a person who pushes, punches, grabs, kicks, and bites to get what he wants. You are either picturing a violent criminal or a perfectly normal two-year-old.*

> —Richard E. Tremblay,
>   developmental psychologist

Maria came in looking flustered. "I'm very upset!" she announced. "I have to tell you what happened this morning. Benjamin was sitting on the couch with a water bottle. Isabel crawled over, pulled herself up, and reached for the water bottle. Benjamin said, 'No!' but Isabel kept on grabbing. So he casually stuck his foot into her chest and shoved her off. She went flying and hit her head on the floor. I yelled at Benjamin to go to his room, and he ran! I spent the next fifteen minutes calming Isabel down. If there's ever a time to punish, isn't this it?"

"I'm with you," said Toni. "You have to draw the line somewhere. It's one thing when a child makes a mistake, but he deliberately hurt her. There has to be a consequence. He can't be allowed to get away with that kind of behavior."

"The way I see it, there already was a consequence," I said. "His sister cried, his mother yelled, he was sent to his room, probably feeling miserable, and now he has a mother who is very upset with him. Not a pleasant outcome. The question is, 'Where do we go from here? What kind of response will get us to our ultimate goal?'"

"Which is?" Toni arched an eyebrow.

"Which is an older brother who feels more tolerant of his little sister, not more resentful. And who has options other than violence to protect himself in the future."

"I don't see how leniency is going to make him behave better," countered Toni. "You're just showing him that he can get away with being a bully. My older brothers used to push me around all the time, and my parents never said *boo* to them about it. There were seven of us, and it was left to us to work out our differences. Good for the older, stronger kids, not so nice for the little ones."

"I'm not suggesting that parents look the other way when one child hurts another," I said. "We need to let our kids know that violence is unacceptable. The challenge is to do it in a way that will allow for loving feelings rather than increasing resentment. That's what will ultimately keep our kids safe from future violence, whether as perpetrators or victims."

The first priority, of course, is to protect. Take action to prevent injury! This may involve grabbing a child. The words that accompany this action are important. We need alternatives to "bad boy" or "how could you hurt the baby like that?" or "don't be mean!" We need words that state your values without attacking the child.

"Sisters are not for pushing!"

The next priority is to attend to the victim.

"Let me kiss that bump to make it feel better. Should we put ice on it?"

But it's not enough to simply draw a line in the sand. You want to head trouble off at the pass so that you don't have to trudge through all that sand in the first place. What can a parent do to make a kid feel more kindly toward a sibling and less likely to attack in the future?

We can help him make amends:

"Isabel needs something to make her feel better. Can you bring her the teddy bear? . . . Thank you, Benjamin!"

And finally we can acknowledge feelings and problem-solve for next time:

"It's not easy to live with a one-year-old. What can a person do when a baby starts to crawl on them or grab their stuff?"

We tell our children not to hit, but sometimes we forget to acknowledge what a challenge that is for a youngster. It can be a great relief to a child to know that he is engaged in one of the great aspirations of civilization—figuring out alternatives to violence!

THE STORIES

Anna's Story: Roar Out a Warning

Anton used to adore his little brother, but now that Luke's two he's getting into Anton's toys and Anton gets furious. He's starting to use his fists. We had a problem-solving session and talked about what he could do when he's mad enough to hit. He liked the idea of roaring like a lion. The next time Luke toddled over to where he was playing, he put his face right next to Luke's and ROARED. Luke burst into tears. Yikes!

I sat down with Anton again. "We have to go back to the drawing board. That was too scary for Luke." We came up with the idea of roaring into a pillow instead of into Luke's face. Anton liked that idea, and he's been doing it when he gets mad. When I hear the roar I run to help him and say, "Thank you for calling me with your awesome roar!" He's not quite ready for tea with the queen but it's a big step. It's a lot better than hitting!

Maria's Story: A Flower for Isabel

After our workshop I decided to try problem-solving with Benjamin. When I told him I wanted to talk about hitting and kicking he got into his bed and wrapped his stuffed monkey around his head. Clearly he was worried!

I sat on his bed and said, "I want to talk about what happened with Isabel the other day. I know it's not easy to live with a one-year-old. They don't understand about not touching your things."

Benjamin didn't answer or look at me.

I kept talking. "I think you didn't want to hurt Isabel, you just wanted to keep her away. You didn't mean for her to fall on her head. That was not the plan! It must have been scary when she started crying and I started yelling. You didn't want that to happen."

Benjamin moved the monkey and looked right at me. "I didn't want that to happen."

"I know. You're a brother who's usually pretty gentle with your sister. We need to figure out what to do when a little kid grabs your stuff."

Benjamin thought, and I waited. "I could put my monkey on her head."

"That might make her laugh and forget about grabbing your stuff. I'm going to write that down."

I got a piece of paper and wrote it and showed it to Benjamin. He gave a little laugh and got up to leave. I was disappointed! I thought we were going to make a long list of ideas, but I guess a three-year-old doesn't always have much attention span. I think he was just relieved not to feel guilty anymore, and he was ready to move on. As he walked away I called after him, "Remember, you can also call me to help, if you feel like hitting or pushing."

A few minutes later he came back with a paper flower he'd made in preschool to give to Isabel to "make her feel better."

The next day, Benjamin was on the couch again and Isabel started crawling onto him. He called to me in a worried voice: "Mommy, move Isabel!" A step in the right direction! Another time he was drawing with markers and she grabbed one. He traded her for a dried-up marker, which she was just as happy with. He's still too rough with her sometimes, but I can see his attitude changing. He's thinking more about how to act around his sister, instead of going straight to violence.

Toni's Story: Cat Fight

I got a call from Thomas's teacher. She said he hit another child during recess and was sent to the principal's office. He wants to be friends with three boys who play together at recess, and I have a feeling they've been trying to exclude him and Thomas isn't taking the hint.

I was steaming when I first got off the phone. I have a zero-tolerance policy for hitting. In my mind I immediately took away his TV time, dessert, his friend's birthday party . . . he was going to learn! Lucky for Thomas, I ran into Anna before school got out, and she talked me down.

When I got to school, the teacher came over and told me about the incident. Thomas stomped out of the building. I walked out and said, "Wow! You seem really angry right now!" He glared at me. "I *am* really angry . . . at *you*, for talking to the teacher!"

"Oh, I see. Your teacher told me that you had a rough time at recess." He buried his head in my shoulder and started to cry. I said, "You're so sad. Something happened."

Then it all poured out. The boys said Thomas couldn't play with them because he didn't own a cat. When he told them he had a stuffed-animal cat, they said that didn't count. And then another boy pushed him, and that's when Thomas hit him.

I kept repeating "Oh" and "Uh-huh" and he eventually calmed down. Then he decided on his own to write an apology note for hitting!

It was very challenging for me not to come down hard on Thomas for acting out like that. But if I'd followed my usual instincts, I don't think he would've told me about the cat game, or decided to apologize.

REMINDER: Hitting, Pinching, Poking, Punching, Pushing

1. Take Action Without Insult

- *Make everybody safe*

  "We need to separate!"

- *Attend to injuries*

  "Let me kiss that bump. Do you want a piece of ice for your head?"

2. Express Your Feelings Strongly

"I don't like seeing Isabel hurt!"

"That makes me very upset!"

3. Help the Child Make Amends

"Isabel needs something to make her feel better. Can you find her a toy? Or do you think she'd like a strawberry?"

4. Acknowledge Feelings

"It can be very frustrating to have a little sister grabbing your things."

"It's not easy to resist hitting or pushing when you're mad!"

5. Give Information

"No pushing allowed in this house. Daddy is not allowed to push me. You are not allowed to push your sister, and she is not allowed to push *you*. And I am not allowed to push *either* of you—unless you need a push on a swing!"

6. Try Problem-Solving

"Sometimes your little sister can drive you crazy! What can a person do when his sister is bothering him? We need ideas."

13

Sleep—The Holy Grail

Joanna

> *The first God that puts her to sleep, I'll convert!*
>
> —Maz Jobrani, comedian,
>   talking about his four-year-old
>   daughter

"Joanna, you keep promising that you're going to talk about sleep, and you keep putting it off!" Toni was adamant. "Food, oxygen, shelter . . . *sleep*. It's one of the basic needs, remember?"

I had tried as hard as I could to avoid this topic. I wanted to maintain my status as a "child whisperer" who could solve any problem my workshop participants threw at me. I feared I would come out of this session with my reputation at least slightly tattered. There are no easy answers here. The holy grail of sleep for a parent of young children often requires a grueling quest.

I still remember the paralyzing fear I felt as a child, waking up from a nightmare, alone in the dark. I would call out for help, literally too scared to move. My mom or dad would shuffle in and take me to their bed. Ah, the sweet relief from terror, to be safe between their warm bodies. I also have memories of being in the kitchen in the middle of the night, with my mom making me warm milk and honey for my sore throat. It was scary not to be able to swallow without pain, but Mommy was there for me with her magic potion to make it better.

I wanted to be that parent. To be heroically available to my kids in the deep, lonely darkness of night. To save them from bad dreams and selflessly attend to their sore throats.

Once I became a parent myself, I realized that it was . . . well . . . complicated. I adjusted my vision of the perfect parent. In my new picture, this flesh-and-blood parent needs sleep of her own to function as that wonderful giving mom-of-the-year. It turns out that I had expected nighttime wakening to be the exception rather than the rule, but somehow my kids didn't get that memo. I discovered that playing  the hero on a nightly basis wears thin fast. It doesn't feel so much like heroism as drudgery. Or sleep deprivation torture. Having my sleep disturbed by needy children several times a night, or taking hours to go through the bedtime routine, was destroying my ability to function as a reasonably pleasant person during the day. I would find myself waking up after a night of many sleep interruptions and gazing upon my children's sweet, rosy faces with a resentful eye and a heavy sigh.

Unfortunately, there is no one-size-fits-all solution for this problem. There are entire books on the topic—shelves and shelves of them—that give advice ranging from letting children cry it out, to maintaining a family bed until the child decides on his own to sleep separately. Some parents worry that their children will feel abandoned if they insist on independent sleeping arrangements. Others have strong feelings about having time to themselves at night. It's not easy to strike a balance between a parent's biological imperative to sleep and a child's desire for unconditional twenty-four–hour service. We wouldn't presume to dictate where you should draw the line. What we can do is share with you what has helped other parents and let you figure out what's right for you.

I asked the group for a brainstorm. "Get out your pens and pencils! We're going to write down what you did with your own children, what you remember your parents doing with you as a child, what your friends or siblings do with their kids. My goal for this session is to create a smorgasbord of bedtime alternatives so that we can all pick and choose the recipes that will work for our own children."

"What, no handout for this topic?" Toni had a dangerous look in her eye. "I come here for answers, not questions!"

I gulped. "We're creating the handout now. Future generations will thank us!"

I passed out paper. The group bent their heads to the task. Fifteen minutes later people were looking up and ready to share. Here are our results.

THE STORIES

Sarah's Story: Story of the Day

One idea that helps Jake relax at bedtime is to have him get under the covers and then tell him *The Story of Jake's Day*. It may not have the same plot twists and illustrations as a regular bedtime storybook, but somehow it helps him let go of the day and relax into sleep. It goes something like this:

"You had a very long and busy day. At seven o'clock in the morning you woke up. You came into the kitchen and asked for blueberry yogurt. But there was no yogurt! You were a little bit sad. But then you decided to have a bowl of cornflakes and milk instead. A little bit of milk spilled but Jango (that's our dog) was very happy about that and licked it up off the floor . . ." and so on. Jake loves hearing the details of his day so much that he forgets to protest about getting into bed.

Julie's Story: Back in a Minute

When Shiriel was two and a half, she'd climb into bed without protest. But the minute I left, she'd pop back up. She needed water, or she heard a funny sound, or she forgot to tell me something. She wanted me to stay until she fell asleep. I tried. I would impatiently wait for her eyelids to droop. Then I'd do the commando crawl to get out of her room, freezing at the slightest rustle. It was not my concept of an ideal evening activity.

I read a book that advises you to insist that your child stay in bed, but you come back to check on them at increasing intervals—five minutes, then ten minutes, then twenty, and so on. If they cry in between you're supposed to ignore it. Well, I put my own twist on that one night, almost by accident. Shiriel wasn't ready for me to leave, but I had to go to the bathroom. So I told her I'd be gone for just a few minutes and then I'd come back to check on her. When I got back I was surprised to see that she was calmly waiting in bed for me. I gave her a little back rub, then told her I needed to finish loading the dishwasher and start it up so that we'd have clean dishes in the morning. But I would be sure to come back to check on her as soon as I was finished, which I did. Then I told her I had to put on my own pajamas and brush my teeth, but I'd come back to check on her after that. By the time I came back she was asleep!

That became our new nightly routine. I'd promise to check on her several times and she'd stay in bed, knowing I'd be back. Better yet, she'd fall asleep on her own. A great improvement over waiting for her to drop off and then trying to sneak out, while she resisted sleep as hard as she could so that I wouldn't leave. I think it helped a lot that she could picture what I was doing while I was gone. One time I even said that I had to leave to read a newspaper article on the couch. A previously unthinkable indulgence!

Joanna's Story: Bad Bunny

When Dan was two he would get very amped up at bedtime. He clearly did *not* want the day to end. Sometimes it was enough to read him a story in bed and sing a few lullabies, but at other times that didn't do the trick. He would deliberately thrash around in the bed, working himself out of a sleepy mood. I was pretty cranky by that time of night, and would tell him he had to lie still and relax and let himself get sleepy. *That* never worked. It took me a while to realize that playfulness would help here. I was not in the mood! But I was desperate enough to try.

Dan had a stuffed animal, a little bunny we called Peter Rabbit. I tucked Peter Rabbit in beside Danny, snuggled under his chin, then I made Peter wiggle and jump up and push off the covers. I sternly scolded the bunny. "Now Peter, it's time for bed. You can jump around in the morning." Peter wiggled out of the covers again. "Peter! Danny needs his sleep! Stop that right now! You *must* stop disturbing my son or he will be too tired to play tomorrow! Danny, can you help me tuck Peter in nice and snug and tight?" and so on.

Dan was highly amused by this drama, and would help me tuck Peter in and calm him down with a tight hug. He got to be the parent figure in charge of a troublesome little hyperactive creature. I think it helped him relieve some of his own stress over making that difficult transition into slumber.

Anna's Story: Lumpy Bed

If I can get Anton into his bed in the first place, that's half the battle. Once he's under the covers he relaxes pretty easily with stories and songs. We have a game for this. I say, "I have to make the bed. I hope it's not lumpy tonight." Then Anton gets in and I start smoothing down the covers complaining about all the lumps. I say, "I don't know how this bed got so lumpy. Every time I try to make it nice and smooth it bumps up again. I'm going to have to write an email to the mattress company and complain. I'm going to try one more time. I've got to smooth out this long skinny lump here!" I press him down all over his body and he snuggles in. He likes the joke, but he also likes the pressure. I've read that physical pressure helps kids who have sensory issues to relax, and it seems to work for us.

Toni's Story: A Bath by Any Other Name

This isn't exactly about sleep, but it's about the bedtime routine. I insist the twins take a bath every evening. If you saw how they eat dinner, sticking their hands in their hair between bites, you'd understand. There's a reason I don't serve fish very often! Anyway, they're usually very resistant to bath time because they know it's the first step to the end of all fun. And I get very cranky because I know it's *only* the first step, and I have such a long road ahead before I can rest.

Last week my mother was visiting and she offered to bathe the kids. Jenna immediately said, "No bath!" I reminded her that she had wiped mango juice in her hair at snack time, but she wasn't impressed. Then Grandma said, "Oh no, of course no bath. There will be no bath under any circumstances. Tonight we are having a *slath*."

I got into the spirit and said, "Do you hear that voice? I think it's your bathtub." I used my high-pitched, sad bathtub voice. "I'm so lonely up here. No one has been in me all day. I miss Jenna and Ella."

The girls scampered upstairs and took off their clothes. When the bath was full, they started to climb in but their grandma said, "Oh no, you don't get into a *slath* the same way as a bath. You have to get in backward." So the girls turned around and backed in. I used my bathtub voice again. "I feel so much better. It's nice to have you to play with. Thank you."

Jenna said, "You're welcome!"

They washed from head to toe, got out, put their jammies on, and climbed into bed. What a lovely night.

Michael's Story: Picnic Breakfast

In our family we have a problem at the other end of the night. Jamie likes to get up early. Really early! Jan and I have begged him not to come in and wake us up before he sees the "7" on the digital clock. (We cover up the minutes to make it easier for him.) Is that asking so much? But he comes in anyway and climbs around on top of us while we try to ignore him. Jamie always says he's hungry. I figured he's just trying for attention. Who can be hungry at 5 o'clock in the morning?

Last Friday evening Jan had an inspiration. She asked Jamie if he wanted a special picnic breakfast. She set out a bowl for him and let him pick the cereal. We put the cereal in a small container. We also filled a sippy cup with milk and put it on the bottom shelf of the fridge. Jamie was ecstatic. The next morning he got up and had breakfast on his own, then went to play with his Legos until 7 o'clock. The table was a little messy, but between mess and sleep there is no contest! Now we do it every day.

Joanna's Story: The Power of Music

When I was a little girl I got a child's record player for my birthday. It was one of the best presents ever. Every night I would choose a record. Sometimes it was music. Some of my favorites were Tom Glazer's *On Top of Spaghetti*, Pete Seeger's *Children's Concert at Town Hall*, and another cherished album called *For Kids and Just Plain Folks*, which included the all-time great song that tickled my funnybone as a kid, "Be Kind to Your Parents." Sometimes it was a record of stories for children. I would drift to sleep listening to those words and melodies. They took my mind off my particular worries—that the shadows were monsters, a robber might come into the house, and a fire could come blazing down the hallway. To this day my brother and I can recite lines, word for word, from those recordings.

Maria's Story: Monster Dust

Benjamin gets scared at night. I've learned that even the most innocent things can set him off. His favorite space book has a page about black holes, which he obsessed about at bedtime for weeks. We don't read that book at night anymore. Last week we let him watch a movie about a little mouse who goes west. In one scene the mouse runs toward his parents in the desert, but when he gets close it turns out they're a mirage and they disappear. Oh, do I regret that movie! Benjamin didn't sleep on his own for the next three nights, for fear we would disappear.

But even without science books and G-rated movies, we still have monster problems. We've made monster repellent out of cornstarch and glitter. We put it in a spice jar and sprinkle it in a line across the doorway for protection. When that idea wore out, we made monster spray out of water with a few drops of lavender oil mixed in. I also got him a feather duster to sweep the monsters out from under the bed. One time my husband helped him build a wall of imaginary bricks around the bed to protect it. We even rearranged the furniture, and that helped a lot, although I have no idea why. We have to keep changing it up, but the main idea is that part of the bedtime routine involves monster management.

I used to tell him that monsters don't exist, and he would say, "I *know*! But I'm still scared of them!" It works better to take his worries seriously. It's more comforting because it makes him feel like we're on the same team—a monster management team.

I was pretty excited. We had produced a rich stew of ideas. But there's no telling whether any of them will work for any particular child. **Problem-solving** is a useful tool if none of these prepackaged ideas do the trick. Here's how it might go:

Step 0. Find a Peaceful Time to Talk with your child (not at bedtime).

Step 1. Acknowledge Feelings

"It's not easy to get used to sleeping by yourself."

"You really like having us lie down with you until you fall asleep."

"Even though part of you knows that Mommy needs to sleep, it's really, *really* hard to resist waking her up."

"It's no fun to be the only one awake in the night."

"It can be scary to lie alone in the dark."

See if your child will talk about how she feels. Reflect back what she says. "Oh, so your toys can look like monsters in the dark." If she doesn't want to talk, you might tell a story about how you were afraid of the dark when you were little. It could be comforting for her to know that her parents had such fears, too.

Step 2. Describe the Problem (Briefly!)

"This is a *really* tough problem. You don't like to be alone when you wake up at night, and Mommy and Daddy need to sleep in their own bed so they can have energy in the morning."

Step 3. Ask for Ideas

"We need ideas. What can a person *do* in a situation like this?"

"What helps put you in a sleepy mood?"

"What *can* you do when you wake up and have trouble going back to sleep?"

Write down *all* ideas without judgment—even the most outrageous ones. ("Buy a pet monkey to sleep with me.") In case you need help getting your creative juices flowing, here are some suggestions that other parents have used successfully.

- Keep a picture book of vehicles by the bed to look through.
- Make a special recording of favorite songs or stories that she can listen to in bed.
- Get a special doll or stuffed animal to cuddle
- Acquire a night-light to stave off fears of the dark.
- Rearrange sleeping accommodations so that the child shares a room with a sibling at night.
- Make three "get out of bed" cards for when she "really, really" needs you, so she doesn't feel stuck. She can help make them.
- Make a recording of Mom or Dad reading a story to her so she can hear your actual voice when she's alone in bed.
- Make a list of special activities that your child can do on her own in the morning before you wake up. Make a special supply box for the activities.

- Hang a two-sided sign on your door that she helps make: "SLEEPING PARENTS" on one side, and "COME IN!" on the other.

There is one very significant caveat to this whole problem-solving process when it comes to the epic bedtime battle. In my experience, no matter how creative you are, it is extremely difficult to compete with the powerful draw of a cozy, parent-filled bed. You may very well find that your child will be willing to consider problem-solving alternatives only if the primary prize is off the table. If you are truly dedicated to defending your sleep space, you may have to draw a firm line in the sand, and *take action* to let your child know you mean business. It is likely that tears will be shed!

That's a deal-breaker for many of our workshop parents. They prefer to come up with some kind of compromise such as getting a bigger bed, adding a "sidecar" to the parental bed, or providing a small mattress on the floor of a parent's bedroom for nighttime wanderers. If you are comfortable with those solutions, more power to you.

For me, those compromises felt like too much of a sacrifice. I treasured the few hours at night that I was not on duty. So did my husband! Once my children got past the baby stage and were able to make it through the night without nursing, I was ready to reclaim my bed. One motivator was that my firstborn took the classic H position at night—head toward one parent and feet toward the other—and energetically kicked his way through his dreams. I was waking up in the morning feeling grumpy and resentful. It wasn't good for my sanity, and it wasn't good for my relationship with my children, either.

If you crave a child-free space at night, please don't feel guilty. We believe that the right to life, liberty, and the pursuit of happiness includes the pursuit of a good night's sleep. The mother (and father!) ship must survive if the crew is to thrive. Think of it as giving your children the gift of a well-rested parent and protecting them from the dangers of the zombie caretaker. We're not suggesting that any parent can expect a perfect night's sleep 365 days a year, but it is possible to create an environment where night duty is the exception rather than the rule.

Here's what *taking action without insult* might look like at night:

THE STORIES

Sarah's Story: Parents Have Feelings, Too

I can't bear the thought of letting my children "cry it out." But I have learned to act a little more displeased at having my sleep interrupted. I used to lead Mia back to bed and go through the whole tucking in, cuddling, and singing rigmarole each time. That led to endless wake-up calls. I finally started expressing my feelings strongly. "Mommy needs to sleep! I don't like waking up in the night! At night we stay in our own beds." I put her back in, gave a brief smoothing of the covers, and went back to my own bed quickly.

The other thing I stopped doing was letting her crawl into bed with me in the middle of the night and stay there. I used to complain but not actually move to evict her. My sleepy brain tells me to avoid getting up at all costs. But I can't get a restful sleep with her wriggling around next to me. In the long run, it's worth it to get up and put her back in her own bed. After a week of forcing myself to get up and lead her back to bed, she stopped coming in—most of the time.

Joanna's Story: A Dark, Dark Night

Three-year-old Danny was in a playful mood. He figured out that getting up again and again after bedtime was a pretty good game. No matter how firmly I spoke to him, he popped up again five or ten minutes later, giggling. After the fourth time I realized that it was going to be a very long night unless I changed my tactics. The fifth time, he popped up to find himself in a decidedly non-fun environment. The house was dark, the door to his parents' bedroom was locked. He cried and pounded on the door. I yelled through the closed door in a grumpy voice, "I need to sleep!"

He yelled back, "Let me in!"

"No! I'm tired. I need to sleep!"

He cried harder. I called out, "You run back to your bed and I'll come tuck you in."

Dan ran back to his bed. I got up and tucked him in. I sympathized briefly. "It's not easy to stay in bed at night! The problem is, I have to sleep. We'll play tomorrow." I opened the doors between our bedrooms again. Peace reigned in the kingdom for the rest of the night.

Not all crying is harmful. In fact, if we managed to protect our kids from every occasion that might cause tears, they probably wouldn't be emotionally healthy. Getting through hard times with the support and empathy of parents can make a child stronger. Sometimes our role is to provide sympathy without giving in to a child's demand, whether that demand is to have candy for breakfast or to keep a parent up all night. Neither one is healthy.

Many parents have found that they have to go through a painful period of "standing their ground" before problem-solving and other methods work for them. Make no mistake, shared problem-solving is still meaningful. You can take heart in the conviction that by problem-solving you are asking your child to participate in conquering a very difficult challenge, rather than arbitrarily abandoning him to weep in the dark.

And then there are those times it seems best to gracefully give in (at least temporarily).

Michael's Story: All Together Now

When Kara was born, Jamie was just barely two years old. He had been sleeping in his own room, but after Kara arrived he started having night fears. He wasn't so happy about having a new baby sister. As much as we tried to reassure him, it was true that he was getting less attention. Here was this noisy little invader in Mommy's arms. And that was just during the day. At night, the three of us—Mom, Dad, and Kara—were in one room, and Jamie was all by himself in another, like an outcast, banished from the rest of the family. It was no use explaining that he had shared our bed when he was a baby. That was ancient history to him. We didn't try any of these other techniques because we didn't know about that back then. So I can't say if they would've helped. What we did do was to put a mattress on our floor so that he could come and sleep in our bedroom.

When Kara was six months old we moved her into Jamie's room, got Jamie a new "grown-up" bed, put up mobiles and posters of dogs and fish and trucks, and generally made a big deal about them having their own special room together. Two kids in one room and two parents in the other. Nobody was alone. At that point Jamie was ready for it. And even though he still sometimes resented his sister during the day, he liked having her there with him at night.

REMINDER: Sleep

1. Acknowledge Feelings

"Sometimes it isn't easy to fall asleep. It can be scary to lie in bed in the dark."

2. Be Playful

"I need to smooth out these terrible lumps in your bed!" (Press down on legs and arms of child.)

3. Try Problem-Solving

"Let's see what ideas we can come up with for staying in your bed at night. A special night-light? A picture book by your bed? A recording of songs or stories?"

4. Take Action Without Insult

"Mommy and Daddy need to sleep! I'm putting you back in your bed. We'll play in the morning."

14

When Parents Get *Angry*!

Julie

> *You can learn many things from children. How much patience you have, for instance.*
>
> —Franklin P. Jones

"The truth is I'm having my doubts about this whole approach," Anna began. "It's not that I don't believe these tools are worthwhile. But I'm never going to be able to remember to use them in the moment. When I get really angry at Anton, all I want to do is smack him. I don't even want to *try* to think of a tool from the workshop. I just don't care! I'm sorry, but I don't have the right temperament to stay calm enough to do this." Anna slumped in her seat.

"Don't be sorry, Anna." Maria looked down as she spoke. "I've been thinking the same thing. The other day I was so furious at Benjamin for intentionally kicking Isabel. I screamed at him, 'What is *wrong* with you? How can you be so hateful? I don't care *what* she did to you, I don't want to hear it. Get out of my sight! I don't even want to be your mother anymore.' I'm too embarrassed to tell you any more details."

I am reminded of a Refresher meeting of my first long-term group. We always went around the room with a five-minute check-in about how we were doing. When it was my turn, I shared with the group how furious I was with Asher. He had been such a horror that morning, mercilessly teasing his brother, that I was ready to give him away. Did anyone want an extra five-year-old?

I worried the group might lose faith in me after my confession. Instead they were relieved to hear I was human. They had imagined that I was infinitely patient and never got angry with my kids. That day I discovered a common misperception about this approach. Parents assume they should be able to remain calm and in control at all times. I have yet to meet a parent who fits that description. And I'm not sure I even want to meet a parent who fits that description! That person would be an automaton, not a real human being.

"Anna and Maria, thank you for sharing your dark feelings. The reality is that normal, loving parents get angry at their kids—even downright rageful. Let's go back to the foundation of this approach. *All feelings can be accepted, some actions must be limited.* That truth must apply to us as well as to our kids. The challenge is to notice and accept our own violent feelings, and at the same time limit our actions so we do no harm. Or, if we do cause harm, the challenge is to reconnect with our children once we've recovered."

Maria ventured, "I've read that you're supposed to take deep breaths, or count to ten, or do jumping jacks when you get really mad at your kids."

"Those things are probably helpful, but the idea that I should try to calm myself down when I'm angry makes me feel irritable! When I get mad I don't want to calm down. It can actually be confusing for children to have their parents talk to them calmly when the kids can tell that they're furious. Talk about mixed messages!"

When I'm angry my voice gets loud. Fortunately for me,

there are plenty of great ways to be loud without doing psychological damage. Stick with the tools. This is where they really come in handy.

Say it with a word.
When I'm driven into a
frenzy by dawdling kids
(and my gentler tools of
playfulness and offering
choices to get them into
the car have failed) I yell,
"CAR!!!" with all my frustration packed into that
word. Chances are the word *car,* even delivered at top volume, will not cause lasting damage to the psyche.

If one word is not enough, you can direct your fury into **giving information**. You can roar, "BROTHERS ARE NOT FOR KICKING!!!"

You can **express your feelings strongly**. Use the word *I* instead of *you.* "I GET VERY UPSET WHEN I SEE A BABY BEING PINCHED!!!"

You can **describe what you see**. "I see people getting hurt!!!"

You can **take action**. "I can't allow sand throwing! WE ARE LEAVING!!!"

None of these words wound. They don't tell a child he is mean or worthless or unloved. They do let him know that his parent is past all patience. And they model a healthy way to express anger and frustration without attack.

Of course, being yelled at by a furious parent can be an upsetting experience in itself. That can't be the end of the story. It's important to **reconnect** after the intensity of anger has abated. Our kids need to know there is a way back into our good graces and a better way to go forward. That can start with **acknowledging feelings** all around. "That was no fun. You didn't like getting yelled at. And I was really mad about ___ (insert your gripe here)."

Then you can go on to plan what to do next time, or help your child make amends. A **problem-solving** session on how to get out of the house in the morning may be helpful. He can **make amends** to his brother by finding a colorful Band-Aid to place on the hurt spot. He may need to talk about what makes him mad at the baby. It's all part of the valuable work of growing up—learning what makes people angry, learning what to do afterward. An angry parent provides crucial feedback in the art of human relations.

"Don't you think you can overdo it, though? I don't think a lot of yelling is good for the kids, no matter what the words are," Maria said. "My mother was a yeller. It felt like we were living with a ticking time bomb. My brother and I were always tiptoeing around in fear of her next explosion."

I had to agree. People do get angry, people do blow up, and the How to Talk tools offer a safer way to release the pressure. But if you feel like you're losing control of yourself, if the kids are getting scared by your frequent outbursts, then it may be a good idea to get outside support. There's no shame in finding a therapist or counselor who can help you figure out alternative ways to relieve your stress. You'll be doing right by yourself and your children.

Anna nodded. "Okay, but before we all go into therapy, can we take a few minutes to share what people in this group do when we feel like we're heading for an explosion? I wouldn't mind a few free tips."

"I yell, 'I feel like hitting! You better get out of here!'" Toni said. "Later I call my sister and tell her about it. She'll commiserate with me, tell me her kids are at least as bad as mine. You might think I could just talk to my husband, but he's one of those guys who's always trying to make suggestions and fix the situation. I'm not ready for that! My sister, she'll let me rant. I do the same for her."

Maria spoke next. "If my husband is home, I go for a run around the block. Two or three if I'm really in a rage. There's something about fresh air and being able to move that helps me calm down."

"I wish I had a partner to take over for me once in a while," Anna said. "I can't leave the kids alone and go for a walk. I lock myself in the bathroom and curse under my breath. The kids bang on the door and beg me to come out. At least I know they're safe, but the door does take a beating."

"After my third kid was born there was a period where I was irritated and overwhelmed all the time," Sarah said. "I finally went to a therapist. It helped me get some insight into what was setting me off. I still get mad of course, but I don't feel like it's out of control, and there are plenty of good times in between. Coming to this group has really helped me, too. Sometimes when one of my kids does something awful, I'll think to myself, 'I can't wait to tell the group about this.' It's nice to know you guys will *get* it. I know we're going to end up laughing about it."

Michael cleared his throat. "I have to admit that I tend to lose my temper if I haven't gotten enough sleep or if I get too hungry. When I say it out loud it sounds pretty obvious, but it's so easy to stay up late to do one more thing. And I'm like that with food, too. Sometimes I don't notice I'm hungry until I'm literally growling at the kids."

"Thanks for making that point, Michael. Sometimes we're so focused on managing the kids we forget to take care of ourselves. Like they say on the airplanes—in an emergency, 'Put on your own oxygen mask first before helping others.' Self-sacrifice is not useful here! On that note, let's wrap this up so we can all go home and get some food and sleep."

THE STORIES

Joanna's Story: You Had to Be There

When my mother and her coauthor finished writing *Liberated Parents, Liberated Children*, she sent a copy to an author whom she greatly admired. He was an observant and creative teacher of children who had written several deeply moving books about his experiences. He responded that he could not recommend her book. He was appalled by the description of parental anger toward their precious young charges. He had spent a lifetime working with children, some of them very troubled, with difficult behavior problems. He could neither imagine nor excuse such violent feelings toward helpless, innocent children.

In all of my parenting workshops, when loving, caring, dedicated parents read that section on anger, they come alive. "I loved that chapter!" "It made me feel so much better about myself." "It was the most helpful thing I've ever read in a parenting book!" I've never once heard a parent who is shocked by the depiction of parental rage in *Liberated Parents, Liberated Children*.

This author was not a parent himself. I can only conclude that you have to have experienced the intense and relentless frustration of being in charge of these precious, sweet, unruly, and infuriating little beings twenty-four hours a day, seven days a week, to truly understand the anger an otherwise loving parent can feel.

Joanna's Story: A Mountain of Trouble

It was a bitterly cold winter day and I was stuck indoors, trying to entertain two-and-a-half-year-old Dan and six-month-old Sam in the living room. Dan was determined to conquer a mountain. If the mountain would not come to Dan, Dan must create his own. He dragged his rocking horse into the living room and hoisted it up on top of the coffee table. He went into his bedroom and dragged out his toddler chair. He reached up and managed to get the chair on top of the horse, balanced on three of the four legs. Then he started to climb.

I grabbed his arm as the whole crazy structure teetered and wobbled. Dan determinedly wrenched himself away from me and headed back up to his homemade summit. No skills came to mind. I didn't accept feelings, give choices, or give him his wishes in fantasy. I simply reacted in alarm: "No! No! NO!" Then I grabbed the chair and horse, undoing his grand design. Dan was outraged. He cried and kicked me, making a solid connection with my shin. Ow! Now *I* was outraged. I grabbed him hard and held him at arm's length, yelling, "Hey, no kicking! That hurts!"

He yelled back, "Stop it!" and continued to struggle and kick.

I shouted furiously, "I won't let you hurt me!" I disentangled myself from Dan, picked up the baby, who was now crying, too, and stormed into my bedroom, locking the door behind me.

Dan was frantic. He kicked at the door and screamed, "Let me in! Let me in!"

"*No*, I won't! I don't want to be kicked!"

"Let me in . . . let me in . . . let me in! I won't kick you!"

"Okay, I'll let you in if you don't kick me."

I opened the door and Dan fell into my arms, sobbing. The baby was still crying. We all got into bed together. Dan snuggled up to me and put his arm around baby Sam. "Evy-boby ty-yi-ing," he snuffled.

"Yes, everybody's crying," I agreed. We pulled the covers up to our necks and snuggled. We were cozy together in our sadness. After a little while we got up and went to get a snack.

There was conflict. There was violence. A child struck out. A mother protected herself and loudly insisted on her rights without striking back. The family reconnected and loving feelings returned. Soon we'll have to talk about how much fun it is to climb, and we'll figure out some safer challenges for Dan. That's life with little kids. Kicking and screaming is part of the territory.

Julie's Story: Road Rage

I got the call that my grandmother passed away in the afternoon, but I couldn't get a flight out to the East Coast for the funeral until the next day. I didn't have the heart for cooking dinner, so I decided to take the kids out for pizza. But the car ride turned into a nightmare. Rashi whined that he wanted to listen to Raffi. Asher told him that Raffi is for babies.

Rashi insisted, "I'm not a baby!"

Asher said, "Yes, you *are* a baby. You listen to baby music."

They went back and forth. Rashi started to cry, and my feeble "Hey, hey!" had no effect.

I couldn't think straight. I couldn't draw up a single tool. I was paralyzed by grief and furious with Asher for taunting Rashi.

I parked the car, and Asher decided to climb into the front seat and search my glove compartment for more "mature" music. I felt a sudden, overwhelming urge to slam the glove compartment on Asher's little fingers. I caught myself in time, but the feeling of wanting to hurt him was so powerful, it scared me.

I learned from that day. When extremely upset, don't get in the car with little kids and drive them around for pizza! Take care of your own emotional needs if you can. In retrospect I should've said, "Kids, I'm very sad tonight. I can't go driving. It's cereal and milk for dinner."

<u>REMINDER:</u> When Parents Get *Angry*!

A. In the moment, if you must yell, use your tools . . . LOUDLY!

1. Say It in a Word

"CAR!!!"

2. Give Information

"BROTHERS ARE NOT FOR KICKING!!"

3. Describe How You Feel

"I GET VERY UPSET WHEN I SEE A BABY BEING PINCHED!!"

4. Describe What You See

"I SEE PEOPLE GETTING HURT!!"

5. Take Action without Insult

"I can't allow sand throwing! WE ARE LEAVING!!"

B. *When the moment has passed and everyone's safe, take care of yourself.*

Do whatever works best for you: run around the block; take deep breaths; take a time-out for yourself (lock yourself in another room); call a friend and vent; email a friend; write in a journal; hug a dog; turn on your favorite music; attend to your own basic needs—sleep and food. . . .

C. *Reconnect and try problem-solving.*

> "That was no fun. You didn't like getting yelled at. And I was really mad about being late. What can we do next time?"

D. *Seek help if you feel the anger is too much.*

15

Troubleshooting—When the Tools Don't Work

Joanna

"I hope you won't take this the wrong way," Toni started, "but sometimes these tools just don't work for me. Maybe my kids are more strong-willed than yours. Or I'm not patient enough. But I thought if I used these tools, I could get my kids to *listen*. Your examples and stories all sound very sweet and amazing, but real life doesn't always have a happy ending. At least not in my family.

"Take the other day, for example. Jenna wanted to go to her friend Megan's house. I had to pick up Thomas from soccer practice and then make dinner. I just didn't have time. I was sympathetic, at least at first. I offered her a choice: 'You can play at Megan's tomorrow, or this Saturday.' She started crying. 'It has to be today! You have to take me!'

"I gave her information: 'I have to pick up Thomas and make dinner. I don't have time to take you to Megan's and back.' I tried putting her in charge: 'What do you want to do instead?' Nothing helped. If anything, I was making it worse. Finally, I couldn't take anymore whining and weeping, so I put her in her room and shut the door."

It's frustrating when you go out of your way to respond to a distressed child with skill and caring, and it doesn't help. It can make you doubt yourself or doubt the whole approach. What's the point of all this if it doesn't lead to cooperative kids?

When "Engaging Cooperation" Tools Don't Work

"When I find myself hitting a wall, my mantra is, **'When in doubt, go back to acknowledging feelings.'** You might try saying, 'This is *terrible*. You don't *want* to go to Megan's house another day. You want to go *right now*! I wish I could take you.'

"There's no guarantee that the storm clouds will lift immediately. This disappointment might be the last straw in a pile of frustrations that have built up over the day. She might need to stomp around or sob on your shoulder before she can finally let go of it."

Toni sighed. "It's true, I didn't think to acknowledge what she wanted in words. I thought that by giving her information, and offering a choice and trying to problem-solve, I *did* acknowledge what she wanted. This is too hard. I'll never get it right."

"Hey," I said, "you got a lot right. You didn't add insult to injury. You also didn't cave in and teach her that she could get what she wanted by whining. You held your ground. I can guarantee you'll get another chance to practice acknowledging feelings when the cooperation tools aren't working."

When Empathy Seems to Make a Child Feel Worse

"But what about when you empathize with a child, and even *that* makes things worse?" Sarah asked. "The teacher told me Sophia had a conflict at school. When I picked her up I said, 'I heard you and Janelle had a fight.' Her eyes teared up. I said, 'That can be so upsetting," and she started to cry. She told me Janelle wouldn't sit with her at lunch or let her play dress-up with the other girls. The more I said things like, 'Oh, wow! That's so hard!' and 'That didn't feel good. That's not what you expect from a friend!' the more she sobbed. I eventually had to leave her crying by herself so I could start dinner. "

Sometimes it can seem as if you made a child feel worse by naming her painful feelings. What's going on?

"Let's try it on ourselves," I suggested. "Imagine that your grandmother died last week. The two of you were very close. You try to put it out of your mind and hold yourself together so you can function at work. Then you run into a dear friend who says, 'I was so sorry to hear about your grandmother. You two had such a special relationship.' You feel your defenses start to crumble and your eyes well up. Your friend gives you a hug and says, 'You miss her.' The tears spill over and you start to cry.

"Did what she said make you feel worse?"

"I think I'd feel better to finally let the sadness out," Sarah said, "and to have somebody know how I feel."

"What if after a few minutes your friend said to you, 'Well, she was old. You can't be sad all night. You have to get over it, so let's go bowling.'"

Everyone groaned. "Okay, I get it," Sarah said. "Just because we say the 'right thing' to our children doesn't mean they're going to cheer up on our time line. It's stressful to have a sad kid. I guess it's hard to accept that we can't instantly heal every wound."

Toni looked skeptical. "So you're saying we have to keep

empathizing for hours and hours until they're ready to move on? That's exactly what I don't have patience for. Especially since we're usually talking about missed playdates, not dead grandmothers."

If your patience runs thin or you run out of time, you can *take care of your own needs without blaming the child*. Instead of, "Come on now, that's enough crying. This isn't so terrible," you can say, "I see how sad you are. I need to start making dinner now. Come to the kitchen and keep me company when you feel like it."

When a Child Gets Mad at You for Naming His Feelings

"But what about when your child actually gets mad at you for accepting his feelings?" Anna asked. "I'll give you an example. Anton has a love-hate relationship with Legos. He adores them, but his fine motor control is not very good, so he can get enormously frustrated. He moans and cries and throws things when something he's been working on falls apart. If I try to acknowledge his feelings by saying something like, 'That is so frustrating,' or 'You look mad,' he gets enraged with me. He'll actually yell, 'DON'T SAY THAT!' It's like I'm rubbing salt in his wounds. He doesn't want to talk about feelings."

When acknowledging feelings isn't helping, here are a few things to check:

Are you *matching the emotion* with your tone of voice, or are you just phoning it in? No child (or adult for that matter) wants to hear a calm, syrupy singsong, "Oh, you are frustrated," when he's extremely agitated. You have to say it like you mean it.

"That's SO FRUSTRATING!"

And don't forget, you're not limited to simply labeling the feeling. There are other ways to let a child know that you're getting it. A *sympathetic grunt* can be comforting:

"Ugh!" "Mmph."

If that's not enough you can *put a child's thoughts into words*:

"Stupid Legos!"

"Someone should invent bricks that will actually *stick together* when you *put* them together!"

"You didn't want *that* to happen!"

Sometimes it helps to *tell the story of what happened*:

"You worked hard on that. You almost had it! You got all the big blue bricks together to make the base. And all the little red bricks for the lights. And you put the alien with a laser on the top. It was almost ready to fly to Mars. And then it exploded! Darn it!"

And sometimes the best approach is to *say nothing*!

There are times when children prefer to be left alone, without any interference at all, *even* when they're struggling. Children (and adults) don't always appreciate a running commentary about how they're feeling. Keep in mind that *kids will cry*, tempers will fly (as will toys and juice cups). We can't shield our children from all distress, nor should we. They can't learn how to handle adversity without wrestling with it a bit.

When a Child Needs Help Climbing Out of a Pit of Despair

"Okay, but what about when the histrionics are truly out of proportion to the problem?" Toni asked. "Aren't we in danger of encouraging a child to wallow in self-pity? What will happen to a kid out in the real world if she's used to endless sympathy at home? She's not going to get that from a teacher with twenty-five kids in a class."

"I can relate to that," I said. "I worried about that very problem with my second child. The thing is, what seems like a minor inconvenience to us can feel like a monumental disappointment to a kid. We can't simply talk them out of their feelings or explain them down to smaller proportions. But there are other ways to help a child climb out of his pit of despair. Let me tell you about Dan and Sam.

A Tale of Two Brothers

My firstborn son would cheer up almost immediately when his feelings were acknowledged. He fell off the swing, banged his head, and broke the plow off his precious tractor that he was holding in his hand (probably the reason he fell in the first place). "Oh dear, that hurts. Let's give your head a kiss. Poor little broken tractor, it'll need some glue." The tears instantly dry, the clouds clear, and the sun shines again. Dan is on to the next misadventure.

In contrast, my second son often needed help to change gears. Sam would cry so long and so hard when he got hurt that I used to worry about what would happen when he went off to school. What teacher would have the patience for his particular extended time line of misery?

I remember once when Sam scraped his knee and cried for such a long time, I wondered if he had broken a bone. But knowing Sam I decided to wait it out. Finally he seemed ready to move on. He said he was hungry and happily munched on the apple I offered. Five minutes later, he looked down at his knee and started crying anew. I was exasperated. "Sam, you don't have to keep crying when it doesn't hurt anymore!"

Sam was outraged. He mustered all the scorn a misunderstood three-year-old can muster and replied, "*Just* because it doesn't hurt, *doesn't* mean I can stop *crying*!"

One thing I learned from having a child who held on to both physical and emotional pain was that it isn't always enough to just acknowledge feelings. You may have to carve some steps into the sidewall of that pit they're in, so that they can see a way to climb out.

"Let me give you a special kiss. You can add your own kiss if you want to." (Sam liked getting involved in the healing.)

"Which Band-Aid should we put on it? The plain one or the one with the dinosaur?"

"It sure is a good thing that our skin knows how to fix

itself. Your body is busy making new skin cells to patch up that scrape. How long do you think it will take to completely heal? Three days? Four?"

This mixture of kisses, choices, and information helped Sam see his way back to good cheer. And by the time he went off to kindergarten, to my relief, he was able to do it for himself. But before he did, there were plenty more occasions for me to hone my tools for the despairing child.

Popcorn on the Pavement

On another tragic occasion, Sam spilled his popcorn onto the pavement of the parking lot as he was getting into the car. I gave him the classic response, "Oh, how disappointing. You were looking forward to eating that. You didn't want *that* to happen!"

Sam sobbed harder. I tried to engage him in a conversation about what snacks we should make when we got home. He was not interested in considering any replacement for his terrible loss. Finally I ventured, "Well, this is really sad and annoying for you. But I know someone who is actually very happy about that spilled popcorn."

Sam's curiosity got the better of him. "Who?" he demanded.

"There is a squirrel who is extremely excited to see all that free popcorn. Right now he's probably running to tell his family and friends the good news, and they're all going to have a big party with that popcorn. Maybe they'll invite the chipmunks, too. Bad for us, but good for them!"

Sam smiled to think of the squirrel party. "Bad for *us*, but good for *them*," he repeated emphatically.

Sam has grown up to be a philosophical young man with a fine appreciation of life's ironies. I can't help but think it may have started with the squirrels.

"Okay. I get it," Toni said. "Sometimes my problem is I'm using the wrong tool. And sometimes I need to be more patient with the tools I have. But aren't there times when these tools just plain aren't going to work?"

It would be nice if we had a tool that was guaranteed to swiftly convert misery to cheer, no matter what the circumstance. We would win a Nobel Peace Prize! (How's that for giving in fantasy what I can't give in reality?) But we may lose something along the way. Kids are not programmable robots. Before they can grow up to be kind, thoughtful, self-directed beings, they're going to have to learn how to manage a range of emotions and experiences, including great sadness and disappointment. That's bound to include some wailing and gnashing of teeth. It's all part of being human.

THE STORIES

Maria's Story: Bathroom Boycott

I was getting my kids ready for bed the other night. Sometimes Benjamin resists going to the bathroom. Either he wakes me up in the middle of the night, which I don't appreciate, or else he doesn't, and we have a mess to clean up in the morning.

I decided to offer him a choice. "Do you want to use the hall bathroom, or the one in my bedroom?"

His response? *"No!* I am not going to the bathroom!"

I tried a different choice, along with some information: "Benjamin, you have to pee before you go to bed so the sheets don't get wet during the night. Do you want to go alone, or do you want me to come in with you?"

"I AM NOT GOING TO THE BATHROOM EVER AGAIN!"

Wow, I used my tools, and the problem got worse. This was looking a lot like failure.

Then I thought, *There must be something else going on.* I remembered that when in doubt, we're supposed to go back to acknowledging feelings, but I didn't know what those feelings were.

I said to Benjamin, "There's something about going to the bathroom tonight that you really don't like."

In response, he stuck out his arms to show me his new dinosaur tattoos. He looked very sad and said, "I don't want them to wash off."

So *that* was it! "Oh, I see. They're very special to you. How about we wrap your arms with towels while you wash your hands so your tattoos won't get wet?" He liked that plan and happily went to use the bathroom.

Michael's Story: Camp Nostalgia

Sunday night I told Jamie that he'd be starting a new camp in the morning. He started screaming and crying. Instead of trying to convince him that it would be great—which is what

I usually would have done—I just kept reflecting his feelings for what seemed like forever.

> **Me:** You don't like that idea. You don't want to start a new camp.
> **Jamie:** No! I'm not going!
> **Me:** You wish you could go back to Adventure Camp! You loved that camp!
>
> (That was his old camp, which he really loved, but it was over.)
>
> **Jamie:** Yeah!
> **Me:** I bet you wish you could go to Adventure Camp forever and ever! They should never have closed that camp!
> **Jamie:** Yeah! They should have it for the whole summer!
>
> (At this point he was still crying, and he climbed into my lap.)
>
> **Me:** And then you would never have to go to a new camp. You would always know what to expect, and you would always have a great time, and you would always have Tom for a counselor.
> **Jamie:** And Andy would be there, too.
> **Me:** It can feel scary going to a new camp. You don't know who's going to be there. You don't know what to expect.
> **Jamie (crying, nods his head):** Mm-hmm.

After twenty minutes of this, I really wanted to say, "Okay, now you're done." It certainly seemed like the more I accepted his feelings the more he would cry. But I stuck with it, mostly so I could tell you it didn't work. After about half an hour he said, "Okay, I don't want to talk about this anymore." He didn't seem to feel better, just tired.

But the next day, when we got to his new camp, he ran off with his counselor as soon as we got there. I guess he really just needed to have a good cry about his favorite camp ending.

Joanna's Story: Candy Clamor

As the youngest of three, Zach was usually happy to go with the flow. Heck, he had two attentive older brothers, three dogs, and a kitten. There was always lots of excitement and distraction. Hardly ever a reason to stay upset about anything. Except for C.A.N.D.Y.

When Zach was two and a half, he was old enough to go trick or treating with the big kids on Halloween. Sure, last year he rode on his mom's shoulders dressed as a Dalmatian to match his dog (who was also dressed as a Dalmatian, with painted-on spots) but that didn't count. This was real. He had a bag full of sweets collected through his own efforts.

He was shocked the next day to learn that there were restrictions attached. I explained that while candy is delicious, it isn't good for your body if you eat too much at a time. The boys agreed that two pieces a day would be reasonable. Three if they were small. We put the bags in the cabinet above the refrigerator so they wouldn't be tempting and they'd be out of reach of the dogs.

Zach agreed with this protocol in theory. But it turned out that a day was longer than he had thought. Whenever the word *candy* was mentioned (and it was mentioned a *lot* after Halloween) Zach got a powerful urge to *have* that candy *in his mouth*—even if he had already consumed the agreed-upon amount. When crying didn't work, he upped his game to kicking and screaming.

Accepting feelings didn't seem to make a dent. Neither did giving in fantasy: "It would be nice to have a mother who wasn't so fussy about food! One of those nice moms who gives you candy for lunch, and isn't all, 'Oh dear, I must make sure my children are *so* healthy'" (said in a syrupy voice).

Brotherly offers of alternative foods simply increased his rage.

I turned my attention to getting lunch for the other boys. Zach eventually wailed himself out and joined us.

Later, I took the older boys aside and asked them not to talk about *candy* in front of Zach. If they needed to say it, they could spell it. The allure of sugar is powerful. Even the thought of it was too much for a two-year-old to handle.

I thought my solution was brilliant. Zach didn't have any more meltdowns, and the older boys used spelling to avoid setting him off. About a week later, I had a friend visiting and Zach asked her, "Do you have any C-A-N-D-Y you could share with me?"

My friend was astonished. "He can spell?? That is the most brilliant two-year-old I've ever seen!"

Turns out Zach was paying attention. It didn't take him long to crack the code when something as important as candy was at stake. But I also realized that he had not thrown another candy tantrum in spite of the fact that he was not fooled by our spelling. He had tested the limit and found it firm.

Sometimes, when a kid really wants something and can't get it, he is going to cry and scream. It doesn't necessarily mean we're doing the wrong thing. The unenviable job of a parent is to stand your ground when the health and safety of your child is at stake, even in the face of a hurricane of emotion that only a toddler can produce.

REMINDER: Troubleshooting

1. When a child is too upset to cooperate, **go back to Acknowledging Feelings**

> "You don't even want to *think* about visiting your friend another time. You were looking forward to going *today*!"

- *Make sure your tone of voice matches the emotion*

> "That's so *disappointing*!"

- *Try a grunt instead of words*

> "UGH!" "Mmph!"

- *Put your child's thoughts into words*

> "Stupid Legos! They should stick together and *stay* together!"

- *Tell the story of what happened*

> "You worked for a long time on that spaceship. You used blue bricks for the base, and red bricks for the lights, and it was almost ready to launch! All it needed was the fins on the rockets. . . ."

2. Give your child **Time to Recover** (and give yourself a break!)

> "I can see how sad you are. I'll be in the kitchen making dinner. Come join me when you're ready."

3. Help a child climb out of the pit of despair by **Acknowledging Feelings, Giving Information,** and **Offering Choices**

> "Oh no, the skin got ripped! That hurts! Good thing skin knows how to repair itself. It's getting busy right now growing more skin cells to cover that poor knee and make it as good as new. How many days do you think it will take? What kind of Band-Aid should we cover it with?"

4. Take Action and stick to your values; if you regularly cave in to whining and complaints, the tools won't work

> "You wish we could have candy for breakfast! I'm putting it out of sight. The choices are cereal or eggs."

5. Check on "The Basics"

> Is your child lacking food or sleep, or feeling overwhelmed? Is your child developmentally ready to do what you're expecting?

The End?

So, we're done here? Every child is now brushing his or her teeth without protest, treating younger siblings and small animals with the greatest gentleness and respect, eating a full portion of greens at every meal, neglecting to poke pennies or peanut butter into the DVD player, and sleeping angelically through the night without interruption?

No?

Ah, we didn't think so. You wouldn't want life to become boring! We hope that you found in our book a wealth of ideas that have helped you survive the daily challenges of life with kids and end the day feeling . . . weary, yes, but more peaceful, connected, and joyful than before.

Onward to new ages and stages, new challenges, new questions and stories. And who knows, maybe we'll go ahead and write another book about that.

We want to hear from you! Please share your stories—your triumphs and calamities, your questions and observations. We can be reached at info@HowToTalkSoLittleKidsWillListen.com or at our website HowToTalkSoLittleKidsWillListen.com. It is our hope to create a community of adults who share ideas and support each other in our most important task: raising the next generation.

—Joanna and Julie

Acknowledgments

To our husbands, Andrew Manning and Don Abramson, who patiently supported and believed in us as we spent long hours tapping away at keyboards while muttering over phone headsets to each other on our opposite coasts.

To our children, Dan, Sam and Zachary Faber Manning, and Asher, Rashi, and Shiriel King Abramson, who challenged us, inspired us, provided tech support, occasional editing, and sometimes even cooked dinner for us while we worked.

To our agent, Bob Markel, and our editor, Shannon Welch, who shepherded our book from theoretical conjecture into actual being and were unfailingly generous and understanding about "stretched" deadlines.

To our artists Tracey and Coco Faber, and Sam Faber Manning, who took our awkward stick figures and made them come alive, even while in the midst of term papers and finals in their senior year at college.

To our parents Adele and Leslie Faber, and Pat and Ed King, for their unwavering faith and abundant wise counsel.

To all the parents, grandparents, teachers, librarians, pediatricians, speech therapists, nurses, physical therapists, day care providers, child life specialists, and preschool directors who shared their stories with us, both their triumphs and their tribulations.

And especially to Adele Faber and Elaine Mazlish, our

founding mothers and our inspiration. We stand on your shoulders!

Finally a shout out to Kazi (Joanna's Belgian shepherd) who would climb up in the chair next to Joanna and dump a chew toy on her head if she and Julie labored too long at the keyboard without getting up for a walk. Vital service indeed.

Kazi at his post

Additional Resources

How To Talk So Kids Will Listen & Listen So Kids Will Talk, by Adele Faber and Elaine Mazlish

Liberated Parents, Liberated Children, by Faber and Mazlish

Siblings Without Rivalry, by Faber and Mazlish

Children Who Are Not Yet Peaceful, by Donna Goertz

Kids, Parents and Power Struggles, by Mary Sheedy Kurcinka

The Spirited Child, by Kurcinka

Playful Parenting, by Lawrence D. Cohen

The Siblings' Busy Book, by Lisa Hanson and Heather Kempskie

The Happy Sleeper, by Heather Turgeon and Julie Wright

Unconditional Parenting, by Alfie Kohn

Punished by Rewards, by Kohn

Uniquely Human: A Different Way of Seeing Autism, by Barry M. Prizant

You Can't Say You Can't Play, by Vivian Paley

Your Baby and Child, by Penelope Leach

Notes

PART ONE

Chapter Two: Tools for Engaging Cooperation

1. For an in-depth discussion of this phenomenon, read chapter three, "Too Much Control," of Alfie Kohn's book *Unconditional Parenting*. And also Donelda J. Stayton, Robert Hogan, and Mary D. Salter Ainsworth, "Infant Obedience and Maternal Behavior," *Child Development* 42 (1971): 1057–69.

Chapter Three: Tools for Resolving Conflict

1. Ministry of Social Development New Zealand, "Publications and Resources." https://www.msd .govt.nz/about-msd-and-our-work/publications-resources/ journals-and-magazines/social-policy-journal/spj27/the -state-of-research-on-effects-of-physical-punishment-27 -pages114-127.html. See also Alfie Kohn, *Unconditional Parenting*. New York: Atria Books, 2005, pages 63–64.

2. https://www.thersa.org/globalassets/pdfs/blogs/rsa-lecture -dan-pink-transcript.pdf.

3. Daniel J. Siegel, MD, and Tina Payne Bryson, PhD,

"'Time-Outs' Are Hurting Your Child," *Time*. September 23, 2014. time.com/3404701/discipline-time-out-is-not-good.

Chapter Four: Tools for Praise and Appreciation

1. Carol Dweck, *Mindset: The New Psychology of Success*, New York: Random House, February 8, 2006.

Chapter Five and a Quarter: The Basics

1. For a good resource about developmental stages, see Penelope Leach, *Your Baby and Child: From Birth to Age Five*. New York: Alfred A. Knopf, 1990.

PART TWO

Chapter One: Food Fights—The Battle at the Kitchen Table

1. Kim Severson, "Picky Eaters? They Get It From You." *New York Times*, Oct. 10, 2007. http://www.nytimes.com/2007/10/10/dining/10pick.html?pagewanted=all&_r=0.

2. Steven Strauss, "Clara M. Davis and the wisdom of letting children choose their own diets." *CMAJ*, November 7, 2006; 175(10): 1199–1201. http://www.ncbi.nlm.nih.gov/pmc/articles/PMC1626509/.

3. Alfie Kohn, *Punished by Rewards: The Trouble with Gold*

Stars, Incentive Plans, A's Praise, and Other Bribes. Boston: Houghton Mifflin Company, 1993.

Chapter Five: Lies

1. Susan Pinker, "Children's Lies Are a Sign of Cognitive Progress." *The Wall Street Journal,* January 13, 2016. http://www.wsj.com/articles/childrens-lies-are -a-sign-of-cognitive-progress-1452704960.

Reminder Index

Reminder Index

Index

Index

Index

Index

Index

Index

Index

Thank you for choosing a Piccadilly Press book.

If you would like to know more about our authors, our books or if you'd just like to know what we're up to, you can find us online.

www.piccadillypress.co.uk

And you can also find us on:

We hope to see you soon!